"David Seelow provides a pedagogical companion for educators which takes us on a journey through a cultural landscape of games, poetry and moving image. The book provides practical suggestions and resources for teachers to engage students in real world issues, such as climate change, the politics of war and even the very topical COVID-19 pandemic. The underlying philosophy of using games in the classroom as transformative experiences is evidenced through a multifaceted narrative, sparking a range of imaginations for teachers and their students."

**Professor Jacqueline Cawston**, PhD, MBA, CEIGHE,
Co-Director, Centre for Postdigital Cultures,
Professor of Immersive Culture and Heritage,
Institute of Creative Cultures, Coventry University, UK

"In my teenage years, games in a classroom would mean playing under the desk during a boring lesson, so having games in classrooms today, serving as an education tool, signals a total shift of perspective. There is so much knowledge that can be drawn from games like *This War of Mine* and other great games and David Seelow's *Games as Transformative Experiences* shows us how games can transform our perspective on education."

**Konrad Adamczewski**, 11 bit studios,
Warsaw, Poland

"David Seelow's newest book, *Games as Transformative Experiences For Critical Thinking, Cultural Awareness, and Deep Learning: Strategies and Resources*, offers educators an accessible and practical way to begin to delve into various aspects of gaming and learning. The book features intertextual examples to address analog and digital gaming related to important contemporary issues, including, but not limited to, equity and inclusion, critical thinking and analysis, and student motivation and engagement. Seelow interweaves anecdotes and personal experiences as he provides practical advice and relevant material for classroom teaching and learning."

**Sandra Schamroth Abrams & Hannah R. Gerber**,
Authors of *Videogames, Libraries, and the
Feedback Loop: Learning Beyond the Stacks*

# Games as Transformative Experiences for Critical Thinking, Cultural Awareness, and Deep Learning

All games are potentially transformative experiences because they engage the player in dynamic action. When repurposed in an educational context, even highly popular casual games played online to pass the time can engage players in a way that deepens learning. *Games as Transformative Experiences for Critical Thinking, Cultural Awareness, and Deep Learning: Strategies & Resources* examines the learning value of a wide variety of games across multiple disciplines.

Organized just like a well-made game, the book is divided into four parts highlighting classroom experiences, community and culture, virtual learning, and interdisciplinary instruction. The author crosses between the high school and college classroom and addresses a range of disciplines, both online and classroom practice, the design of curriculum, and the transformation of assessment practices.

In addition to a wealth of practical exercises, resources, and lesson ideas, the book explains how to use a wide and diverse range of games from casual to massively multiplayer online games for self-improvement as well as classroom situations.

# Games as Transformative Experiences for Critical Thinking, Cultural Awareness, and Deep Learning

## Strategies & Resources

David Seelow

### CRC Press
Taylor & Francis Group
Boca Raton  London  New York

CRC Press is an imprint of the
Taylor & Francis Group, an **informa** business

Cover design and art by Carlijn van der Leede

First Edition published 2023
by CRC Press
6000 Broken Sound Parkway NW, Suite 300, Boca Raton, FL 33487-2742

and by CRC Press
4 Park Square, Milton Park, Abingdon, Oxon, OX14 4RN

*CRC Press is an imprint of Taylor & Francis Group, LLC*

© 2023 David Seelow

*Library of Congress Cataloging-in-Publication Data*
Names: Seelow, David, author.
Title: Games as transformative experiences for critical thinking, cultural awareness, and deep learning : strategies & resources / David Seelow.
Description: Boca Raton, FL : CRC Press, 2023. | Includes bibliographical references and index.
Identifiers: LCCN 2022030037 (print) | LCCN 2022030038 (ebook) | ISBN 9781032062679 (hardback) | ISBN 9781032062662 (paperback) | ISBN 9781003201465 (ebook)
Subjects: LCSH: Video games in education. | Virtual reality in education. | Simulation games in education.
Classification: LCC LB1028.75 .S44 2023 (print) | LCC LB1028.75 (ebook) | DDC 371.33/7—dc23/eng/20220810
LC record available at https://lccn.loc.gov/2022030037
LC ebook record available at https://lccn.loc.gov/2022030038

ISBN: 978-1-032-06267-9 (hbk)
ISBN: 978-1-032-06266-2 (pbk)
ISBN: 978-1-003-20146-5 (ebk)

DOI: 10.1201/9781003201465

Typeset in Minion
by codeMantra

*This book is dedicated to Beth Ellen Tedford in gratitude for her extraordinary friendship and support and to Roderick, the little the pug whose presence brings my greatest happiness.*

# Contents

## Part II  **Games as Transformative Classroom Experiences**

# In Memoriam

INEVITABLY, AS ONE REACHES the late stages of life, loss becomes promi-nent. Parents, mentors, former teachers, and sometimes even friends and colleagues. I want to honor four people here who had a tremendous impact on me as a person, and an educator. I have acknowledged them before, but their memory deserves special attention.

## HAROLD WILLIAM BRIGHTMAN, J.D., PHD (10/4/1939–1/23/2017)

Harold William Brightman, lawyer and professor, a man of extraordi-nary intelligence with expertise in literature, philosophy, linguistics, lan-guages, and the law. Considered a little eccentric, which must be why the Humanities secretary at State University of New York, Old Westbury, Pat Ryan, thought we would get on so well when introducing us in 1991. She was right. Harold was a dear friend, who would talk to me about D.H. Lawrence for hours and provide me much comfort and support including appearing at my bedside following my heart attack and surgery, as a spirit of hope and encouragement.

## RANDALL SCOTT DAVIS (5/17/1954–11/19/2021)

The best of best friends, I met Randy in first grade. I was a shy new stu-dent sitting in the back corner of the room. His jocular attitude and wel-come spirit helped established an immediate friendship that never ceased, never even dipped. It was all good, all the time. He provided me house and hearth when I was at my absolute lowest and helped me climb out of the abyss of despair. Soon after this personal crash, Randy introduced me to Joe Gross (the two shared a love of sci-fi), Professor Harvey Gross's son, and that introduction led me from a near-death experience to a PhD where Harvey Gross served on the my oral exam committee. We obtained our B.A.s the same day at the same university. When Randy passed, our condos were within walking distance of each other. We were never far from each other. Really, I cannot say enough about his friendship. I miss him every day.

## HUGH J. SILVERMAN, PHD (8/17/1945–5/8/2013)

I first studied with Hugh as an undergraduate in Comparative Literature, then, later in my doctoral seminars on deconstruction. Hugh was a very rare person, a gentle soul whose support of students was unwavering. Students would sit the floor outside his office for over 2 hours to ask his advice or insight. Hugh never left until every student was seen for as long as each student needed to be heard. When a less than supportive chairman forced me to give up a much-needed part-time job to commit everything to the program, Hugh intervened in my favor. I worked with Hugh as his teaching assistant in a terrific year-long course on Western Civilization. Later, he edited my dissertation, and soon after introduced me to Leo Duroche, scholar of German literature and Men's Studies, who helped launch my publishing career. Cofounder and Executive Director of the International Association of Philosophy and Literature, Hugh provided a graduate student van to bring students at no cost to IALP's annual conference. When I lacked money to fly to Edmonton, Canada, for the 1991 conference, he paid me to run the book exhibit, allowing me to make the trip, present a paper, and see my good buddy Ciro Sandoval. Hugh's house in Port Jefferson was always warm and welcome. I am deeply indebted to Hugh's kindness and generosity which extended for over 30 years.

## EDWARD W. TAYLER, PhD, LIONEL TRILLING PROFESSOR EMERITUS IN THE HUMANITIES, COLUMBIA UNIVERSITY (3/13/1931–4/23/2018)

Dr. Tayler was one of the most honored of all Columbia's illustrious teachers. He was a brilliant scholar of 16th- and 17th-century literature, especially John Milton and John Donne, but his great scholarship did not match his charismatic, transformative teaching. From profound graduate seminars to new ways to teach writing and the core curriculum, Dr. Tayler made ideas come alive, what one former student called "time bomb teaching." Even more than such stalwart scholarship and teaching, from the Vietnam protests in the late 1960s to his retirement at century's end in 1999, Professor Tayler supported and inspired students to be citizens of integrity. Dr. Tayler was the primary reason a shy kid from a tiny village in upstate New York, an average high school student, was able to attend one of the world's finest universities. I am deeply grateful for that opportunity and have never forgotten our first meeting in Philosophy Hall, way back in 1978.

# Author

**David Seelow** has taught in higher education continually since 1989 at both public and private colleges ranging from top tier research universities to community colleges. He has also taught several years in public school and holds four permanent education licenses from New York State, which has the most rigorous licensure requirements of any state in the nation. Dr. Seelow founded the Center for Game and Simulation-Based Learning based in Albany, New York, as well as an award-winning Online Writing Lab. Dr. Seelow has taught online courses for 15 years, designed several online courses, and developed entire online programs, all of which give the book an added appeal during a time when many schools rely on virtual and blended learning models. He has a certificate in game design and has published and presented nationally and internationally on games in learning, humanities, and education. His previous books are *Radical Modernism and Sexuality* (Palgrave MacMillan, 2005), the well-reviewed *Lessons Drawn: Essays on the Pedagogy of Comics and Graphic Novels* (McFarland, 2019) and *Game Based Classroom: Practical Strategies for Grades 6–12* (Routledge, Eye on Education series, 2021).

# Introduction

*The Power and Potential*
*of Games for Learning*

## GAMES AND EMPOWERED FACULTY

Over a decade ago Danish game scholar Jesper Juul published an important book called *The Casual Revolution* (2009). Revolution with a small "r" since the book described only a revolution in the games industry; however, this small revolution had a large cultural impact. Juul argued that casual games revolutionized a game industry that privileged expensive large-scale AAA games by major studios targeting a largely adolescent male audience. These games favored First Person Shooters, racing, and fighting games that appealed to young males. The games were complex with stupendous graphics and required hours of dedicated game play, often at consoles, to master the game's many levels. On the contrary, casual games, as Juul described them, could be played on mobile devices, especially smartphones, making them ready at hand any time of the day at any location. You could play them on a subway, doing laundry, or waiting at the dentist's office. The games were free or inexpensive. They could be learned in a matter of minutes and played for short bursts of time with no loss of quality play. You could experience success quickly, but the games also allowed for more advanced play as progressive levels demanded increasing skill. Such games appealed to a broad, much more inclusive audience than traditional "hard core" games. This broader audience, in turn, led to an explosion in the game industry to the point where video games exceeded Hollywood as the top-grossing entertainment medium (Witkowski, 2021). Casual games made this success possible.

As games catapulted to the top of the entertainment pyramid some scholars, educators, and designers looked to their educational value, whether education in the classroom, or for improved health and a better society. However, designing games for specific learning outcomes remains a major challenge. First, the cost of development requires a return on investment. Maybe not best sellers, but companies still need to be solvent. Thus, a game needs an audience and K-12 schools, colleges, and universities have different curricula, different instructors, different philosophies, and so forth. A game designed for Algebra would have to reach across multiple school districts and geographic regions to be successful and that proves rather difficult to pull off. Purchasing decisions are also made by professionals who usually have little knowledge of games and even less of their educational benefits. College professors can require whatever material they feel benefits their students, but many, like their K-12 counterparts, are also unfamiliar with the learning value of games. *Call of Duty* might be a mega hit but proves a hard sell to history professors. Designing a game for a specific history class would not be economically feasible in the way a textbook, however dull and unengaging, might be.

## FROM GAME FIELDS TO CLASSROOMS

Rather than argue specifically in favor of learning games, on the one hand, and for casual games as learning opportunities, on the other hand, I propose to argue in favor of games as transformative experiences that can help us reimagine education. All games are potentially transformative experiences because they engage the player in dynamic action, i.e., learning by doing, in response to other players, in a complex system made up of challenges whose overcoming bring the player into a new zone of possibility. If games are used in a learning situation, inside and outside formal classrooms, guided by an instructional presence requiring critical thinking in a cultural context, then games are very likely to enable transformative experiences.

Of course, transformative experiences can be either regressive or progressive. Franz Kafka's Gregor Samsa wakes up a roach. That's not a pleasant transformation, but all too often such a transformation characterizes formal education. The playful joy of kindergarten squeezed out of kids before they reach middle school. That's why we have too few scientists and engineers. This book focuses on the positive, or progressive, potential of transformative experiences using games. Such experiences do not have to be extraordinary epiphanies like Saul's on the road to Damascus. They simply need to move the learner forward on the road in the direction of improved learning and well-being, which will be different for every learner.

Let me take a simple example from my own life. As a child, I played on a village Little League team. At first, I was a bench warmer who helped keep that bench very warm for the older kids who played in the field. During practice, I would hang out in right field, the baseball equivalent of a wall-flower, dreaming of Mickey Mantle, as practice carried on. By chance, and randomness plays a significant role in most games, I threw a ball that had somehow made its way to the no man's land of deep right field, on the fly to home plate. For a ten year old that was an Olympic throw. Apparently, I had some ability hidden underneath the shell of my low self-esteem. The coach noticed the throw; good coaches have a knack of seeing the little, off-center aspects of a game. As I moseyed into the batting team's position to the right of home plate the coach asked me, "Have you ever considered pitching?" I thought to myself, are you crazy, but sheepishly responded, "No." I mean come on coach, pitchers are the stars. They are positioned in the center of the magic diamond glittering for all to see. I'm a loser out in right field. Let me nap. No responsibility out there, far from the action. The coach couldn't hear these thoughts run through my brain. He promptly had me pitch the very next inning and start the very next official game.

There I was on that elevated mound in the middle of the diamond. No confidence to speak of, but the coach believed in me. I ended the season winning every game I pitched, never, so far as I recall, giving up more than three hits over the duration of our seven inning games. The older kids grumbled under their breath about the younger kid being allowed to pitch but winning has a way of taming bullies. They enjoy the accolades and ice cream sundaes of success.

This minor experience had a transformative effect that still ripples throughout my life in different ways. The game's effects translated from the baseball diamond to the square box of classrooms, but only after a lengthy time delay. I made no effort in my classes. No teacher observed what the Little League coach observed, and so my potential hid under the desk. I still dreamed of Mickey Mantle not William Butler Yeats. School had no magic, no fun, and no game. However, when I wandered into the right field of college way out on Long Island the confidence lit by my success in Little League resurfaced. A handful of professors became my coaches and my fastball became thoughtful papers delivered as consistent strikes across the instructor's desk. Eventually I became the only kid from my high school class to obtain a degree from an Ivy League school.

The game of Little League gave me the belief that I could be a leader, a quiet leader, but no less, a leader, other kids looked up to. For the first time, I had experienced genuine success. A game not a classroom enabled that success which has stayed with me for decades. Certainly, I have thrown more than my share of wild pitches, but I have always bounced back from defeats, the losses of everyday life, deserved and undeserved, to win. Failure in games, unlike school, is temporary. You learn from them and gain an extra life. Pac-Man running through the maze eating up the enemy Nay Sayers. A transformative experience does not have to bring immediate results. The benefits can be the gradual outward ripples that expand your belief in yourself, your horizon, and your understanding. "Know thyself" not "no self" speaks the Delphic oracle. Games are the platform, the field of dreams, which help make possible deep and enduring learning all the way to Level 256 and beyond.

## APPLIED GAMES OR DESIGNING FOR TRANSFORMATION

Traditionally, games that are designed for educational or other non-entertainment or commercial purposes are referred to as serious games. This adjective does not serve anyone well. What does serious mean with respect to games? When you sit down to play *Scrabble*, I feel relatively certain that you are serious about beating your opponent. Even if your opponent is a much more experienced player, you will try your best and will attempt to form the best words possible in an earnest fashion. No one wants to play a spoil sport—meaning a person with no seriousness about the game. When two chess grandmasters face each other in international competition they are very serious. When Serena Williams steps on the tennis court, LeBron James, the basketball court, Aaron Judge, the baseball diamond, or Tom Brady, the football field, they are approaching their respective games with the utmost seriousness. Let's dispense with the overdetermined serious adjective. I reserve serious games for wargames played by active military in preparation for actual battle where real lives not avatars or on the line.

Applied Games are designed specifically to affect transformative experiences in non-entertainment situations such as the classroom, health conditions, behavioral issues, social or political impact, empathy, and other prosocial attitudes and behaviors. These are games that are designed to have an impact on learning, attitude, behavior, or society. I divide these games into two general classifications or types. There are custom learning or health games designed to meet a specific targeted outcome. These games often have grant funding and are part of a research project that measures their effectiveness at meeting well-defined outcomes. The well-known Project Evo and The *NeuroRacer* game coming out of Dr. Adam Gazzaley's research at the University of California, San Francisco, would be one example.[1] These games target Autism and Attention Deficit Disorder in the young and cognitive decline in the elderly, respectively. My colleagues at Yale University's College of Medicine produce very targeted health games. For example, *Invite Only VR: A Vaping Prevention Game* targets teen vaping and the dangers of e-cigarettes. Their success has been reported in the professional journal *Addictions* (2021) (Figure I.1).

Similarly, Hope Lab and an interdisciplinary team produced *Re-Mission*, a health game targeting forms of pediatric cancer, which was also written about in a professional journal (2008). Other applied games do not have

FIGURE I.1  Invite only VR game. (Image courtesy of Kimberley Hieftje Yale University play4REAL XR Lab© Used with permission.)

such clearly defined outcomes and are less likely to be part of controlled studies, but, nonetheless, these games have educational, behavioral, affective, or social goals and frequently feature supporting curricula. These games are based on solid academic research. Like *Re-Mission*, *That Dragon Cancer* addresses childhood cancer, but with a more general goal of creating empathy for families living with children suffering from cancer. *The Mission US* series of games targets middle school students by featuring important moments of United States history with the objective of increasing student understanding of these historical moments. These games are all based on historical research and have extensive supporting curricula. *Dragon Box Algebra 5+* and *12+* target the general mathematical skills of solving algebraic equations. *Portal 2* has application to learning physics. All these types of applied games have tremendous potential for improving student learning.

## ALL GAMES CAN BE TRANSFORMATIVE EXPERIENCES

Applying games, refers to any game-commercial or not, video, board, athletic, card, etc., that can be deployed in some fashion to a learning situation. Applying games is akin to using a film, song, or novel in a classroom not specific to that media. For example, a professor might use Michael Moore's *Bowling for Columbine* (2002) in a sociology class to examine mass shootings or Bob Dylan's song "A Hard Rain's a-Gonna Fall" (1962) in a history class explaining the context and aftermath of the Cuban missile crisis or social change more generally. In virtually all cases, I argue creative products or works of art are superior to standard, non-engaging textbook fare.

In some instances, the use of commercial games makes common sense. Sid Meier's classic *Civilization* has long been used in social studies classes. The *Assassin's Creed* series from Ubisoft also makes perfect sense for social studies and history classes. On the other hand, games that appear to have no benefit to the classroom, either because of their casualness or the perceived inappropriate content, also have tremendous value in a wide range of classes. The fabled *Bejeweled* franchise—a simple match three game for killing time—has significant learning benefits at both ends of the learning spectrum, young children, and elderly adults (2011). Esports games like *League of Legends* (2009) teach a range of important skills including teamwork, communication, hand eye coordination, critical thinking, and sportsmanship.

*Monopoly* presents a fascinating mix of applied and applying games at the same time. *Monopoly* began as *The Landlord Game*, designed and self-published by the underappreciated woman designer Lizzie Magie around 1904. Magie designed an applied game with the specific intention of teaching players Henry George's economic theories. Her outcome was well defined. Players would learn that wealth creation needs to be shared for society to prosper in an equitable fashion. When Charles Darrow purchased rights to the game, ripping off Lizzie in the process, what he sold to Parker Brothers was a very different system of values (Figure I.2).

Magie's left-leaning anti-monopoly game ended up its opposite, a game of exploitation and self-interested wealth creation. Sadly, as I discuss later in Chapter 12, *Monopoly* has reinforced a value system that promotes not

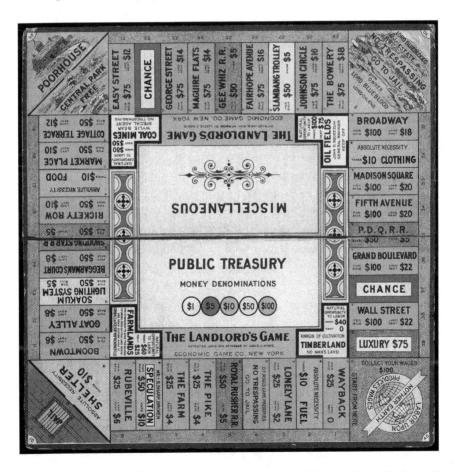

FIGURE I.2 The landlords game. (Image courtesy of Thomas Forsyth. https://commons.wikimedia.org/wiki/File:Landlords_Game_1906_image_courtesy_of_T_Forsyth_owner_of_the_registered_trademark_20151119.jpg.)

the free market, but market domination, a reality we face with increasing ferocity at the expense of the consumer. Genuine competition is swallowed up by endless mergers and acquisitions. In this sense, the game can be applied to teach about the dangers of corporate aggrandizement.

The much-reviled *Grand Theft Auto* series might seem wildly out of place in the classroom, but my colleague Paul Darvasi (2021) has clearly demonstrated how valuable and rich this game proves in an English classroom. The game allows for vibrant discussions of race, gender, urban life, inequality, and more. The game would be an asset in sociology, especially urban sociology, gender studies, cultural studies, social studies, feminist studies, and social psychology. In other words, both applied games and applying games, from the most evidence-based game to the most casual, dentist's office time killer are invaluable resources for contributing to a dynamic, interactive learning environment that motivates all students and connects their lived experience outside of school with their formal learning inside of school.

## CRITICAL THINKING AND CULTURAL AWARENESS

Operationalizing games cannot be conducted according to a formula. You don't just apply game A to class B lesson B1 and expect success. Like all other art forms—literature, film, music, games require context, and that context includes the social context or learning ecosystem for using the game. Critical thinking demands this contextualization for genuinely deep and enduring leaning to occur. Successful use of games in the classroom depends in large measure on effective teaching. However, when I discuss games those games are discussed, for the most part, in a larger social-cultural context where they can impact student learning in a significant way. A lesson idea or ideas follow each chapter along with substantial resources pertaining to that chapter's topic. Additionally, every chapter has a list of the game(s) and other primary texts discussed in the chapter with their respective publishers and dates.

## THE NECESSITY OF CRITICAL THINKING FOR A DEMOCRATIC SOCIETY

Critical thinking eludes any simple definition, but as a competency, critical thinking crosses every discipline. You cannot be a successful biologist, chemist, mathematician, sociologist, businesswoman, etc., without practicing critical thinking. Likewise, critical thinking proves essential to living a well-balanced life. Students need to learn how to read food labels for proper nutrition, medication labels for potentially danger-ous side effects, and fine print for privacy and contractual reasons. They must think critically to be effective citizens and support genuine democratic forms of government, which means, voting for candidates based upon the candidate's voting record and integrity, not their expen-sive and meaningless campaign speeches and advertisements. Students must trust science and evidence while being aware evidence grows and changes over time as does the state of science, but that science will always be superior to opinion and Monday morning quarterbacking. If the quarterback knew his pass would be intercepted, naturally he would not have thrown it, but not one of us humans can predict the future with total certainty. As Mallarmé wrote, "Un coup de dés jamais n'abolira le hasard"/a throw of the dice never abolishes chance.[2] Games involve chance, a degree of randomness. Like life, uncertainty is fundamental, but good decision making based upon sound evidence is much better than a flip of the coin as a guide to life.

Today the need for critical thinking is urgent. Students live in a social media saturated world filled with misinformation. Social media, and much of the Internet, lack formal gatekeeping, so often ridiculous, at times delu-sional ideas, float around masquerading as research-based evidence. Can students distinguish a news entertainer, like Sean Hannity, from a cred-ible journalist, like Bob Woodward of *The Washington Post*? Even elected, national political leaders make statements that can only be construed as uninformed and dangerous.[3] Ignorance may be a state we all inhabit at different points in our journey, but responsible people do not accept igno-rance as an excuse. We have an obligation to teach our students the impor-tance of learning, of searching out information, of thinking critically, and turning our ignorance into a quest for knowledge—whether about the ingredients of the food we eat or why e-cigarettes are potentially ruinous to one physical health.

This book argues for the transformative power of games as a tool that supports critical thinking, which in turn, with deference to Socrates, who thought more deeply than any of us, promotes a life based on the pursuit of wisdom.[4] If education is anything of value, education should be the pursuit of wisdom, a ladder to knowledge, not a trampoline to a big house and luxury car far away from the suffering of others less fortunate than many of us.

## A NOTE ON MAKING GAMES

This book focuses on the use of games for learning learning, including having students make games. The popularity of *Minecraft* shows how student creativity and world building can transform learning in powerful ways. The maker culture (Niemeyer and Gerber, 2015) of today's youth thrives through creative action, whether making comics, games, clothes, music, Tik Tok videos, or many other products. Likewise, faculty can make their own games as well. Today's authoring and game-making tools allow for non-programmers to design fully versatile and dynamic games. For instance, I developed a pilot online program across diverse disciplines ranging from nutrition and history to nuclear technology and public administration. In the history class on World War I, the professor used Muzzy Lane Author, a tool from Muzzy Lane Software, who specialize in higher education games, to create a series of historical role-playing games. There are a few chapters in my book listed below (Seelow, 2021) by contributors who describe the power of student game making, and I urge all readers to explore this pathway. Also, a few of the game-making tools are listed under the resources section below.

## THE BOOK'S DIVISIONS

The book divides into four relatively equal divisions. The chapters are grouped for the reader's convenience and overlap between chapters and divisions can be expected. Some chapters are quite long, some very brief, the content drives the chapter and nothing else. The book has an organic structure just like a well-made game. Part I, "Games as Transformative Classroom Experiences," stresses the primacy of intrinsic motivation, personalized learning, the strength of storytelling, and the social and political power of games to transform students, classes, communities, and, to an extent, nations. No, I do not think games will change or save the world, but I do argue games can help make us better informed, more active, and responsible citizens of the world, and more empathetic of others with a sense of gratitude that we have the very opportunity to do better.

In Part II, "Games as Transformative Experiences for Community and Culture," I focus on how specific groups of games contribute to personal transformation through their cultivation of positive character traits and encouraging the freedom to explore one's identity. Additionally, I show how games can promote community building and cultural understanding.

Part III, "Casual Games as Transformative Online Learning Experiences," puts emphasis on virtual learning. COVID-19 forced nearly all educators and students to move classes online. For a connected world, where the web has a pervasive impact on many of our lives, online and blended learning must be far more effective than the dull pre-packaged Learning Management System delivered courses of today are. Sorry, but I will take a Ferrari for my learning not a Ford. No disrespect to Ford, but assembly lines do not serve students well. Many of the games that I discuss in this section are inexpensive or free, easily played on mobile devices, and therefore ideal for learning 24/7. Often the games can be effective from elementary school all the way through higher education. In addition to games for academic skills, I talk about games for the "real world," meaning outside the classroom and following graduation. Moreover, I stress the value of games for self-improvement. Total self-mastery is impossible, but we can always improve.

Lastly, the final part "Playing across Boundaries: Interdisciplinary Instruction with Film, Games, and Literature" echoes President Reagan's imperative to the Soviet Union in demolishing the Berlin Wall.[5] The continued isolation of disciplines diminishes learning in every possible way. Interdisciplinary instruction must be made central to formal education, or we will never solve the major problems facing the global community. COVID-19 and its variants cross all boundaries. Trying to defeat this epidemic simply through science will not be sufficient. We need bipartisan policy, behavior change, effective communication, social support, international cooperation, private-public partnerships, and so on. I do not attempt to solve such monumental problems, but I show how interdisciplinary approaches to teaching about pandemics, wars, and human diversity are the right method for attempting to solve our most urgent problems.

Finally, I think of Muhammad Ali, hand trembling from Parkinson's disease, lighting the cauldron at the 1996 Summer Olympics in Atlanta, Georgia, and I think how inspiring games can be.

So, Let the Games Begin.

## NOTES

1. Dr. Adam Gazzaley and his colleagues at the University of California, San Francisco, have been at the forefront of using games and neuroscience to explore possible treatments for cognitive disorders. In addition, to *NeuroRacer* and cognitive decline among the elderly, in Project Evo they have

studied attention deficit disorder, and Sensory Neurodevelopment & Autism. *Endeavor Rx* is an actual video game app approved by the FDA for the treatment of ADHD. These are examples of designed games in the health field.

2. Mallarmé's approximately 20-page poem was published in 1897, just before his death. The lyric remains one of the most inventive, complex pieces of poetry ever written. Its use of the printed page resembles a comic book/ graphic novel, and the poet plays with typeface, layout, and even the linearity of reading in a way that anticipates current visual storytelling, but with a depth that has no bottom. The notion that randomness or chance plays a foundational role in human experience strikes me as central to game design as well as central to how we think about ourselves within a system we can never master. An entire, exhilarating book has been written just about this poem, see *One Toss of the Dice: The Incredible Story of How a Poem Made Us Modern* by R. Howard Bloch, Liveright, 2016. Top of Form.

3. The entire experience of COVID-19 has demonstrated both great and deplorable leadership in the country. Tragically, several prominent politicians such as the governor of Florida have made incomprehensible statements. Although citizens may have a right not to wear a mask, they do not have a right to defy public health policy. Individual rights do not supersede the rights of the community and when you make a choice that harms another citizen you are acting not only in violation of mandates, but in an irresponsible fashion. A politician that promotes irresponsible action and jeopardizes the health of children certainly requires scrutiny. Critical thinking will enable citizens to act as informed people not uninformed people risking the public's health. An example of what can only be called dumb is Senator Rand Paul from Kentucky arguing with Dr. Anthony Fauci over medical research on July 20, 2021. If one practices critical thinking, we can take issue with an expert, but only using evidence supported by credible research and other experts. We cannot dispel medical science in favor of political opinion proffered by individuals with absolutely no training in either science or medicine.

4. Socrates' justly famous statement, "the unexamined life is not worth living," appears in Plato's *Apology* (38a). The statement has tremendous complexity, but ultimately suggests truth as the value driving Socartes's life even at the very trial that sentenced him to death. Philosophy is "love of wisdom" and that should to a primary purpose of education. If there is an ideal historical exemplar of critical thinking, that would be Socrates.

5. President Reagan made his famous speech with the imperative, "Mr. Gorbachev, tear down this wall!" at the Brandenburg Gate in Berlin on June 12, 1987.

## LESSON IDEA

Critical thinking can be easily assessed on the fly by asking some very basic questions about a topic. Student responses will inevitably expose a number of preconceived ideas, many generated from media reports that distort information. For example, I start the semester with questions like, "What do you think is the average age of a gamer?" or "What percentage of gamers is male and what percentage is female?" You can write down the range of responses on the board and then show the latest "Essential Facts" report from the Entertainment Software Association. Students are typically very surprised that the average age of gamers is over 30. You can then take this essential fact and explore with the class what this fact suggests about our perceptions, our culture, the game industry, and so forth.

## GAMES

*Assassins Creed* (franchise/series)

> Developed and published by Ubisoft Montréal, 2007_____.
>
> Historical fiction, open-world action adventure.

*Bejeweled* (franchise/series)

> Designed and published by PopCap Games, 2001.
>
> A classic match three game that benefits cognitive skills like pattern recognition.

*Civilization* (franchise/series)

> Developed by: MicroProse, Activison, Firaxis Games. Published by: MicroProse, Activision, Hasbro Interactive, Infogrames, 2K Games. Created by Sid Meir. 1990_____.
>
> A franchise of civilization building games based on a pioneering 4X model: Explore, Expand, Exploit, Exterminate.

*Dragon Box Algebra 5+* (ages 5–8) and *12+* (ages 12–17)

> Designers: Jean-Baptiste Huyuh and Dr. Patrick Marchal, originally from We Want to Know in Norway, now owned by Kahoot DragonBox AS and published by Kahoot DragonBox AS.
>
> Games for teaching Algebra through metaphor and designed by a math teacher based in Norway. Full support is offered for the games.

*Grand Theft Auto* (franchise/series)

> Designed by Rockstar North. Published by Rockstar Games. Original creators: David Jones and Mike Dailly, 1997_____.
>
> Open-world game for mature audiences, senior high school, or college. Ideal for sociology, English, social psychology, urban sociology, race, and gender studies.

*Invite Only VR*

> Yale University College of Medicine play4REAL Lab, 2019.
>
> Vaping prevention game for late middle school and high school students. Research based and supported by a teacher's manual.

*The Landlord's Game*

> Designed by Lizzie Magie, 1904. Self-published.
>
> Board game with a socialist perspective on wealth.

*League of Legends*

> Developed and published by Riot Games, 2009.
>
> A massively popular online team battle game very popular in Esports competition.

*Mission US*

> A series of games sponsored by public media, WNET Thirteen addressing transformational moments in United States history:

*1770: The American Revolution, 1848: The Antebellum Era, 1866: Westward Expansion, 1904 The Immigrant Experience, 1929: The Great Depression,* and *1941 World War II.* Each game has a full curriculum.

### Minecraft

Developed by Mojang Studios. Published by Mojang Studios, Microsoft Studios and SONY Interactive Entertainment, 2009.

A brilliant sandbox game, something like a digital LEGOs. *Minecraft* is a treasure trove for teachers and students. Chapters by Katie Salen (pp. 33–40) and Douglas Kiang (41–51) in my book (Seelow, 2021) describe ways to use Minecraft in education.

### Monopoly

Adapted by Charles Darrow. Published by Parker Brothers and Hasbro, 1935.

Famous pro-capitalist board game.

### NeuroRacer

University of California, San Francisco, under the direction of Dr. Adam Gazzaley, 2013.

A cognitive therapy-based game focusing on cognitive skills in elderly adults.

### Portal 2

Developed and published by Valve, 2011.

A puzzle teleportation game that has proven very effective in teaching physics (see "Teach with Portals" under resources below).

### Scrabble

Famous board game and inspiration for the Facebook game *Words with Friends.*

Published/Manufactured by Mattel and Hasbro. Designer: Alfred Mosher Butts, 1938.

*That Dragon Cancer*

Developed and published by Numinous Games. Designer: Ryan Green, 2016.

An empathy, storytelling game about Ryan and Amy Green's experience raising their son Joel, who was stricken with terminal cancer and passed away at age 5.

## RESOURCES

Select Websites/Organizations/Curricula

*Able Gamers*—https://ablegamers.org/

The able gamers charity promotes inclusivity in the game industry and community. They are strong advocates for people with disabilities and stress the necessity of designing games for accessibility and the use of adaptive technology.

*Connected Learning Alliance*—https://clalliance.org/about-connected-learning/

Connected learning stresses the importance of connecting youths' personal interests with partners, and real-world experience, in a supportive and guided fashion, using digital technology. The alliance's network has an extraordinarily rich membership. Connected Learning Lab, directed by Professor Mimi Ito, is based at the University of California, Irvine, and sponsors a Connected Learning Summit every year in addition to Connected Learning Camps. The alliance also publishes many valuable reports and research related to youth, learning, and technology.

*Entertainment Software Association*—https://www.theesa.com/

ESA is the primary organization for promoting and supporting the computer and video game industry. Among many of their projects are the video game ratings system and essential facts about the industry. This site would be a key place for finding up-to-date statistics and facts about video games.

*Entertainment Technology Center Press*—https://press.etc.cmu.edu/

Based at Carnegie Mellon University's Entertainment Technology Center, ETC Press features many games-related publications. Founded by Dr. Drew Davidson, the press publishes open access, digital first work, which means you can download for free digital versions of all the outstanding work published by the press.

*Filament Games*—www.filamentgames.com

One of the premiere educational game companies, based in Madison, Wisconsin, Filament Games has a full support plan for implementing their excellent games, including: Warm Up, Pre-game Activities, Exploration, Pause and Think, Labs, and Hands-on games.

*Game Developers of Color*—https://www.gamedevsofcolorexpo.com/

A recently formed organization for promoting diversity in the game industry. They hold an annual conference in September that showcases the excellent work of designers of color.

*Games for Change*—https://www.gamesforchange.org/

Since 2004, Games for Change (G4C) has been a leading force in the support of using games to promote positive social change, deep learning, healthy behaviors, civics education, and STEM skills. The organization empowers youth, contributes to the use of progressive technology to create games, and holds a sensational summer festival in New York City. The current president Susanna Pollack keeps the organization at the forefront of social change and justice.

*iCivics*—www.icivics.org/games

This exceptional site supports the many short icivics games and the teaching of civics. The organization was founded by Supreme Court

Justice Sandra Day O'Connor in 2009. There are links to all the games, lesson plans, and excellent curriculum units on all aspects of civics and the three branches of government.

*International Game Developers Association (IGDA)*—https://igda.org/

An important organization dedicated to game developers across the globe. The local chapters are a terrific resource for teachers and students who want to learn more about games. They will often provide speakers to visit schools and run workshops for students.

*International Society of Technology in Education (ISTE)*—https://www.iste.org/

The largest K-12 educational technology organization has many publications, events, and professional development opportunities. They also publish educational technology standards for using technology that is equitable, sustainable, and scalable. The current president, Richard Culatta, has been a major advocate for games-based education for many years.

*iThrive Games*—https://ithrivegames.org/

An organization dedicated to helping teens thrive through games and gameful experiences that promote social-emotional health and deep learning. Led by social psychologist Dr. Susan Rivers, iThrive offers a wealth of resources including original games, game guides, curriculum support, learning tools, and research.

*Mission US Teach*—www.mission-us.org/teach

The site offers Mission Guides for each of their history games. The guides include Classroom Activities, an Overview, Classroom Videos, Historical Background, Primary Sources & Resources.

*Neuroscape Center*—https://neuroscape.ucsf.edu/

Dr. Adam Gazzaley's center at University of California, San Francisco, where you can learn the latest about neuroscience and games as they related to various cognitive issues.

*Penny Arcade Expos (Pax)*—https://www.paxsite.com/

Like Games for Change, Penny Arcade Expos started in 2004 and have expanded to a few regional sites and Melbourne, Australia. Evolving out of a web comic, the various Pax conferences are game-focused cultural events and well worth attending.

*The Serious Play Conference*—www.seriousplayconf.com

Founded by Sue Bohle, this conference stands out among the many annual conferences on games and play for its range of offerings, workshops, and professional development opportunities.

*Short Sims*—https://www.shortsims.com/

An eLearning pedagogy developed by Clark Aldrich with whom I have worked several times. Clark is the country's leading expert on learning by doing and a pioneer in serious games and simulations. Short Sims can be made using a variety of tools like PowerPoint, BranchTrack, and others. They are highly effective, interactive scenario-based simulations for any learning situation, and ideal for online and blended learning. Clark also published a book on *Short Sims: A Game Changer* in 2020 with CRS Press.

*Teach with Portals*—https://developer.valvesoftware.com/wiki/Teach_with_Portals

A community of educators centered around the use of the Portal games for teaching physics, problem solving, and critical thinking.

*Tech with Kids*—http://www.techwithkids.com/

If you work with younger kids—pre-school and early elementary age, this site has expert reviews of video games and technology apps that empower parents, grandparents, and teachers of the very young to make smart decisions about kids' technology use.

*Yale Center for Health and Learning*

Led by Lynn E. Fiellen, MD, a specialist in public health, general medicine, internal medicine, and much more, the Yale Center features the play2PREVENT Lab and the 4REAL Lab (VR) as well as For A Girl program. The games are evidence based and further ongoing research in games for health.

## Select Game Maker Software

I only mention a handful of game-making resources because this is not the book's focus, but I urge faculty to explore these tools for themselves and their students. The two best software programs for making games are Unity and Unreal Engine. Both these programs can be used to make highly sophisticated 3-D games, and they are used by professionals, but the high learning curve makes them primarily beneficial for faculty with significant time to invest in the game-making process. All programs listed here have extensive tutorials that you should avail yourself of. I also recommend taking workshops whenever possible. A basic knowledge of programming is always helpful in using game-making software. Learning JavaScript, HTML 5, and C# are especially helpful to know or be familiar with.

### *Construct 3*—Scirra

Easy-to-learn visual scripting and development environment for making games in a variety of genres including platformer games, puzzle games, and shooters. A great tool for HTML5 games.

### *Dreams*—Media Molecule

Winner of the 2020 Games for Change best game award, this game is actually a game creation tool that allows players to make and share games and user-generated content. It is marvelously creative, but currently restricted to SONY PlayStation.

### *Game Maker Studio 2*—YoYo Games

A highly proficient relatively easy-to-learn development environment for making games capable of playing on multiple platforms. Different subscription tiers allow for different levels of support and creative possibility.

### *Inklewriter*—Inkle Studios

A U.K.-based program for writing interactive fiction. This is very easy to learn and an effective tool for students. A chapter in my book by

Hap Asiz and Joy Baker (Seelow, 2021, pp. 92–103) describes how students can create historical based text adventures to gain a better understanding of history.

## *Muzzy Lane Author*—Muzzy Lane Software

I have worked closely with this excellent Massachusetts-based company. Author allows for collaborative authoring and creating rich simulations. The tool has excellent support for analytics and assessment.

## *Roblox*—Roblox Corporation

An online game platform especially popular with elementary and middle school students for making and sharing games and interactive experiences. Roblox is now an entire community and culture that allows for socialization. Beware of microtransactions and the purchasing of items.

## *RPG Maker/ RPG Maker MZ*—ASC II and others

A Japanese toolkit for making role-playing games and visual novels. Support for JavaScript allows for more complex games.

## *StarLogo Nova*—MIT Game Lab

This program uses blocks-based programming to construct games and simulations. It is especially useful for creating simulations to explain complex concepts in science and mathematics.

## *Twine*—Chris Klimas

Free open source tool for writing nonlinear interactive fiction. You publish stories to HTML. The tool also allows for CSS and JavaScript if you desire more advanced functionality. The excellent game *Depression Quest* was made with Twine.

## Books

Burack, Asi and Parker, Laura. *Power Play: How Video Games Can Save the World*. St. Martin's Press, 2017.

A book from a founder of Games for Change. Chapters address key games in the games for change movement including crowdsourcing games. An excellent introduction to the power of games for change and how these games are developed and deployed.

Cassie, Jonathan. *Level Up Your Classroom: The Quest to Gamify Your Lessons and Engage Your Students.* ASCD, 2016.

An excellent guide to using gamification strategies in the classroom stressing the common principles of risk-taking, experimentation, community building, positivity, and meaningful choices. The Association of Supervision and Curriculum Development (ASCD) also has a helpful study guide for faculty using the book.

Faber, Mathew. *Gaming SEL: Games as Transformational to Social and Emotional Learning.* Peter Lang: 2021.

A terrific practitioner of game-based learning Matt Faber's book shows how games can help teach the invaluable social and emotional competencies necessary for student success inside and outside the classroom. The book is full of practical ideas.

Gee, James Paul. *What Video Games Have to Teach Us About Learning and Literacy.* Palgrave Macmillan, 2003.

The classic book that launched the serious application of games to learning. This is an indispensable starting point for those interested in games for learning.

McGonigal, Jane. *Reality is Broken. Why Games Make Us Better and How They Can Change the World.* Penguin Books, 2011.

A pioneering book by futurist and game designer Jane McGonigal, this book shows how the principles behind successful mega games can be harnessed to improve both ourselves and the world we live in. She focuses on Massively Multiplayer Online Role Playing Games (MMORG) and Alternate Reality Games (ARG).

Portnoy, Lindsay. *Game On? Brain On! The Surprising Relationship Between Play and Gray (Matter).* Dave Burgess Consulting, Inc., 2020.

Dr. Portnoy's fascinating and practical book applies cognitive science to games and shows how play makes for deep and enduring learning. Dr. Portnoy is also a co-founder of the game design studio Killer Snails which designs excellent STEM-based games supported by cognitive science and research.

Schrier, Karen (Kat). *100 Games to Use in the Classroom & Beyond.* Learning, Education & Games, Volume 3. ETC Press, 2019.

Each chapter in this eminently practical book applies a particular game to different learning situations.

_____. *We the Gamers: How Games Teach Ethics and Civics.* Oxford University Press, 2021.

An excellent well-balanced and practical book on how games teach ethics, critical thinking, and inquiry to improve civics education and more.

Seelow, David. Editor. *Teaching in the Game-Based Classroom; Practical Strategies for Grades 6–12. Routledge,* Eye on Education series, 2021.

My edited collection includes chapters on all aspects of game-based learning from setting up a gameful classroom and using Minecraft to empower youth to learning about cells through virtual reality and conducting playful assessments.

Sheldon, Lee. *The Multiplayer Classroom: Designing Coursework as a Game,* 2nd Edition. CRC Press, 2020.

A pioneering book by game designer and author Lee Sheldon gives level-by-level guidelines as well as case studies for turning your class into a game where all student-players are winners.

Squire, Kurt. *Video Games and Learning: Teaching and Participatory Culture in the Digital Age.* Teacher's College Press, 2011.

An important early book on the value of games in the classroom and after-school programs with extensive discussion of Sid Meir's *Civilization.*

Toppo, Greg. *The Game Believes in You: How Digital Play Can Make Our Kids Smarter.* St. Martin's Press, 2015.

President of the Education Writers Association Board of Directors Greg Toppo's book describes how pioneering teachers are using games as game changers in K-12 education.

# I

## Games as Transformative
## Classroom Experiences

# CHAPTER 1

# My Favorite Game

## *The Power of Personal Learning*

O VER THE LAST TWO decades, no lesson has served me better than my adaptation of Robert Pinsky's "My Favorite Poem Project."[1] Pinsky launched the project while serving as the country's Poet Laureate. People from all over the United States, diverse in age, race, ethnicity, gender, and class, named their favorite poem and read that poem aloud in addition to explaining why the particular poem they chose made such an impression on them. The people were recorded, and the videotape was placed on the project's website. Most people do not read poetry once they leave formal schooling and yet each person had a moving story to tell about their favorite poem and its impact on them. Why not? Across culture and time, poetry has represented the most richly textured, emotionally resonant, and spiritually transcendent (think of the Biblical Psalms or *Rg Veda*) use of language possible.

Around 8 years ago, the college where I was working held their own "My Favorite Poem" event at a local community arts center. Employees ranging from admissions counselors to senior vice presidents introduced and read their favorite poems from the stage to the college audience. The event boosted college morale and proved to be an immensely positive experience. Each reader's story added value to the poem just as the poem added value to the reader's life.

DOI: 10.1201/9781003201465-3

My experience with this project impressed me so much that when I started teaching a fully online course called "Secrets: A Cyberculture Mystery Game," I adopted the "My Favorite Poem" activity for the unit on games. Students were asked to name their favorite game and explain why the game they identified was their favorite. This was an online course, so students shared their games via the Learning Management System's Discussion Board. The course served an adult student body ranging in age from their mid-twenties to late fifties. Most of the enrolled students self-identified as gamers. This activity helped unify a geographically diverse group and genuinely contributed to forming an online learning community.

## THE ONLINE CLASS: NONTRADITIONAL STUDENTS' FAVORITE GAME

The discussion board prompt read as follows:

> Identify any game you have played as an adult: video, console, mobile, card, athletic, role playing, board etc. Briefly describe the purpose and rules of the game to your peers. Explain why you play this game and what the game contributes to your sense of well-being then reflect on two of your peers' games. Have you played them? Would you like to play them? Why or why not?

One expected pleasure a game provides is an escape, but escape means more than just drifting off into another world. In talking about *The Sims* (Entertainment Arts), a student talks about how she "would play this game because it was *fun to create a world* and characters of my choosing." In other words, the game offered not just escape from the world, but world building as an imaginative activity akin to writing a novel or play. This world building "contributed to my sense of well-being." Fantasy, fun, and satire offer another type of escape, which a student describes in playing the *Stick of Truth* (South Park Studios). "It is a role-play based fantasy war involving humans, wizards, and elves, all who want to possess the Stick of Truth. It is further complicated by aliens, Nazi zombies, and gnomes." Most important to this seasoned veteran, but novice game player, was the game "makes me laugh."

Several students, including those on active military duty, talked about how games created community, and kept them connected with friends and family when living apart or on deployment. "I enjoy playing this game [*Rainbow Siege Six* (Ubisoft)] because it is thrilling, and I like playing video games with my brothers. *We all live far apart, so playing games on the Xbox is what keeps us connected.*" This student also stressed how the game [a competitively played game] "requires a great amount of teamwork." Similarly, in *Clash of Clans* (Supercell),

> You also become a clan with other players and work together to defeat other clans. I like this game because I can create my base however I want. I can work with others to conduct attacks. *Also, I have friends from all over the world in my clan. And I'm not talking friends that I met online but my actual friends from playing the game.*

The most surprising game named to me turned out to be a student's love of *Friday the 13th* (III Fonic).

> *I play this game because of the social aspect of it.* If you are near another counselor, you can talk to them but if they are across the map, you must get lucky and find a radio to be able to talk to them. This game also has a true fear factor to it. You will be alone in the woods and then suddenly Jason will appear, and you must survive.

What an intriguing way to learn survival skills, battling Jason Vorhees, a one-man army of the night!

Another student, a lifelong gamer from the old Atari 2600 days, talked about "*the visceral nature of the storytelling* [which] forces me back for another playthrough," in the game *Fallout: New Vegas* (Obsidian Entertainment).

Let me conclude this section by quoting a handful of students' extended comments about their favorite game.

> I like to play a mobile game called *Plague, Inc.* You are playing as some disease (bacteria, virus, prion, fungus, etc.) and the purpose is to infect and ultimately kill everyone in the world before a cure is developed and distributed. I enjoy playing this game as some of the levels are challenging, i.e., to to completely kill everyone before there is a cure. Also, sometimes it's fun to have control over how things are going especially when real life seems so unpredictable and uncontrollable. I get some perverse pleasure when I complete a level and I know I just killed everyone in the world.
>
> I play this game as a kind of release of pent up frustrations and when I feel helpless in a situation. Being a military family can be

challenging and there are many times where what happens in our lives are based on the needs of the military; even then things can change 500 times before anything happens. It can be extremely frustrating to live that way, so I like to play games which let me be in complete control.

*Leanna*

One of the games I have played as an adult is *Chess*. *Chess* is mainly a board gamse, but it can also be played [over] the internet. ... I play *Chess* because it improves my critical thinking skills. ... It [playing chess] means that my thinking and ability to come up with solutions quickly is improved.

*Caroline*

As I [have] got[ten] older, I don't play as many games as I used to. ...So, I will go ahead and reflect on a recent board game I played with a few of my peers called *Secret Hitler*. I know the title itself says a lot, but it honestly was a fun and amusing game if you have people who truly get into it. The game is made up of two groups, one being fascists and the other being liberals. You get thrown into groups when a card is handed to you. You don't know who is a liberal or fascist and the point of the game is to pass enough liberal laws before the fascists pass fascist laws. There is one player who is Hitler, and no one knows who [Hitler] is, not even the other fascists. The other fascists figure out who each other are when the whole group closes their eyes and only fascists keep [their eyes] open. I think this game is fun because you get to see how good of a liar people can be or how easily you can deceive someone and how people turn against each other when it comes to [wanting to] win the game.

*Stephanie*

I have played *World of Warcraft* (WOW) on and off for over a decade. It is a massively multiplayer online role playing game (MMORPG). The purpose of the game is to provide a social environment, a virtual kingdom, where players play together. Warcrafters can join guilds and engage in epic battles to overcome various challenges. Players, such as I, can play against others in competitive player versus player (PVP) game modes.

There are many reasons why I play this MMORPG. First and foremost; my friends are playing it. I have made new friends and met countless new people along the road as well. The feeling when we overcome challenges in the game contributed to some of my fondest memories. The game's incredible complexity is also one of the aspects of *WOW* that attracted me. As an example, I had 38 key binds to control my character.

The game's vast open world where you can go anywhere is mesmerizing. The feeling of playing against skilled opponents could only be comparable to some of my athletic competitions. Winning feels just as exhilarating in this virtual world as in the real world.

Overall, I can only recommend *WOW*. Be aware though, it will pull you in, and you will have a tough time doing homework instead of playing.

*Gabor*

Strategy, concentration, decision making, teamwork, friendship, world building, and laughter are key reasons nontraditional students play games.

## THE TRADITION CLASSROOM: YOUTHFUL COLLEGE STUDENTS' FAVORITE GAMES

Three years after teaching the online course to adult students, I taught a nearly identical course called "Cyberculture and Identity" to traditional age college students (18–23) in a traditional brick-and-mortar classroom. Unlike the earlier class, this course was not listed as a game-based course. Consequently, only one of the 18 enrolled students self-identified as a gamer.

As before, in the unit on games, I asked these younger students to report to the class about their favorite game. The results, along with the students' major, class year, reason for playing the game, and where they typically play or played the game are listed in Table 1.1. This information provides a small window into the world of largely non-gamer students and the games they play. Such snapshots can help educators think about some of the mechanics that might engage students born and immersed in our digital, touch screen culture.

Eight of the 18 total students agreed to use their names and provide feedback (I have eliminated last names for privacy reasons). Interestingly,

TABLE 1.1  Undergraduate Students' Favorite Games

| Student | Year of Study | Major | Favorite Game | Where I Play the Game | Reason for Continued Play |
|---|---|---|---|---|---|
| Bianca | Junior Psychology | Communications | Spot It | Dorm Room | Fun, Fast Paced, Stimulates my brain |
| Patricia | Sophomore | | Kings Corner | With Family | Brings my family together, requires strategy and focus |
| Caitlyn | Biology | Junior | Tiny Zoo | Everywhere on iPhone | Entertaining and an alternative to social media |
| Conor | Business Management | Senior | PlayerUnknown's Battlegrounds | Personal Room | Enjoy survival games, easy to play |
| Nicholas | Criminal Justice | Junior | *Dark Souls III* | Every other day on Play Station 4 | A fun and challenging RPG; allows extensive customization of your character; increasing difficulty as you progress through levels |
| Alexandra | Forensic Psychology | Junior | The Sims | All the time on iPhone and tablet | Allows for designing and creativity; mimics life |
| Justin | Political Science | Junior | Super Mario Odyssey | In room on weekends | The thrill of adventure |
| Jessica | Medical Technology | Senior | Uno | Dining Room during vacations or college breaks | Great family activity |

of these eight only one can be considered a gamer, Nick, a junior Criminal Justice major. Consequently, that Nick identified *Dead Souls III* as his current favorite video game comes as no surprise. The *Dead Souls* video games are highly immersive, big-budget action role-playing games that require skill, strategy, and hours of game play to play well. What Nick's response tells me is that players value customization, which translates to personalization in learning situations. Additionally, players of immersive games like continual, progressively more difficult challenges.

Three of the seven non-gamers favorited card games. I think this speaks to the continued value of board or tabletop games even in a digital world. *Uno*, of course, is one of the world's best-known games. It is inexpensive, portable, and easy to play for ages 6 and up. In a world of mobile game play, keep in mind, card games are also portable, and can be played almost anywhere, by two or more people. The basic game play deals players seven color-coded cards. The players' objective is to match colors, symbols, and numbers of their cards with cards in the discard pile. The first player to discard all his or her cards and yell Uno wins the round, but with a catch. The person must remember to call Uno when he or she has one card remaining. A player wins the game by accumulating 500 points. Points are earned by counting the card values of each losing player in any given round. What really makes *Uno* fun in addition to the fast pace are the action cards like skip, reverse, and draw 4. These cards introduce the surprise element which can bring about an immediate change in a player's fortune. That helps keep all players engaged. Think about how you can bring about a reversal of fortune for your struggling students. *Uno* now has a special *UNO*—Susan G. Komen® Special Edition that donates proceeds to fight breast cancer. That is another noble reason for playing games (Figure 1.1).

*Kings' Corner* is another easy-to-play card game that uses regular playing cards. Using a standard 52 card deck, each player is dealt 7 cards. Four cards are placed around the center deck forming a square. Each player draws a card in turn and attempts to place the card under one of the four existing columns by maintaining consecutive numbers/values. If the top card of a column is 10, the next card in that column must be a 9. If the top card is a 4, you must place a 3 underneath and so on. Drawing a King changes the entire game play. The King is placed in a corner, hence the game's name, and you build out from that corner with a Queen and so on. However, you can move cards from existing columns under the King

FIGURE 1.1   Uno card types. (Public domain.)

which then opens a clear space to begin a fresh column. As with *Uno*, the first player to discard all cards wins (Figure 1.2).

The final card game, *Spot It*, offers quick and easy game play that focuses on pattern recognition. The game is a great learning tool in early elementary grades. In *Spot It*, players are dealt a round card with pictures on it. The goal is to match your existing card with a card drawn from the deck that has a picture that matches a picture from your card. Just like yelling Uno, you must yell Spot It as you grab the matching card. Two things appeal to me about this simple game. First, you can mod the game just like you would mod a video game by inventing your own version of the game or playing the game in variant ways. For instance, instead of the objective being to score as many cards as you can, reverse the objective so that the person who discards all cards wins. Second, you can purchase different versions of the game. You can buy special editions of *Spot It* like Major League Baseball where the cards include pictures relating to America's pastime. This does not add anything to the play but appeals to different audiences and checks for knowledge about the sport.

Although designed for elementary school kids, the mechanic translates to any subject. You could match plays and playwrights, inventors and

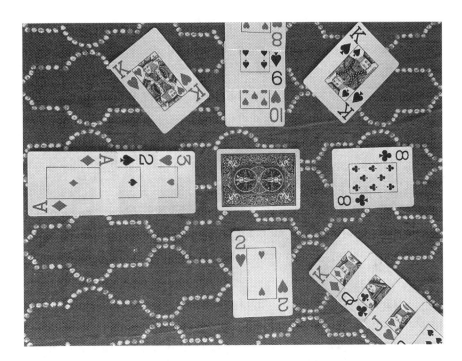

FIGURE 1.2    Kings corner. (Photograph by Beth Tedford © used with permission.)

inventions, or whatever matching option your discipline calls for. Finally, as both Jessica and Patricia mention, these card games bring family members together. In a world where so many family members are glued to screens, card games require face-to-face play and conversation!

*Tiny Zoo*, the only digital game played by Caitlyn, a member of the college's soccer team, is a solitary game. Caitlyn plays as an alternative to using social media. A nurturing game in the tradition of Facebook games like *Farmville*, playing *Tiny Zoo*, tells me students can learn and develop empathy through such simple games. Additionally, in a world where boredom seems intolerable, young people can play for fun, and disengage the gossipy, at times, destructive and obsessive practices of social media.

The best-known games mentioned, *The Sims*, designed by the great Will Wright, a simulation game, and *Super Mario Odyssey*, a game that echoes the early arcade games and traces its lineage to the early 1980s, have components that make the games appealing both to avid gamers as well as casual gamers like Alexandra and Justin. Originally, Wright designed *The Sims* as an open-ended, sandbox-type game with similarity to a virtual doll house. *The Sims*, in a sense, preserves that doll house play style with players interacting with the characters they design, dressing them the way, a child might dress and play "make believe" with a doll. What the enormous success of *The Sims* suggests to me is exactly what Alex points out, *The Sims* encourages and thrives on the player's creativity. This translates into an educational practice whereby students should be given much more room to explore in their classes. Teachers might consider the benefit of less emphasis on prescribed curriculum, or, at least, provide opportunities within a course for a student's personal expression and his or her original voice to emerge. Traditional exams and research papers do not always allow such voices to emerge on the undergraduate or lower level.

As a recent incarnation of the Mario Brothers franchise, *Super Mario Odyssey* (the Odyssey is Mario's hat-shaped steam punk style ship), designed by Futoshi Shirai and Shinya Hiratake, takes advantage of Nintendo's innovative new platform Switch. This console allows players both a stationary, arcade-like experience and the flexibility of mobile gaming (perfect for college students moving between dorm rooms and dining halls). In this game, Mario has a new ally—Cappy—yes a hat or cap, as he travels across various kingdoms including the beautifully realized New Dong City in the Metro Kingdom to save Princess Peach from her evil abductor Bowser. As Justin says, and many others would concur, he plays *Super Mario Odyssey* for the "thrill of adventure," and few games have provided more entertaining adventure than the Mario franchise (the character Mario first appeared way back in 1981's classic *Donkey Kong*). Like with the Sims franchise, this *Super Mario Odyssey* game allows players first and foremost the freedom to explore.

Finally, Conor's choice *PlayerUnknown's Battlegrounds* was a tad surprising to me. It is an immersive shooter-style game popular with many young males. However, the assumption only avid or hard-core gamers play shooters is doubly false. Conor is not an avid gamer but plays this shooter often. Females also play such "violent" games. In fact, although Jessica selected *Uno* as her favorite game, she also often plays *Call of Duty*. *PlayerUnknown's Battlegrounds* is a twist on First-Person Shooters (FPS), combining shooting with survival-type game play. Up to 100 players parachute onto an island, search for guns and weapons with the objective of being the last man or woman standing. It is a kind of video game dodgeball with simulated bullets. The actual game traces its roots to a weird Japanese cult-type film *Battle Royale* (2000) directed by Kinji Fukasaku, that in turn, adopts a lesser-known 1999 novel by Koushuu Takami.

This game designed by modding expert Brendan Greene initiated a genre or subgenre of game called "Battle Royale." This genre now has millions of followers.

## THOUGHTS ON ADAPTING STRATEGIES FROM "MY FAVORITE GAME" TO CLASSROOM LEARNING ACTIVITIES

The main purpose of this opening chapter has been to provide a snapshot into which games a mixture of traditional and nontraditional college students play so that instructors can think about and experiment with new ways to engage students. As students talk about their favorite game, they are speaking about something they are passionate about, which is a key step in tapping intrinsic motivation and capturing interest-driven learning. Once you have harnessed interest-driven learning, you will discover students will write and speak about the topic more effectively. I write much better about poetry than I ever would about chemistry. You also learn about students by eliciting their passions. In terms of students, when they reflect on something they love they are also deepening self-understanding which goes a long way toward success in the classroom. Finally, the principles behind this lesson translate into more general learning principles that can be applied to any classroom. Here are a few concrete lessons you can draw from and apply in your classroom regardless of the discipline.

- Find ways to encourage student creativity and help unlock or tap into the non-analytic side of their brains. This will boost motivation and have a ripple effect across other more traditional academic assignments. In other words, creativity should not be the sole province of arts departments.

- Allow students to explore and discover throughout a course and don't adhere to rigid schedules or inflexible syllabi.

- Provide space for team and group learning.

- Allow for personalization or customization for some assignments since interest-driven learning has more enduring benefits than top-down curricula.

- Board and tabletop games still have value and appeal (see Chapter 3).

- Design lessons for learning in short bursts (especially true for online lessons).

- Use the wild card mechanic of surprise to keep classes lively.

Adapt the ideas discussed in this opening chapter and turn your classroom into your students' favorite class, or if class is already their favorite—probably true—make the class one they cannot wait to start and hope does not end.

## NOTE

1. Robert Pinsky launched the My Favorite Poem Project (http://www. favoritepoem.org/about.html) in 1998 the year after he was named the country's Poet Laureate. During the 1 year call for submission, 18,000 people contributed their favorite poems. This is a wonderful project and website. I always ask students to watch at least three of the videos where citizens read and discuss their favorite poem and the impact the poem has made on them. Students are always moved by the videos. Without exception, this poetry experience has been positive for my students, and I highly recommend the website with its accompanying videos.

## LESSON IDEA

One effective way I use this activity in class is to hold a "My Favorite Game Contest" where students have a set period of time to make two arguments that are evaluated in two different ways. First, they must make the case that their game is the game the rest of the students need to play. You create a rubric to assess how to pitch a game for personal enjoyment and entertainment purposes. All the students would assess the presentation from this perspective. The second challenge would be for the students to also pitch the game as the one the professor should use the next time he or she teaches the course. This is a different slant to the challenge that requires thinking about the value of using their game in a formal classroom. This aspect would be assessed by the professor or teacher. This evaluation would have no impact on any formal grade; the teacher can do that separately based on separate criteria. The winner or winners are awarded a prize organic to the activity such as a gift card to Google Play or the iTunes store. What better game than one where you cannot lose?

## GAMES

*Clash of Clans*

    Strategy: Mobile game.

    Developer and publisher: Supercell, 2012.

*Dark Souls III*

    Action, role playing

    Developer: From Software, Inc. Publisher: Bandai Namco Entertainment. Designers: Shigeto Hirai, Yaya Kimijima, Hiroshi Yoshida, 2016.

*Fallout: New Vegas*

    Post-apocalyptic action role playing

    Developer: Obsidian Entertainment. Publisher: Bethesda, 2009.

*Friday the 13th: The Game*

    Survival horror (inspired by the movie franchise)

    Developer: Ill Fonic with Black Tower Studios. Publisher: Gun Media. Designer: Dan Russet, 2017.

*Kings Corner*

    Card game, solitaire style. 2–6 players, age 7+

    Publisher: Jax Ltd. Developer: Exact origins unknown.

*Plague, Inc.*

    Real Time strategy: Mobile game.

    Developer and Publisher: Ndemic Creations with Miniclip, 2012.

*PlayerUnknown's Battleground*

Multiplayer, Battle Royal

Developer/Publisher: PUBG Corporation. Designer: Brendan Greene, 2017.

*Rainbow Six Siege (Tom Clancy series)*

Multiplayer online First Person Shooter and Strategy.

Developer and publisher: Ubisoft. Designer: Daniel Drapeau, 2015.

*Secret Hitler*

Social deduction board game: 5–10 players (ten best). Mature ages.

Developer: Goat Wolf and Cabbage. Producer: Breaking Games. Distributor: Blackbox. Designers: Max Temkin, Mike Boxleiter, Tommy Maranges. 2016. There is a Trump expansion pact.

*Spot It*

Pattern recognition card game: 2–8 players, ages 7+.

Publisher: Asmodee and many others. Designers: Denis Blanchot, Jacques Cottereau, Guillaume Gilles-Naves, Igor Polounchine.

*The Sims*

Life simulation.

Maxis/ Sims Studios- Published by Electronic Arts (EA). Designer: Will Wright, 2000 and up.

*Stick of Truth* (inspired by the animated television series)

Role playing, satire. Developer: Obsidian Entertainment and South Park Design Studios. Publisher: Ubisoft. Designer: Matt MacLean.

*Super Mario Odyssey*

> Platformer.
>
> Developer and publisher: Nintendo. Designers: Futoshi Shirai and Shinya Hiratake

*Team Fortress 2*

> Multiplayer First Person Shooter (part of a franchise).
>
> Developer and publisher: Valve Corporation, 2007.

*Tiny Zoo*

> Zoo simulation.
>
> Publisher: Swipe Forward, LLC., 2011.

*Uno*

> Card game: 2–10 players. Ages 7+.
>
> Publisher: Mattel. Developer: Merle Robbins, 1971.

*World of Warcraft*

> Massively Multiplayer Online Role-Playing Game
>
> Developed and published by Blizzard Entertainment. Designers: Rob Pardo, Jeff Kaplan, and Tom Chilton, 2004.

# CHAPTER 2

# Ask the Sphinx

*Power Up Student Motivation
with Superpower Challenges*

## INTRINSIC MOTIVATION: FOR THE LOVE OF THE GAME

One of the most impressive and motivating features of role-playing video games is the potential to increase one's abilities or improve one's standing vis-à-vis the game world through everything from health points to better armor. Players, operating through their choice of an avatar or character, can also earn trophies, discover valuable collectibles, inflict damage points on one's opponents, unlock secret locations, and trigger new Boss Battles that catapult one to higher levels of the game. These opportunities can be part of the game's primary narrative line, or they can be side quests. Side quests, which extend game play, have their own intrinsic motivation based on the player's curiosity to explore, discover, and engage new challenges for the thrill of the challenge.

For example, the recently released game *Assassin's Creed Odyssey* can run up to 100 hours of play with various side quests. The game has a plethora of opportunities for the player to earn, unlock, achieve, collect, and otherwise enjoy his or her experience for these many hours of play. *Assassin's Creed* has three large skill trees or sets: hunter, warrior, and assassin. Each class includes numerous skills under its general domain. As an example, a player's general progress through the game could unlock Nikloaos' sword. This sword has a special engraving that adds power to your Sparta Kick ability. In another example, you can discover Atlantis after completing a main quest titled United Front, and then succeeding in a side quest called, "A Family's Legacy." Once you reach Atlantis you can engage one of literature's greatest battles, the game's Boss Battle with the mythic Cyclops.

Riddles are also fun. In *Assassin's Creed: Odyssey*, when players complete a quest called Lore of the Sphinx, they are asked questions in the form of riddles (Figure 2.1).

- At night they come without being fetched and by day they are lost without being stolen." – **Stars**

- What is large, yet never grows; has roots that cannot be seen, and is taller than the trees?" – **Mountain**

The Sphinx serves as a perfect vehicle for almost any class and would provide a great tool for delivering riddles and challenges that empower

FIGURE 2.1 Oedipus and the Sphinx, 1861, Gustave Moreau, Watercolor. (Metropolitan Museum of Art, New York, New York. Public Domain.)

students. The ancient Greeks adopted, transformed, and mythologized the Egyptian monument into a guardian of cities. The story of Oedipus represents the most famous example of the Sphinx. Guarding Thebes, the only way travelers can pass through the gate is to solve the Sphinx's riddle. Failure to provide the correct answer results in the person being devoured. "Which creature has one voice and yet becomes four-footed and two-footed and three-footed?" Oedipus answers correctly, "Man." The myth and drama of Oedipus, simultaneously hero and villain, goes beyond this chapter's purpose, but the idea that a riddle or puzzle proves to be the enigma of our species, shows how powerful puzzle solving can be. In using this mythic trope, of course, you drop the fate of giving the wrong answer, keep the riddle mechanic, and reward the solver of the riddle with a power worthy of the King of Thebes in the small kingdom of the classroom.

Now imagine a class, where students want to go on side quests or extra class activities that extend class time, even double class time, for the love of adventure and exploration, i.e., the love of learning. Well, this wild possibility becomes real when you start thinking of class activities as game quests where students can gather collectibles, earn special weapons, protect from harm, and boost their abilities to succeed. What kind or trophy or collectible you ask? Use your imagination. In my class "Superheroes and the Millennial" an *English 106: Texts and Contexts* class, perfect attendance last term earned free comic books. A minor reward, at $4.99 each, but eight students had perfect attendance (about 45% of the class), when I ordinarily have two. These are not just extrinsic rewards. The small token really reflects students' intrinsic motivation to win at an aspect of the game where there are potentially multiple winners.

## WINNING WITHOUT LOSING: DEFINING A SUPERPOWER CHALLENGE

In terms of superpower challenges, the outcome does not count for students' grades or experience point total. In other words, the challenge is inside the game or class, but also outside because it does not "count" as a traditional quiz would. You can only gain from the challenge, never lose. That is the point. A quiz frequently generates frantic study and memorization, in quest of a high grade, and soon thereafter, the material is forgot and lost. The superpower challenge generates whole class excitement, a winner, and fun. The winner wins, and that student's victory has an immediate and lasting benefit on the student's progress and success in the course (hence the motivation), but no one in the class loses. The fact there are no losers in the traditional sense of a bad grade, liberates the student's enthusiasm to take up the challenge. In each superpower challenge my entire class participates with genuine excitement. They rush, like a pro football team's defensive line, toward me, the quarterback, wherever I am seated, to show me their solutions. When they do not solve the puzzle the first time, they go back to their desk and work on an alternative solution soon returning to me with another proposed solution. Rarely does a student solve the puzzle on the initial effort.

Admittedly, a class on superheroes makes the choice of superpowers a bit easier than other classes might, but instructors simply need to think which powers or skills enable success in his or her discipline. The superpowers are metaphorical. Why not a telescope for an astronomy class that allows the winner to see into distant lands, i.e., this student can get a preview of an exam a week before any other student. In criminal justice, the superpower can be access to a special witness to a crime no one else has, or, perhaps, an informer. This student gets an inside peek at a few upcoming questions that other students do not. The instructor can be creative and his or her creativity also models creative thinking for the class.

I usually offer three superpower challenges and spread them throughout the semester, but this can vary by instructor. An instructor can make the challenge individual or team based. Even in individual challenges I have noticed students often talk and help each other for fun. If the challenge is team based, then all members of the team earn the superpower. Whether or not the instructor allows the use of digital assistants is a personal choice, but I do not. For me, students need to abandon Google and Wikipedia, and use their own brain power the entire time, but that's my preference.

A few game mechanics/rules are critical for the challenges to work, but each mechanic or rule can be modified in a wide variety of ways to fit an instructor's preference. First, the challenge must address course content that has been covered up to the point of the challenge. The challenge is a learning activity, and success depends upon both a student's attentiveness in class and to the course material. Second, a time limit. If you do not want an extremely strict time limit, keep the challenge within the class period. I prefer 20 minutes as a limit. The time factor plays a significant role in many game environments and adds to the students' excitement as well as their serious approach to finding a solution. Third, the reward must have a strong and immediate impact on the student's success in the course.

This reward should motivate students throughout the course. It can catapult a strong learner upward to new heights as well as pull a student off to a slow start out of a trench and toward success. In jump starting a struggling student you want that new beginning to sustain itself, and a superpower needs to stay with the student. You do not generally lose something you earned. Spider-Man's agility is always with him. It does not guarantee success in every battle, but it sure improves his chances of success over a Peter Parker without the spidey's skills. Let me now provide concrete examples of superpower challenges that I use in class.

## A MEANINGFUL MAD LIB

This example uses the comic book *Doomsday Clock* (DC, 2017–2019) and the CW TV series on *Supergirl* for the content. If you can wrap the challenge with a narrative or story related to the course so much the better. That is what I have done here. This challenge is a form of Mad Libs—a word game students find enormously fun.[1]

Superpower Challenge # 1: Superpower of Healing

> Power Up Capabilities: The winner can heal and improve his or her score on an individual mission within a week of receiving his or her score. If you take a challenge where you can earn 20 XP and you obtain 16, you can go back and redo the two incorrect responses and change your score to a perfect 20! You must heal within a week, but this counts for every individual mission throughout the duration of the semester.

*Task*

The Opioid Crisis, Climate Change, and other global problems have their own Doomsday Clock and the minute hand keeps moving toward global disaster. It seems we need superheroes more than ever to overcome our ordinary citizens' inertia. The Directors of the National Institute of Health and the Center for Disease Control (CDC) have called on ten superheroes to fight the opioid public health crisis. The CDC has called up superheroes from the DC Universe and NIH has called up superheroes from the Watchmen Universe (i.e., *Doomsday Clock*, Issues 1–7). Use the below mad lib and name the nine superheroes and one wild card villain. The first student to name and evenly divide all ten super characters into their appropriate teams will win the power of superhealing.

*Alert: One superhero was trapped and replaced by a notorious supervillain, so your success will require an extra-large challenge.

Use SMS [_____] to contact 2 birds of the dark _____ and _____ for your eyes and ears to discover who pulls her strings _____ as she plays with the big grinning puppet _____, but this show is no joke, so read the ink blot _____ for a clue to understanding the Bible's first man's shadow self _____ who plans to build an empire greater than the greatest king of ancient Egypt _____ and rule the world through the processing and dissemination of the poppy plant everywhere on earth.

*Each blank represents one and only on superhero. There are no duplicates. We have read, watched, or discussed each of these superheroes in class.

Here is the answer with clues italicized:

> Use SMS- Simple Message System [**Superman Mime Supergirl**] to contact 2 birds of the dark [Nite **Owl** and **Bat**man] for your eyes and ears, respectively, to discover who *pulls her strings* [**Marionette**] as she plays with the *big grinning* puppet [**The Joker**], but this show is no *joke*, so read the *ink blot* [**Rorschach**] for a clue to understanding the *Bible's first man's shadow self* [**Black Adam**] who plans to build an empire greater than *greatest king of ancient Egypt* [**Ozymandias**] and rule the world through the processing and dissemination of the poppy plant everywhere on earth.

Students next break the characters into teams. DC would include Superman, Supergirl, Batman, and Black Adam with the rest belonging to the Watchmen Universe created by Alan Moore and Dave Gibbons. The Joker belongs to DC—a true wild card!

This challenge is not just motivating and fun it genuinely deepens the class discussion. For example, the above team allocation allows for further challenge as you can continue class by talking about the gray nature of superheroes, especially the Watchmen characters who are deeply flawed, along with Black Adam, a complex DC antihero.

## Superpower Challenge # 2 Double Your Power

In the game *Scribblenaughts*, Doppelganger is the evil twin to the superhero Maxwell. A doppelganger is a twin or shadow self that psychiatrist Carl Jung argued many of us carry around with us, but doubles can, like with the character Domino, bring good luck too. Rolling doubles in dice and drawing two aces in poker generally result in good outcomes. For the late great Stan Lee, naming his many characters with the first initial for both first and last names helped him remember their names. Peter Parker, Reed Richards, Brue Banner, and the like are also easy for us to remember because the human memory works best through associations, and, researchers tell us, remembering first consonants is easier than remembering any other letter. The following are the initials of people associated with superhero comics discussed during this course. They can be actual superheroes, supervillains, writers of those comics, artists, or even editors and executives who helped make superheroes possible.

For this challenge identify who the following initials—first letter of their first and last names—belong to and show how they fit into the below hint-filled scenario. The first one (or first team) with the correct answer can double their Poster Mission XP (Experience Points).

This **independent author** has created a new superhero team to battle one of comic book history's most **notorious villains** who has already imprisoned this **scientist and his wife** in a secret location. This **teenage nerd** has applied to be one of the team and brought a new **Muslim teen crush** with him. The **Daily Bugle's editor** has borrowed **Clark Kent's colleague** to join the **villain's sister** at mayor Mitchell Hundred's press conference about the missing superhero couple. The major will be joined by his **chief scientist** who will try and explain why the public needs to control their *anger* and find evidence before attacking this genius foe.

**LL, MM, BB, SS, JJ, PP, RR, LL, KK**

For those few non superhero fans, the answers are:

Lex Luthor, Mike Magnolia, Bruce Banner, Sue Storm, Jonah Jameson, Peter Parker, Reed Richards, Lois Lane, Kamala Kahn.

## Superpower Challenge # 3: A Puzzle

*Super Strength*

All superheroes or supervillains have appeared in a comic we have read, watched, or heard reported on up to this point in class. Once you have identified each character or team assemble them into either superheroes or supervillains. For the superhero teams, one should be made up of Marvel characters and one of DC characters, and one will be independent. The independent figure can help either Marvel's or DC's team. Just be able to explain why you assigned this person to the team you assigned him or her to. The winner can power up and add 5% to their score on every individual mission and challenge for the rest of the semester. The first person to correctly assemble the two teams and the enemy (enemies) wins.

***Answers are in parenthesis.

**Clues**

Many heads are stronger than one

Strong as Steel

Speak softly and carry a big hammer

He might go nuclear on you

Strong as a brick shit house

Giant size strength of Biblical proportions

Postgraduate Brain Power

Stones can break your bones if you have 6 of them

Here are the answers. The superhero or supervillain is named first followed by their publisher. How many did you get right?

**Answers**

Many heads are stronger than one (**Hydra, Marvel**)

Strong as Steel (**Superman, DC**)

Speak softly and carry a big hammer (**Thor, Marvel**)

He might go nuclear on you (**Doctor Manhattan, DC**)

Strong as a brick shit house (**The Thing, Marvel**)

Giant size strength of Biblical proportions (**Goliath, Marvel**)

Postgraduate Brain Power (**Cat or Abigail from** *My So-Called Secret Life*, Independent)

Stones can break your bones if you have 6 of them (**Thanos, enemy**).

In conclusion, superpower challenges deepen the connection between games and learning, engage the entire class, and promote student motivation, whether to spur high achieving students to new levels, or pull struggling learners out of the pit and back on the track to success. So, power up student learning and design some superpower challenges.

## NOTES

1. The origin of Mad Libs in the 1950s as a word game collaboration between Leonard Stein and Roger Price makes fascinating reading. I am especially fond of the initial spark being set off by Stein's working on a script for the legendary comedy show *The Honeymooners*. Mad Libs is primarily a zany

and humorous game as befits its comedic inventors, but like any game, you can make slight mods to suit your own learning objectives. Having students compose their own Mad Libs works best as a learning activity.

2. Noted comic book author Gail Simone started a website listing women characters and female superheroes who had been abused in various ways in comics. She started the site in 1999, and the list has grown considerably. That fact should trouble all of us. She takes the title of her list from the cover of a notorious Green Lantern issue, which you can view with the actual list and its history at the following site: https://www.lby3.com/wir/.

## LESSON IDEA

One challenge that addresses, but also transcends comics, focuses on women in comics. It is called *Women In Refrigerators*, after Gail Simone's famous list.[2] Adapt the below challenge for your discipline: which women have been oppressed or kept silent in Hollywood, in history, in Chemistry, and so on.

Open the Door to Female Equality

Women are tired of being trapped in the refrigerator of comics' masculine bias. Help spring these freezing women and embiggen (a power of Kamala Kahn, Ms. Marvel) your XP with 75 bonus points.

Students identify the oppressors of female superheroes and then discover weapons to help defeat the oppressors and tear off the door of the sexist refrigerator. You can adapt this challenge to any subject matter given the transcultural and long-standing oppression of women, whether in government, science, or any other field. The refrigerator is a symbol of discrimination, enclosure, abuse, and so on. What women have been fridged in your discipline? What superpower relevant to your discipline will you award the winner or winning team skill?

## RESOURCES

Games

1. *Assassin's Creed*—Developer and publisher: Ubisoft, 2018.

2. *Scribblenaughts Unlimited*—Developer: 5th Cell. Publishers: Warner Brothers, Entertainment and Nintendo, 2012.

Website

*Center for Self-Determination Theory*

https://selfdeterminationtheory.org/

This membership center based in Florida provides ample material about self-determination theory including research, case studies, videos, and applications of the theory to different fields.

Book

Rigby, Scott and Ryan, Richard. *Glued to Games: How Video Games Draw Us In and Hold Us Spellbound, Illustrated Edition.* Prager, 2011.

This excellent thoroughly researched book examines why video games are so compulsively appealing to young people. The author's findings support the self-determination theory as the best account of video games' appeal. Self-determination theory claims three factors contribute to video games appeal: autonomy, relatedness, and competence. If you design any user experience with these three goals as part of your design the chances, you will elicit the user's intrinsic motivation. In terms of education, you want your lessons designed to give students choice or options, when possible, work in teams or with partners and provide the opportunity to share their work with others, and make sure students can succeed.

# CHAPTER 3

# Gen Con in the Classroom

## Board Games for Learning

ONE OF THE RIPPLE effects of the explosion in video game popularity has been a renewed interest in board games. With the assistance of crowd source funding several new board and card games have had significant commercial success. *Exploding Kittens* and *Cards Against Humanities* are two of the most notable examples of this success. Many cities now play home to board game cafes that bring residents together over both cooperative and competitive games. Retail stores devoted to entertainment host game nights. For instance, Zombie Planet near me hosts a game night for *Dungeons and Dragons* as well as *Magic the Gathering*. The City of Troy, birthplace of Uncle Sam, hosts the Bard and Baker Board Game Café (Figure 3.1).

This brings me to Gen Con, where *Magic the Gathering* launched into phenomenal success (in 1993), and the learning value of board games.

In some ways, the success of modern board games can be measured by the growth of Gen Con. Gen Con stands as shorthand for the Lake Geneva Wargames Convention inaugurated by *Dungeons and Dragons* co-creator Gary Gygax in 1968. Gygax, a wargame enthusiast, held the inaugural convention at the Horticultural Hall in Lake Geneva, Wisconsin, where he spent his summers. The convention cost $50 and about 100 people

DOI: 10.1201/9781003201465-5

FIGURE 3.1 The Bard and Baker Board Game Café in Troy, New York. (Photograph by the author.)

attended. The convention has since moved to Indianapolis, Indiana, and attracts around 70,000 attendees, a remarkable growth that testifies to the enormous appeal of tabletop gaming. The annual event now has live action role playing, an ongoing *Dungeons and Dragons* game, a huge exhibition hall, and the launching of new games, including the previously mentioned *Magic: The Gathering* in 1993.

Board games have also benefited from the international spread of German designed board games. Following the Allies victory in World War II American board games favored military style games based on aggression and expansion (e.g., *Axis and Allies*). On the other hand, as a defeated nation, German designers and manufacturers moved decisively against military style games toward games with pacifist themes, community building, and cooperative game play (e.g., *Catan*, *Agricola*). The birth of Germany's Spiel des Jahres ("Game of the Year") award and the annual Internationale Spieltage ("International Game Day" fair in Essen, Germany (many times bigger than the American Gen Con) helped bring German-based board games with their creative, cooperative strategies and mechanics to prominence. German games, awards, and events have led to a movement of board game design loosely referred to as Eurogames. The highly successful *Ticket to Ride* franchise being a prime example.

Ian Livingstone captures the essence of Eurogames,

> ...the term encompasses any game, no matter where it was designed, that follows the school of game design pioneered in Germany in the last half-century. It should have easily grasped rules, depend on strategy rather than luck, lack direct confrontation, and require collaboration for progression. It should also have high production values that often include lovely wooden pieces, such as meeple (p. 134).[1]

Inevitably, any popular success attracts attention for possible profit-making purposes and Gen Con is no exception. There are local versions of the convention, pop-up conventions, and even international versions. The business was bought by the giant toy company Hasbro, before being sold to Peter Adkison (former CEO of Wizards of the Coast) in 2002. The annual convention can rightly be called an event like Super Bowl week or San Diego Comic Con and I recommend all faculty attend at least once during their active years. However, for pure learning value, I prefer the original, low end, smaller, Horticultural Hall type event. In my own field of literature, I always prefer the regional versions of the Modern Language Association to their behemoth annual convention after Christmas. One learns better in a seminar than a large lecture hall, so I urge teachers and professors to use their classroom as a mini Gen Con every so often to spur deep learning, social bonding, and community building with students.

In elementary school, teachers often design the classroom with learning stations that students rotate between. For older students, instead of stations, you have tables, and each table serves a different tabletop game. Students move around the room so that each student plays each game.

In an elementary class you can play any number of games with learning value. In the later grades, you can easily organize the tables with games that serve different disciplines. Keep in mind that the games do not have to be discipline specific to be of value. Games also teach competencies, which over the long run often prove more valuable than disciplinary or content knowledge. For example, in social studies or history you can play a content-based game like *Freedom-The Underground Railroad* where students play abolitionists fighting against the slave economy. This game perfectly suits a unit on the Civil War. However, you could also play the popular game *Catan*. In *Catan* students develop key lifetime competencies like strategic thinking, managing resources, and building settlements—an activity that assumes many skills.

My primary purpose in this short chapter is to bring faculty members attention to the immense learning value of tabletop games. They are even cost effective. A computer game often requires purchasing a class license, but a board game is a board game. Buy one and use it for years. Now let me give two examples of mini Gen Con classrooms, one for the quite young (primary school grades) and one for older students (secondary school and undergraduate college). I will list five games with annotations that can be used in a mini Gen Con with learning stations (i.e., tables that students rotate between). Each game could also be used when covering the subject matter most relevant to the game.

## IT'S ELEMENTARY, MY DEAR WATSON: BOARD GAMES FOR THE YOUNG

***Trekking: The National Parks, Second Edition*** (Science, Environmental Science, Geography, Conservation), Designer: Charlie Bink. Publisher: Bink Ink LLC, Underdog Games, 2018, 2–5 players.

In this game students are introduced to the beauty and value of the United States' National Parks. We have 61 in the United States. In the game, players trek along different routes to park destinations. Your objectives are collecting different colored stones and using Trekk cards numbered 1–4 in 5 suits. The suits are used for Park cards and for moving across the board. A player can take two actions from among four possibilities: draw a Trekk card, move, occupy a major park, or claim a minor park.

What matters to me is less the competition for Victory Points than the actual trekk or the structure of the game, which enacts the very nature of games: exploration. The game encourages exploration or trekking outside of the game, whether through family vacations to national parks, camping in forests, or hiking and biking trails. Additionally, the game's cards are beautiful photographs of national parks that also provide essential facts about the various parks. How much better to learn geography through playing a game instead of reading an encyclopedia entry (Figure 3.2).

Games that can push kids out into the world where play becomes a learning experience with lifelong benefits. Let nature be the playground and students will learn conservation skills as they play.

FIGURE 3.2   Game board and pieces. (Image from Trekking the National Parks. Used with Permission of Underdog Games ©.)

### *Tri-FACTa* (Basic Math)

Publisher: Educa Korea, Learning Resources, 2–4 players.

This basic math game has both an addition/subtraction version and a slightly more advanced multiplication/division version. An equilateral triangle makes up the board game. Game play consists in making families of three, i.e., triangles, which the game calls fact families. The game board helps young players visualize operations. TriFACTa is an excellent game for developing numerical literacy.

A family fact requires using three numbers in addition-subtraction equations. For example, if the vertex of the triangle is an 8 and the base points are a 1 and a 7, you complete the following operations: addition, $7+1=8$; and subtraction: $8-1=7$ and $8-7=1$. The game teaches general problem-solving abilities in addition to mathematical thinking. Students build equations as they would build a sentence with figures as a substitute for words. Helping students develop a syntax for math has long-term benefits this game facilitates.

***Engineering Ants*** (Building, Cooperative Learning, Creative Problem Solving, Engineering, Math,)

Designer: Peggy Brown, Don Ullman. Publisher: Broadway Toys LTD, Peaceable Kingdom, 2015, 2–4 players.

Engineering Ants brings the early primary grades exposure to engineering principles. Ants are extraordinary species humans simply step on. Perhaps, only Marvel's Ant Man brings these industrious little creatures the respect and attention they deserve. In the game players move ants and their arch enemy the anteater around the board. Your objective is to rescue three ants before the anteater reaches the ant hill. There are red obstacle cards placed face up, and green obstacle cards placed face down. You cannot move past a red obstacle course without rescuing the blocked ant. Rescuing an ant requires cooperative effort where players use material provided in the game to build a structure around the obstacle, i.e., a bridge over troubled water (there are 36 pieces of building material and 36 hardware pieces to make use of).

Using creative problem solving as a team to rescue a generally ignored species right under our feet has deep value for young kids. It teaches them respect for a species that has tremendous capabilities. Also, if you want to attract girls to engineering, what better place to start than first grade!

***Covalence: A Molecule Building Game*** (Science, Chemistry)

Designer: John Coveyou. Publisher: Ediciones MasQueOca, Genius Games, 2016, 2–4 players.

Perhaps, my least favorite class in school was chemistry. Covalence would have helped spark some interest in the subject if I had played this game years ago. In the game, like *Engineering Ants*, you are building, but in this case, you are constructing molecular structures. You can play as a Knower, who has knowledge of the hidden structure, or a Builder. Knowers pass out structural and number clues. The builders can use a guess token to identify the structure. Each Builder then takes a set of Element Tiles that bear a variety of elements and bonding patterns.

The Knower must study the Secret Molecules designated for each Builder and then give each Builder clue cards that relate to their specific Molecule!

Each Builder must interpret these clues as they arrange and rearrange their individual Element Tiles, attempting to deduce the structure of their Secret Molecule. If they are correct in their identification, they receive a clue token and move on to the next challenge. Like many of the games targeting primary school players, game play is cooperative. Covalence belongs somewhat in the deduction game genre but applied to science instead of society (Figure 3.3).

FIGURE 3.3   Covalence game components. (Image courtesy of Steve Schlepphorts. Used with permission of Genius Games ©.)

Like video games, *Covalence* has different difficulty levels (indicated on the Molecule Cards), and thus allows for game play in elementary school as well as high school. The highest difficulty is to add chlorine into the mix as well as a greater variety of molecules. The game makes chemistry engaging and introduces some complex principles of organic chemistry to young students which will help prepare kids for a subject many students abandon in high school.

***Castle Panic*** (Cooperative Play, Problem Solving, Strategic Thinking)
Designer: Justin De Witt. Publisher: Fireside Games, 2019, 1–6 players. There are many expansions of this game, but I suggest the Big Box which includes three expansions.

*Castle Panic* uses a medieval battle setting to stress strategic thinking. Players defend the castle against the onslaught of monsters. The castle sits in the middle of the board and a series of concentric circles move outward from the castle. They are called arcs and each arc includes three colored rings: archers, knights, swordsmen. Damage can only be included within the ring designed for that castle defender.

*Castle Panic* has both the features and the look of a video game fighting fantasy game, but here players can play together in proximity as they make decisions based on consensus. Any battle or military genre game requires strategic thinking: where to move, when to attack or counterattack, anticipating the enemies' movements and actions. As in chess, players need to think about future moves in advance and hypothesize about their enemies possible moves. Although game play is basic these skills are fundamental for later competencies necessary in achieving school success. Best of all, unlike the popular Battle Royal last man standing genre, here you win together or lose together.

## LONG-TERM LESSONS IN GAME PLAY FROM THE PRIMARY GRADES

The five games discussed above bring forth some lessons that persist throughout a student's academic life and beyond. First, games engage students in fun questions and tasks that engage their active learning modality. Engagement builds persistence. Nothing frustrates persistence more than the ridiculous testing regime implemented by the federal government under the totally mistaken notion that forcing students in elementary school to take standardized math tests will do anything good whatsoever for them. Second, introducing young students to subjects with high attrition rates like math and chemistry provides a foundation and interest base that serves as a gateway to more engaged learning in middle school, high school, and beyond. Third, if you want more girls in engineering, start them in first grade.

Let me make a slight detour to explain the benefit of telescoping primary school activities. When I ran a mentoring program between college students at the State University of New York, Old Westbury, and Roosevelt Middle School on Long Island, the mentoring between college students of diverse backgrounds and majors and the almost entirely minority middle school students achieved much more success than a professional tutoring company could ever have achieved. In fact, students who did not have an assigned mentor wanted one, and word spread across the district. The principal of the Harry D. Daniels School (Grades K-2, closed in 2007) heard the talk and asked if I could arrange for her second grade class to spend a day at the college. My first reaction was second grade? She explained these were all minority kids whose parents, for the most part, did not attend college. Many were low income and lived in a segregated, almost entirely minority populated town. She strongly believed that having these kids on a college campus would plant the idea of college as a realistic goal in their head and help stir the kids' aspirations. I proceeded to arrange a day on campus with the kids going to the computer lab, a Spanish class, and the college gym. Over the course of the day kids interacted with a very diverse college population. The day ended with a group photo taken on the steps of the administration building with Vice President of Student Affairs, Dr. Ruben Gonzalez, a highly accomplished Hispanic male. Over 20 years later, that day remains one of the most memorable of my teaching career.

Similarly, allowing for some mixed age or mixed grade learning can be immensely beneficial. This typically happens, like many useful activities, only after the formal school day. A third grade student can mentor a first grade student. This builds the third grade student's self-esteem. At the same time, you will find the first grade student responds much better to his older peer than an overpriced professional tutoring company. This fact reflects how much monied interests not genuine learning drives education.

Finally, most of the games discussed here empathize cooperative play. That needs to happen much more throughout formal education. We cannot solve today's complex, national or international problems as individuals. We need to work together, or we will suffer together, which COVID-19 has driven home in the most deadly fashion with over 900,000 U.S. citizens dead (as of February 2022) from the virus, many preventable. Let's also work on group and team assessments and slow down the individual testing mania which only produces nothing but anxiety and stress.

## THE COLLEGE PATHWAY: BOARD GAMES FOR OLDER STUDENTS

My expertise is literature and humanities, which I discuss in other chapters, so here I will use five science-related board games ideal for high school and college classes.

### Killer Snails: Assassins of the Sea

Designer: Nicholas Fortugno. Publisher, Killer Snails, 2016, 2–5 players.

*Killer Snails* share some of the scientific detection skills of *Covalence*, but here rather than chemical structures you detect cabals (groupings) of peptides released by the eponymous snails. You play a research scientist collecting snails for their valuable toxins. Sounds strange, but true. Killer or cone snails release peptides when they harpoon (from the tip of their tongue) a prey with poison. In game play, you build your deck by killing appropriate prey through attack values v. defense values. Once you

FIGURE 3.4 Killer snails. Game components and box. (Image courtesy of Jessica Ochoa Hendrix. Used with permission of Killer Snails ©.)

capture and kill a prey the peptides (little flat round objects) are released with the player's goal being to detect the three peptides of a cabal. You need to detect all three cabals to win (Figure 3.4).

The peptides released by cone snails have been found to have compounds with powerful healing effects. The toxins have been used to make a drug called Prialt (trade name for Ziconotide) that targets cancer cells and provides the same pain relief now only possible through the administration of highly addictive opioids. Imagine a drug that manages pain but prevents what has become a deadly pandemic of opioid addiction. These killer snails are a true pharmakon.[2]

A major value of this game would be having students further research these cone snails. Dr. Baldomero "Toto" M. Olivera, a Distinguished Professor of Biology at the University of Utah, has done extensive and pioneering work on these snails (Telis, 2014). Also, as a researcher at the Howard Hughes Medical Institute Dr. Olivera has developed a program that brings biochemistry to elementary school grades along with a full curriculum to support the program. Games help support this bridge between college and primary grades by erasing barriers our ossified formal educational systems continue to prevent.

Finally, once students recognize how nature provides the material for many advancements in medical science and therapeutics, they will begin to develop an understanding of how interconnected the earth's living systems are, and why, as future leaders and active citizens, they must fight to perverse the natural world from human onslaught.

***Wingspan*** (Biology, Bird Watching, Ornithology, Resource Management, Science, Strategic Thinking)

Designer: Elizabeth Hargrave. Publisher: Stonemaier Games, 2019, 1–5 players.

An aesthetically beautiful board game featuring 170 different species of birds, *Wingspan* introduces players/students to the world of birds. The bird cards are magnificently illustrated by Ana Maria Martinez Jaramillo, Natalia Rojas, and Beth Sobel (Figure 3.5).

You learn about nests, eggs, feeding, and habitats. You begin with five bird cards, food cards, along with information about the birds' nests, feeding, habitats, and eggs. Every turn there are four actions to choose from:

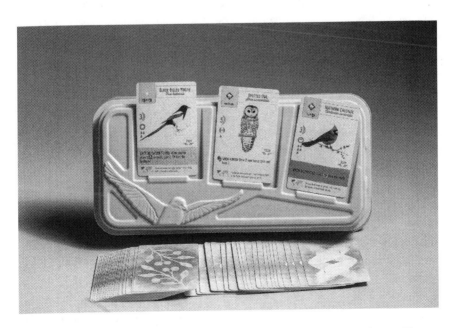

FIGURE 3.5  Bird cards from Wingspan. (Photograph courtesy of Tim Chuon, Used with permission of Stonemaier Games ©.)

play a bird, gain resources in the forest, lay eggs in the field, grain cards in the wetland. The more birds you play the more success you have in the game and the more you learn about birds. There are four rounds with quick turns that decrease each round from 8 turns, to 7 and so forth. The game demands considerable strategic thinking where players must think of the long-term consequences and possibilities extrapolated from their current move.

I have six bird feeders ranging from large platforms to custom Oriole feeders. Learning about birds and their habitats as you play makes this a classroom treasure that just might motivate students to bird watch or at least notice and appreciate the richness birds add to the world as they walk around campus or their neighborhood.

**Gut Check** (Health Care, Public Health, Economics, Business Management)
Designers: Digitalmill, Tiltfactor. Publisher: Tiltfactor, 2018, 3–5 players.

All students have been a patient at some point, trying, quite logically, to find the best treatment possible for their ailment. This game requires students to play concerned patients, but also flips the tables, and has them play hospital administrators. This role switch gives students a deeper perspective on the harsh realities of health care. In the United States, medical care often comes at a premium and not all patients/clients can access the best care. Hospitals are very cost conscious. Today, many hospitals, like their corporate counterparts, practice merger and acquisition as a business strategy more than a medical practice. How do patients know if they are getting the best health care possible? Play the game and they will find out.

Each player is dealt five face-down department cards. Each card has a quality value on its face-down. Every turn one player takes on the role of the patient, and all other players take on the role of providers. The patient declares which of her remaining conditions she is seeking treatment for, and the providers each do one of three things to convince the patient to visit their department: research—secretly peek at the quality value of any provider's face-down department cards; publish—reveal the quality of one of her own face-down department cards value to everyone; or improve—replace one of her current department cards with a new one from the supply. Providers simultaneously set their prices. The patient wants to visit the provider who gives the highest quality care at the best price. You win by achieving the best quality care, but also making the most money as a provider. That's the catch. How do making money and quality care work together? How often do patients benefit? Patients on mandated Medicare know the mediocre quality of U.S. health care. Medicare offers seniors no dental coverage without paying a steep premium. Medication prices are exorbitant and largely uncontrolled. Treatment options limited by high copays. If students learn about these insurance inadequacies in the United States early in life, then there is a chance for meaningful change that benefits all citizens not just the wealthy

*Lovelace & Babbage* (Computer Science, History of Science, Woman Studies)

Designer: Scott Almes. Publisher: Artana, 2019, 2–4 players.

A fast paced game that gives students a fun taste of computer science. Computer Science is a subject that should be taught as a core subject in every high school. Excluding the subject from students does them an immense disservice. The game has a planning phase and an execution phase. You are also able to execute subroutines and learn some basic computer science principles.

The game embeds a tangential, but invaluable history lesson by bringing students attention to two brilliant individuals they most likely have never heard about (none of my 20 students had heard of them). Charles Babbage was a Victorian genius with exceptional abilities in engineering, math, invention, and philosophy. Babbage's design for an Analytic Engine with its computing and storage capacity that we now associate with programming can be seen as a prototype for the first computer. Ada Lovelace, an extraordinary scientist too often ignored by history, added footnotes to her translation of a scientific paper from the French in 1843. The footnotes constitute the first documented computer program. Together the two scientists made an unlikely friendship separated by some 37 years in age (Babbage 45 and Lovelace 18). Students' lives are enriched by studying this wonderful friendship between two brilliant figures from the history of science.

*Tesla vs. Edison: War of Currents*

Designer: Dirk Knemeyer, Artana Games, 2015.

Two more great inventors are the subject of this exciting board game, but now rivals rather than friends. Virtually all American students will know who Thomas Edison is (General Electric was only miles from my childhood home), but few will have heard of Nikolas Tesla. This game provides a gateway to the history of science and invention as well as an exciting showdown between players. In the game, the two players duel by building a company that has projects spread across the states, fight a public relations battle over the superiority of DC or AC current, and strive for financial success. The winner will be the player with the most valuable stock.

Each player has stocks and players want stock prices to rise. To attract investors or stockholders you need to build in different cities. Cities have different levels for different values. You build either an AC or DC company developing technology, promoting your technology, and increasing your financial wealth.

On the one hand, the financial aspect of a game about competing inventors seems overdone, but on the other hand, finances, including attracting and keeping investors, had as much to do with these respective geniuses as their actual inventive skills. Edison pioneered the entire process of innovation in Menlo Park, New Jersey with his subdividing work into expert teams. A process that led to numerous patents, but, whereby Edison, at times, (many times) took credit for others work. The Serbian immigrant Tesla was the more visionary and brilliant of the two figures. Tesla's ideas prevailed in developing the modern power grid, and the first hydroelectric plant in Niagara Falls, New York. Tesla also developed ideas for wireless technology and communication over 100 years ahead of his time.

Historical extension activities are a critical off shoot of this game. What a contrast. Edison was a cutthroat capitalist, a robber baron who operated totally independent of any ethical framework. His ego was gargantuan. Tesla, on the other hand, was a humanitarian. Edison was extrinsically motivated, in large part, by wealth and fame, while Tesla was internally motivated by a love for science. Edison was wealthy and powerful, Tesla died alone, virtually penniless. In fact, during the current wars, Edison, a sore loser and reality denier, conducted a vicious disinformation and smear campaign against Tesla, whose success at the 1983 Chicago Worlds Fair and partnership with George Westinghouse, Edison could not stomach (Zakarin, 2017). Edison's despicable tactics should not be ignored, and students need to think deeply about the ethical dimensions of science when they play and discuss this game.

## FROM BORED TO BOARD

Board games are an overlooked and invaluable component for any classroom. Board games bring students together in proximity where genuine bonds can be formed, and communities built. These games are for the college classroom just as much as for the primary school classroom, In fact good games bridge age groups in many creative ways. For instance, Professor Elizabeth George uses *The Game of Life*, typically played as a family game with small kids, in her college course on Renaissance and Reformation (2017). She modifies the game to reflect everyday life during the Renaissance and has students develop historical avatars that reflect the period. The cooperative nature of many German-inspired board games betrays the stereotype of games as competitive winner takes all experiences. Also, games embed assessment and as such are far superior to tests, especially standardized tests. As you progress in the game you are necessarily learning from setbacks. In cooperative play you measure group learning, something our current testing regime inadequately assesses. Finally, board games can be a springboard to learning outside the restricted space of traditional classrooms. Let games help bring students into the laboratory and out into nature where exploration is fundamental, authentic, and transformative.

## NOTES

1. A meeple (me+ people) is a meticulously crafted wooden game piece or figure used in board games. Its exact original is not definite, but many consider the game *Carcassonne*, to be the first game to use meeples.

2. A good discussion of how natural products derived from plants have served as sources for medicine would be, Veeresham, Ciddi. "Natural products derived from plants as a source of drugs," *Journal of Advanced Pharmaceutical Technology and Research*, Vol. 3, No., 4, Oct–Dec. 2021 2, doi: 10.4103/2231-4040.104709. Web, and Wong, Kate. "Mother Nature's Medicine Cabinet." *Scientific American*, April 9, 2001, retrieved from: https://www.scientificamerican.com/article/mother-natures-medicine-c/.

## RESOURCES

Websites/Organizations

*American Ornithology Society*

https://americanornithology.org/tools-for-studying-birds/

Full of information for birth watchers, hobbyists, students and the curious. Pay special attention to "Tools for Studying Birds."

*National Audubon Society*

> The preeminent organization for the study and watching of birds. You can sign up for *Audubon Magazine*, join a local chapter, and download an excellent Bird Guide App (like the one in "Alba, A Wildlife Adventure" discussed later in the book). Make sure to visit and engage your students with "Get Outside."

*National Parks Service*

https://www.nps.gov/index.htm

This government site makes the important declaration that nature is our largest classroom. They have programs for young rangers, urge "every kid outdoors," and have an excellent, searchable database of lesson plans for educators.

*Purdue University INSPIRE Research Institute for Pre-College Engineering.*

https://engineering.purdue.edu/INSPIRE

An institute at the College of Engineering dedicated to bringing engineering thinking to pre-college students. As the website outlines:

INSPIRE has three strategic focus areas:

- Integrating engineering with science, technology, mathematics, computational thinking, and language arts
- Characterizing engineering thinking for pre-college settings
- Promoting the participation of underrepresented populations in engineering

*The United States Department of Energy*

https://www.energy.gov/edison-vs-tesla

This government site has an exceptionally informative guide to the Tesla vs Edison history with facts, questions, historical background, interviews, and videos.

Board Game Resources
*Board Game Geek*

> https://boardgamegeek.com/

> The most comprehensive site devoted to board games. It includes a massive database of games, professional and fan reviews, hot topics, videos, up to date news, and more. You will refer to this site often if you use board games in learning.

*Games in College Classrooms*

> https://www.facebook.com/groups/1773710516258929/permalink/2641190799510892/

> An exceptional private Facebook group created by Patrick Rael, a noted History Professor at Bowdoin College in Maine. Dr. Rael is an expert on board games and this site is an excellent resource and networking space for any teacher interested in the use of board/tabletop games in the classroom.

*Gen Con*

> https://www.gencon.com/

> The largest tabletop/board game event in the United States. It is held every summer in Indianapolis, Indiana except for COVID-19 years. The event attracts up to 70,000 attendees.

*Howard Hughes Medical Institute*

> https://www.hhmi.org/science-education/programs

> The institute's Science Education Alliance integrates students into professional research projects. The professors' program features distinguished science professors who model innovative ways of teaching research and science to undergraduate students.

*iBiology*

https://www.ibiology.org/speakers/baldomero-toto-olivera/

This site hosts talks by stellar biologists including the above series on killer snails by Distinguished Professor Baldomero Olivera discussed above.

*Internationale Spieltage SPIEL*

https://www.spiel-messe.com/en/

The world's largest tabletop/board game event/fair held in Essen, Germany. New games are premiered here, prestigious awards are given, and the best game play on tabletop is to be had. There is also an excellent educator's day. This is a truly international event and must be visited at least once in your lifetime if you are a board game player.

*Killer Snails*

https://www.killersnails.com/

A small game design company that specializes in research based science games using the best principles of cognitive science.

*Spiel des Jahres*

https://www.spiel-des-jahres.de/en/

The German Game of the Year award is the Oscar of board games. The site lists the exceptional winners and games nominated for the award since the award's beginning in 1978. There is also a Kennerspiel or connoisseur game (something like serious game or classic literature or art film and a Kinderspiel or Children's Game of the Year). If you want a quality board game go here first.

*Tilt Factor*

https://tiltfactor.org/

An exceptional game design "lab" based at Dartmouth College and led by Distinguished Professor of Humanities Mary Flanagan; the group specializes in games for social change. They have designed numerous educational board and card games.

## Books and Primary Media

*American Genius. Edison vs. Tesla, Director: Paul Abascal. Documentary, TV Miniseries, 2015.*

An engaging eight-part television series on the rivalry of two tremendous inventors and scientists who have had an incalculable influence on modern society.

Donovan, Tristan. *It's All a Game: The History of Board Games from Monopoly to Settlers of Catan.* Thomas Dunne Books, 2017.

A sweeping and engaging history of board games by a British journalist.

Livingstone, Ian, and Wallis, James. *Board Games in 100 Moves: 8,000 years of Play.* DK; Illustrated edition, 2019.

Ian Livingstone, founder of the Games Workshop in London, has been a visionary in the game industry for decades. This beautifully produced book gives an excellent, highly readable account of 100 top board games over the centuries.

Zakarin, Jordan. "Why Thomas Edison and Nikola Telsa Clashed during the Battle of the Currents." *Biography,* May 13, 2021, https://www.biography.com/news/thomas-edison-nikola-tesla-feud.

# CHAPTER 4

# Video Games in the English Classroom

## Supercharging Critical Literacy

## CLOSE READING AND THE POWER OF ANALYTIC THINKING

### Why Close Reading?

One of the chief benefits of taking a literature class continues to be the development of deep reading skills. No discipline fosters deeper and more attentive reading than literature precisely because no form of writing represents more multilayered, complex, and nuanced use of language than good literature. In an era where so many people, including students, read from the web, deep reading becomes an even more valuable skill than in my long past student days. As the skill becomes rarer, its value increases.

Literary criticism is the art of close reading. One of my mentors, the late renowned theater critic Jan Kott, taught a graduate course called *The Art of Interpretation* and criticism was one of the five areas of my oral examination, so I have a finely calibrated appreciation for the art and science

DOI: 10.1201/9781003201465-6

of deep reading. A class steeped in reading great literature can serve as a model for the study of video games. For avid gamers, stepping back from game play to examine what makes a game work well will give the player a new appreciation and understanding of a game. At the same time, literature students can apply their skills to a form of new media that has increasing importance in students' lives. Being able to closely analyze a text, whether a poem, a film, or now, a video game, has clear relevance to a student's ability to think critically in multiple contexts.

In the game world, the idea of well-played, as in a journal of that name: *Well Played: a journal of video games* published by Carnegie Mellon University's Entertainment Technology Center Press, serves as the video game texts version of literary close reading. This journal's mission clearly situates the concept of well-played in close relationship to what we in literary studies call close reading or practical criticism.

> *The Well Played Journal* is a forum for in-depth close readings of games that parse out the various meanings to be found in the experience of playing a game. It is a reviewed journal open to submissions that will be released on a regular basis.
>
> Contributors are encouraged to analyze sequences in a game in detail to illustrate and interpret how the various components of a game can come together to create a fulfilling playing experience unique to this medium. Through contributors, the journal will provide a variety of perspectives on the value of games.

The description perfectly fits one of the goals of many literature courses and programs. Even the journal's name *Well Played* echoes Cleanth Brook's classic text *The Well Wrought Urn: Studies in the Structure of Poetry* (1947). Brooks' work can be considered the seminal work of new criticism and his close reading of richly textured, famous poems like John Donne's "The Canonization" (a line in this dense poem offers the title for Brooks' text) or W.B. Yeats' "Among School Children." Close reading, of course, is only one of the many forms of literary interpretation, but I would argue students of literature, games, and film would do best to begin with the theory and practice of close reading. It provides a foundation or scaffolding for understanding other critical theories and developing acumen for interpreting all kinds of texts.

I pursued graduate study during the explosion of post-structuralist thought, and my first book (Seelow, 2005) used many contemporary theories in reading D.H. Lawrence; however, I started my inquiry with Lawrence's prose and lyrics. I knew no critic writing about Lawrence could ever approximate the beauty and power of Lawrence's own words (such critics commit what Cleanth Brooks would call "The Heresy of Paraphrase"). During the 1980s I sometimes became disillusioned with English professors who would write and talk so intelligently and passionately about theory, but, ironically, seemed to have less passion and less understanding about the literature they were theorizing about. Perhaps literary theory needs to be considered independent of literary criticism, but criticism, which I advocate here, begins and ends with literature or the text proper. Close reading is primary.

In reading a video game, like reading a poem or short story, you look at all the interconnected parts: narrative, voice, setting, plot, characterization, symbols, themes, irony, meter, or music in the case of a game, imagery or game art, genre, and game mechanics or rules, which in literature can be thought of as conventions (a sonnet's 14 lines, an ode's elevated tone, etc.).

After practicing close readings of a game, the students can move on to interpret video games through the same variegated lens that they would use to interpret a short story or film: psychoanalytic, Marxist, feminist, post-structuralist, queer theory, and so on (Parker, 2008). Each theory will disclose something different and valuable about a game and any theory can be applied with value to any game, though some theoretical lens might be a better fit for certain games. The *Grand Theft Auto* series strikes me as ripe for almost all major theories, which, in turn, shows how even an incredibly popular and controversial game yields rich material for critical thinking.

## Classroom Implementation

An aesthetic object demands close attention to detail. Analyzing the minutiae of a game, or a poem or film brings about a deeper appreciation for the object and a realization that the final poem or game or film is more than the sum of closely examined parts. Student choice is always an important factor asking which game a student should analyze. Unless everyone is playing the same game, I would suggest letting students analyze and report on a game of their choice. For example, in my class on cyberculture, I asked students to analyze a game of their choice related to some aspect of cyberculture and identity. Given how often the course addresses artificial intelligence, most students have no trouble selecting an interesting game. Choices included *Bioshock Infinite*, which, though set in 1912, represents current and future class conflict; *Fallout Vegas* a great post-apocalyptic survival game about future war between nations; *Xenogears*, a Japanese, animie-flavored role-playing game with a strong religious/metaphysical foundation and machine-man theme.

Although I preferred a written analysis for this assignment, I still gave students an alternative whereby they could offer a close reading through a walk through or video blog. Walkthroughs are a form of close reading on the fly as the player comments about the game during play. Walkthroughs are perfect for millennials who can easily learn the technology or software needed to make them. (There are numerous examples at the website Game Anyone.) One student did a walkthrough of *Half Life 2* and another student, a female, did a walkthrough of the cyberpunk side scrolling game *Dex*. The latter provides an interesting feminine perspective on the protagonist's sexuality. Another female student offered a video blog commentary on gender in *Deus Ex: Human Revolution*. As background to this assignment, I had shown the class examples of Anita Sarkeesian's superb Feminist Frequency blog, which clearly made a positive impression on some of the female students as indicated by their choice of games.

Feminist Frequency brings me to another important point. The professor or teacher should model a close reading of a poem or video game before asking students to do the same. Modeling gives students clear parameters on what to look for, and how to perform a solid close reading. Reading an article is a fine supplement, but not a substitute for live modeling by an instructor. Finally, I recommend you focus close reading on a game that can be played during a single class period. This allows you to model a reading and gives students a manageable text to work with.

## Classroom Activities

One potentially illuminating activity would be to conduct a version of I.A. Richard's (1929) early practical criticism experiment on reading poetry by substituting reading video games for reading poetry. Richards, a professor of English at Cambridge University, would give his students (mostly honors students) sheets of anonymous poems to read over a 1-week period and ask them to keep track of their close readings on note paper. Richards considered this a psychological experiment because he was studying how students thought about poetry. It was as much about the reading process (what we now call reader response theory) as poetry interpretation. The anonymity allowed students to demonstrate their own thought process without relying on scholars' critical readings. In the age of the Internet such original readings are important. Today's students first, habitual response is to look at Wikipedia or some other website and use the interpretations (often professional, though not always illuminating) they find there as the meat for their own readings, which then end up being highly derivative. Consequently, I allow students to approach a text with fresh eyes and play a video game in class that they are unlikely to have played beforehand.

Let me pause momentarily to clarify common student misconceptions about opinions and correctness in close reading by briefly talking about what E.D. Hirsch, Jr. calls validity in interpretation (1973). Students must learn that not all interpretations are equally valid. I.A. Richards' argument maintains, as the subtitle of his book indicates, that interpretation is a judgment about distinguishing between good and bad, effective, and ineffective writing. There are well-wrought poems and there are ill-wrought poems (many more of the latter). The same can be said of video games, some are well designed, and many are not. Students need to know what makes one poem or game well-wrought and another ill-wrought. Part of being educated requires the ability to make clear judgments and evaluate artifacts and products with acumen. The ability to judge and value will extend across many domains in the student's life, so poetry or games are perfectly good places to begin developing this ability.[1]

In learning what makes a well-wrought poem or a well-wrought video game a student will also learn the same degree of validity applies to their close readings. Interpreting is not just stating one's "opinion" and not all readings are valid (in Richards' experiment only 30% of his honor students made what he considered valid readings of the poems). In describing a valid reading Richards does not therefore maintain that there is a single correct or true interpretation, which many students and some professionals continue to misunderstand. On the contrary, new critics argue that no correct or final interpretation of a poem is possible. Brooks emphasizes over and over that the "inner essence of a poem" (261) always eludes any single reading. A poem can never be reduced to a prose statement or translation. This is the nature of art. Learning this fact will help students both appreciate the art of art and the art of interpretation, i.e., deep reading at its best.

Richards' experiment revealed some disconcerting findings (Richards, by the way, was one of the 20th century's finest readers of poetry). Students at one of the world's best universities, studying a major that featured poetry, produced miserable results. Richards' book, based upon his classroom experiment (which we today call action research), outlined ten problems (pp. 12–15) students seem to experience when reading poetry and he addressed each of these ten at length in his book. Richards overwhelming impression concerned his honor students' "mental inertia." If Richards was a touch distraught by the poor reading habits of honors students at Cambridge in the 1920s, I suspect, he would be much more so today. My experience over the last 15 years has been that students read less now and that reading less, much less in many cases, results in a serious decline in skills. However, a decline can always be reversed, and that's one reason for my writing this chapter.

Richards used his findings to argue for the value of a course or program in the art of interpretation. He ends the book with a dire prognosis about the negative effect of technology on reading skills and a call for the value of the Humanities (this well before the web was even imagined):

> We defend ourselves from the chaos that threatens us by stereotyping and standardizing both our utterances and our interpretations. And this threat must be insisted, can only grow greater as world communication, through the wireless and otherwise improve (319).

I would argue we are on the verge of that chaos now because of the decline in reading, especially attentive reading. Stereotyping our response to poetry after all goes hand in hand with stereotyping the people and documents we encounter on a daily basis. Our unwillingness to see beyond our own stock response to the world of the text closes off genuine interpretation. If students learn to read well, they will play well. A well-played game like a well-read poem makes all the difference.

## PLAYING AND READING, CONTRASTING EXPERIENCES OF "THE DARK KNIGHT"

Another helpful activity for teaching close reading and critical thinking focuses on comparisons between a game and film or a game and a novel that have a similar or identical subject or even a game adaptation of a film or film adaptation of a game. In assigning such comparisons I avoid asking students to make a judgment about whether a video game is better than a comic or film about say Batman. These cross-media judgments strike me as pointless. They are better left for late night bull sessions or talk radio. I feel the same about the dumb conversations about "I like the book better than the movie." "Well, good for you," I say. That's a matter of taste not informed judgment. A movie about Hamlet is entirely different than a play about Hamlet. They have different technologies, performers, audiences, etc.

The comparison between a video game and a work of literature pushes students to learn what makes a work meaningful within its medium while also giving students a different appreciation and understanding of the other media. What makes a great game will differ from what makes a great novel even though both can excel in their respective forms. Once students have made an extended comparison, they can say which medium they prefer and make that an informed statement, though a statement of taste not value. Baseball is not better than basketball, but I prefer the former based upon these reasons. In comparing a work of literature with a video game, students are comparing reading with playing as differing experiences of a text. A comparison can also be made with films, but as I strongly believe students need to read more, I prefer the fiction and game comparison.

A comic book or graphic novel is an ideal work of literature to compare with a video game since comics also have a strong visual component. Moreover, students are more often familiar with comic books than traditional novels.

## BATMAN: EXPERIENCING THE SHADES OF HEROISM

Virtually all students today will be familiar with the character Batman, most likely from Christopher Nolan's Dark Knight Trilogy. You can frame the assignment by discussing the students' general familiarity with the character and how they arrive at their knowledge base. Comparing Grant Morrison's 1989 graphic novel *Arkham Asylum: Serious House on Serious Earth* with the 2009 video game of the same name, *Batman: Arkham Asylum*, an assignment from my class, will serve as my model for this activity.

Both novel and game take place in Arkham Asylum and revolve around the old fear, "the inmates are running the asylum." Batman is called upon to liberate the psychiatric hospital from the hands of his rogue's gallery of villains and their commander, the Joker. Making the comparison between game and novel students will need to focus on characterization and how the respective media highlight certain aspects of Batman.

As superhero comics primarily use action sequences (possibly 70% of the panels) and superhero video games are action adventure in style, students have much common ground for their comparison. However, in Grant Morrison's story, students will encounter an emphasis on Batman's interior life, a focus one would expect to find in a traditional novel not an action packed comic book. Setting his novel in a psychiatric hospital allows Morrison to explore Batman's psyche and the fine line that separates sanity from insanity. Students usually note this overt difference between story and game immediately, "The graphic novel seems to focus more on the psychological themes of Batman opposed to the game, which offers a more dynamic gameplay and action filled experience."[2] Morrison uses a mythic journey to the interior to frame Batman's entrance into the asylum, along with a parallel between the present and an account of the asylum's founder Dr. Amadeus Arkham. Thus, the story serves to tie Batman's psyche in some deep sense with the historical origin of the asylum. The institution is symbolic of Batman's state of mind or, perhaps, even his very character. To capture the psychological nature of the story, artist Dave McKean uses symbolic art and makes significant use of expressionist and surrealist techniques, which many students will find to be a new experience especially in the context of a comic book.

One male student nicely describes the eerie nature of the art and typography to evoke characterization, "The Joker's artistic representation also creates an atmosphere that is scrambled and blood-chilling as all dialogue is written in a strange bright red script and his own depiction is very blurred and chaotic. The internal battle that Batman faces as he is subjected to the Joker's mind games mess with his head and truly disturb his own mental capacity."

A female student also observes how the art serves Batman's shadowy sense of self and the psychological struggles he faces in contrast to a brighter more confident Batman depicted in the video game,

> The graphic novel focuses on the mental health issues that the villains suffer from along with Batman's own trauma. The art style is very dark and experimental as well. The graphic novel is very sketchy in the sense there are [few] definitive bold lines, …some pages don't have panels, [and other pages have] a lot of

vertical panels on other pages, as opposed to the video game which includes brighter colors and defined characters.

Here you can see how the student notes the elimination of the gutter, i.e., the space that separates two panels, as a structural element in comics and how that device contributes to characterization.

Overall, students did an excellent job identifying the differences between the novel and game and how these differences led to their very different endings:

> In the video game, Batman's main test is a titan who has been enhanced from toxins provided by Bain. Batman fights more prisoners and villains in the ultimate battle in the video game than in the comic. In the comic, Batman is released by a flip of a coin by Two Face. Also, in the comic, The Joker taunts Batman by providing him with a message indicating that if life gets too hard for him [...] then he always has a place in Arkham. In the video game, The Joker kills himself. As you can see both the video game and graphic novel took two totally different routes in the end. The ultimate battle in the comic leaves room open for further interpretation, the video game not so much in my opinion.

The above comment indicates how each art form takes a different approach to closure, and this difference will have an impact on students' preference for one medium over the other.

How students expressed their preference or represented their artistic taste seemed consistent with their actual experiences, "I personally enjoyed playing the game more than I liked reading the graphic novel. Playing the game helps you interact and [complete] a challenge ... based off skill whereas reading a book just takes you through the story step by step and has very minimal interaction." For this student game interaction appealed to him, but that appeal also disclosed a very honest confession that might indicate a student's heavier investment in game play as opposed to reading. Another student comments,

> The plus of reading the novel over playing the game is that you get to use your imagination to help create part of the story that might not be entirely written. I personally don't have the best imagination, so I do prefer the mission based interaction that you get from playing a video game as to reading even a graphic novel.

In this comment you have a declaration of taste, but also a finer appreciation of reading as a spur to imagination.

A female student also notes the interactive nature of controlling, i.e., playing a character, but reaches a profound conclusion that disputes a frequent presupposition that a video game is more immersive than a novel,

> Most people would say that video games are more immersive than graphic novels, but I would disagree; I think that they are immersive in separate ways. This graphic novel is a good example of that ideology. It makes you connect to the villains as people and gets you involved in in their back stories as opposed to in the video game where you just beat them [the villains] up.

One student describes that difference between an action-oriented Batman and a psychological Batman. The student prefers the more physical character which, in turn, reflects a need for a more resolute story ending brought about by a clearly heroic and victorious Batman,

> Playing the Batman in my opinion was more enjoyable. [It was] fun to use his powers and defeat villains. It gives the player a different sense that is satisfying and hopeful toward [...] the end goal of defeating the main evil character, the Joker. Reading about Batman in this comic shows us a different angle, shows us a more broken-down character who is trying to prove to himself he is different than these psychopaths while the conflict is driven with the idea that he could be more alike than different from the psychopaths such as The Joker.

This comment reflects a clear sense of where the student's preference comes from while appreciating the different qualities of two different mediums of expression.

## OUT OF THE ASYLUM: SOME BAT LESSONS LEARNED

This comparison between reading and playing will most likely disclose new discoveries for both teachers and students. For example, the obvious is not always so obvious. Students will make the obvious comment that video games are interactive and that's the primary difference between a video game and a novel. That's a given, but consider stopping students to ask them if they think a work of literature is really a static object? No, the minute you turn a page you are interacting with the text and constructing meaning. Students will reach this discovery on their own as, for example, when the above student explains how reading requires his imagination to complete a scene. He does not name that action as interactive, but you, as teacher, can name his discovery. In fact, Scott McCloud (1993) talks at length about how comics are built around closure wherein the reader closes the space created by the gutter between panels through her imagination. Students can be encouraged to think about interactivity as more than the point and click of a mouse, the shift of a body to sensors, the manipulation of a controller, and the touch of a screen. Ask them to describe how these forms of interaction impact the game. For instance, how does playing Batman change his character based on different inputs such as the use of Detective Vision?

The common observation that the video game focuses more on physical action than psychological drama is accurate but help students keep in mind that just as a video game can explore psychological depths and rich characterization, a written text, even one without pictures, can be chock full of battles and action. Homer's *Iliad* comes immediately to my mind. In other words, differences between the two media are relative not absolute.

Nonetheless, in the case of *Arkham Asylum*, students came up with excellent descriptions of how the physical action of the video game, which ends with a strong, victorious Batman, and squarely defeated Joker, differs from the graphic novel with its open ending, and the lingering feeling that Batman may not be all that different from the Joker. Perhaps, this difference explains differences in taste, and that differences in taste, perhaps, represent a difference between players and readers. In my class, the preference for the video game Batman reflects a preference for victory and decisiveness, a need to win and beat the villain. That's a comforting feeling. Ending a story with the toss of coin is unsettling, not at all comforting. This difference in endings reflects a difference between wish fulfillment and realism which may reflect a difference between how the two mediums approach to representation. As I grew up reading stories not playing video games my preference remains with graphic novels; nonetheless, this kind of comparison activity allows me to learn more about what this generation values in games and allows this generation to learn more about what I value in reading stories. A student provides the prefect concluding statement to the activity, "In my opinion, both the video game and graphic novel are great in their own unique ways." After all, Batman is a top-notch fighter, skilled detective, master of gadgets, and an unfathomable mystery, the dark knight.

## NOTES

1. The need to evaluate is ever present. Is the news report real or fake? If we are fortunate enough to dine at Nobu in Manhattan we expect a well-wrought, i.e., well-prepared meal, but when grabbing a meal from the tray at McDonalds, we expect no such careful preparation, and we will not receive it. If students don't learn to make valid judgments, they might wind up with a house of straw not a house of brick in very windy city.

2. The Elizabeth Arkham Asylum for the Criminally Insane was introduced into the Batman universe back in 1974 during author Denny O'Neil's famous run. The institution has been an integral part of Batman's world ever since. Arkham Asylum also introduced the now celebrious character Harley Quinn as psychiatrist Dr. Harleen Quinzel.

## LESSON IDEA

1. "Young Goodman Brown's Night in the Woods"

   Practicing close reading with a game, film, or story works best with short texts or scenes from larger works. In terms of games, there are many excellent story driven games to choose from. Many of these games are released in episodes one at a time on the STEAM portal. In some cases, the initial episode or installment is free. When comparing texts across media I would stay within the same genre—horror, detective, comedy—for easier comparisons. One example would be to compare the highly regarded narrative game *Night in the Woods* (2017) with Nathaniel Hawthorne's "Young Goodman Brown" (1835). Both stories fit the horror mystery genre and share some aspect of setting and theme, but from dramatically different time periods and storytelling styles.

   In *Night in the Woods*, a female protagonist Mae returns to her magical hometown of Possum Springs when she gets drawn into the woods by a lingering mystery. Her experience in the woods has supernatural overtones and the entire narrative alludes to Mae's possible mental illness or delusions. Dreams, a Halloween setting, paganism, cults, all play a role in the story. Likewise, Goodman Brown travels into the woods, meets a stranger with hints of the devil about him, and ends up observing a midnight rite. The story also suggests that Brown suffers delusions and dreams up the entire event.

Ask students look at typical literary elements like point of view, setting, characterization, symbolism, imagery, and theme, but add in the key question about how does playing the protagonist in *Night in Woods* affect your experience of the story and how does that compare to the pure reading experience of the Hawthorne story? Comparing these stories should prompt very deep reading and critical thinking as students unpack the importance of symbolism and imagery to setting and character.

2. Persuasive Writing and Argumentation

Another challenging assignment would be to have everyone read Ian Bogost's provocative *Atlantic* essay, "Video Games are better without stories." *Dr. Bogost is both a noted game designer and Distinguished Professor at Georgia Institute of Technology with expertise in literature.* Break the class into a few groups and assign the groups a different game which Bogost talks about, e.g., *Bioshock* or *What Remains of Edith Finch*? Have each group debate the strength of Bogost's argument with respect to their assigned game. This exercise promotes argumentation, communication, critical thinking, and comparative analysis. Finish the assignment by having all students write a persuasive essay supporting a clear well-argued position with respect to Bogost's claim.

## GAMES

*Arkham Asylum*

Developer: Rocksteady Studios. Publisher: Eidos Interactive and Warner Brothers Interactive Entertainment, 2009.

*Bioshock Infinite*

Developer: Irrational Games. Publisher: 2K Games. 2013.

A First Person Shooter (FPS) with a science fiction setting strong story components and multilayered themes with social and political ramifications. The game is far superior to most FPSs and well worthy of literary attention and close reading.

*Fallout: New Vegas*

> Developer: Obsidian Entertainment. Publisher: Bethesda Softworks. Designer: Josh Sawyer, 2010.

> A spin off the Fallout franchise, this action role-playing game has a science fiction post-apocalyptic theme set in the year 2077. Excellent for teaching strategy and the science fiction genre.

*Half Life 2*

> Developer and publisher: Valve, 2004.

> Another FPS with strong storytelling. Like *Bioshock Infinite*, this game would be excellent in a science fiction class.

*Dex*

> Developer and publisher: Dreadlocks Ltd. Designer: Jan Jirovský, 2014.

> A side scrolling cyberpunk game with a female protagonist. Like many games mentioned here there is a political conflict between a powerful, authoritarian organization and a resistance movement making the game ripe for Marxist, new historicist, and, in this case, feminist perspective.

*Deus Ex: Human Revolution*

> Developer: Eidos Montréal. Publisher: Square Enix. Designers: François Lapikas, Antoine Thisdale, Pierre-Francis Lafleur, 2011.

> Second game in a franchise, this game has rich themes, settings and characterizations that provide an excellent text for discussing posthumanism and bioethics.

*Night in the Woods*

Developer: Infinite Fall. Publisher: Finji. Designers: Alec Holowka, Scott Benson, Bethany Hockenberry, 2017.

A story-based game with the depth and range of any good short story. An excellent choice for literature classes using horror or mystery as genres.

Primary Texts

Hawthorne, Nathaniel. "Young Goodman Brown," originally published in *The New England Magazine*, 1835.

A classic short story about puritanism, the pagan Salem environment, and faith. It is allegorical in style with an immense range of interpretations. The story can be found in numerous editions and anthologies.

Morrison, Grant and McKean, Dave. *Arkham Asylum: A Serious House on Serious Earth*. DC Comics, 1989.

## RESOURCES

Website/Journal

*Well Played: a journal on video games, value and meaning*-https://press. etc.cmu.edu/index.php/product/well-played-vol-1-no-1/

*The Well-Played Journal* is a forum for in-depth close readings of video games that parse out the various meanings to be found in the experience of playing a game (from the website).

Books and Articles

Bogost, Ian. "Video Games Are Better Without Stories," *The Atlantic*. April 25, 2017. Retrieved from https://www.theatlantic.com/technology/archive/2017/04/video-games-stories/524148/.

A very provocative essay by a distinguished game designer and scholar that argues video games are a poor medium for delivering stories in comparison to film, television, and literature. He discusses several of the games mentioned in this chapter. It is a terrific thought provoking essay everyone should read.

Chess, Shira. *Ready Player Two: Women Gamers and Designed Identity*. University of Minnesota Press, 2017.

> This book has several good feminist readings of video games and the assumptions that form the basis of games targeting women. It is a good example of a feminist reading, cultural analysis, and media criticism.

McCloud, Scott. *Understanding Comics*. William Morrow Paperbacks, Reprint edition, 1994; originally published in 1993.

> The standard book for reading comics and graphic novels composed in comic book form by a practicing writer/illustrator. McCloud discusses the structure and forms of comics in a clear, well organized fashion.

Norton Critical Editions

Norton publishes these excellent editions of important texts with considerable primary source material, biographical data, top-notch critical essays, and helpful editorial material. They are great editions to use for close readings of a text. I have used them in this book for my discussion of Daniel Defoe's *Journal of the Plague Year*.

*Woke Gaming: Digital Challenges to Oppression and Social Injustice* edited by Kishona L. Gray and David J. Leonard. University of Washington Press, 2018.

An excellent collection of essays that present readings of games from diverse theoretical positions that address inequality and inequity.

# CHAPTER 5

# Playing through Stories

*Teaching Interactive Narrative*

S TORYTELLING HAS EXISTED SINCE the beginning of culture when prehistoric nomads illustrated hunts on the cave walls in Lascaux (Campbell, 1992). Stories pass on a culture's history and traditions. They also convey the nuance of humanity better than any other product or form of communication. Video games present a new, postmodern way of telling stories that stress interactivity. Readers play and help determine the course of the story. Students will not encounter stories with the richness and depth of a Dickens or Proust novel; however, video games represent the storytelling today's students are most likely to encounter on a regular basis. In other words, teaching the storytelling power of games meets students where they are instead of pretending they are where you want them to be. At the same time, reading, analyzing, and discussing game-based stories can be a gateway that leads students to more traditional stories that everyone's lives are enriched by. You can begin with *The Last of Us* (2013) and end up with Cormac McCarthy's *The Road* (2006).[1]

Game narratives have improved significantly over the decades. Even blockbuster, sprawling open-world games can feature powerful storytelling, as the just mentioned *The Last of Us* shows. Nintendo's *Legend of Zelda* franchise launched in 1986, designed by the legendary Shigeru Miyamoto and Takashi Tezuka, provided a template for using the action-adventure fantasy to tell stories of mythic proportions. The game's

DOI: 10.1201/9781003201465-7

hero Link, the Kingdom of Hyrule, Princess Zelda, and the evil Ganon provide the archetypal scaffolding more recent open ending game storytelling can build upon. These games combine rich storytelling without sacrificing the dynamic and engaging action and exploration of the open-world environment. For example, *Red Dead Redemption 2* provides the sprawling canvas of the Wild West in 1899, just as the century turns and the frontier's twilight casts its shadow over a vanishing world. Outlaw Alex Morgan traverses the land on a series of adventures that collapse three seasons worth of a classic TV series Western into a single game. The game includes everything from exploring the wilderness and gunfights to the meticulous care of horses and the gradual, irrevocable shift from the American frontier to an industrialized country. Although open-world games are not feasible for in class, they provide excellent research assignments, homeschooling opportunities, individual study projects, and extended project-based learning opportunities. To teach game narrative in the classroom, begin at the beginning, the very beginning with *Dungeons and Dragons* and its oral storytelling, modeled after the ancient singers of preliterate cultures.

## THE REINCARNATION OF THE BARD: THE DUNGEON MASTER AS STORYTELLER

Storytelling in games begins most prominently with a tabletop game that has exerted enormous influence on video games, especially role-playing fantasy games that have massive numbers of players and a giant fan base. Co-created by Gary Gygax and Dave Arenson, *Dungeons and Dragons* (D&D) created in 1974 provides a prototype for game-based stories. First, players take characters derived from fighting-based fantasy games (Conan, the Barbarian being the biggest impact on Gygax Kushner, 2017). Players customize the characters based on various classes such as Elves or Paladins. The use of dice contributes to each character's various abilities, i.e., a form of character definition. Characters go on campaigns, which can be predefined sketches, or they can be entirely original. Typically, the setting is medieval, but there are no limitations. In essence, the game master or storyteller, referred to as a Dungeon Master (DM), runs the game. The DM tells the story or campaign, by setting scenes, describing characters, and detailing combat and challenges in the same fashion an oral storyteller from the days of Gilgamesh would.[2]

The storytelling or singing, as the oral tradition calls the tribal bards, allows players to create scenes in their imagination.[2] Players are presented with choices and these choices influence the nonlinear direction of the story. These choice-driven stories are the text adventures and branching narratives the computer afforded soon after *D&D*'s launch. In principle, the story has no ending, and the open world of *D&D* frequently results in games extending from months or even years.

## TEACHING ORAL NARRATIVE

Teaching oral storytelling helps develop students' listening skills. Although students listen to music all the time their listening skills regarding information are inadequately assessed. The New York State English Regents used to begin with an assessment of listening skills, but that has gone by way of lowered expectations. Consequently, I begin my lesson by acting as a Dungeon Master. First, I ask students to design their own avatar, a key feature of games being players ability to customize avatars. Additionally, I give them an Adventure Sheet and rules from Ian Livingstone's and Steve Jackson's *Fighting Fantasy* game book series discussed below. Their character's attributes will play a part in later storytelling and battle scenes. Next, I set the scene and provide choices. Students make one of three choices which I follow with a description of the results of each choice. At this point, the students are handed the storytelling role.

In this example, I adapted elements from Celtic myth in setting a scene that mixes in medieval Irish history.

## *THE MISTS OF IRELAND*

### Characters

First, I have students create their own medieval characters as described above. The students' heroes will then face the scene I describe below.

### The Scene

The Tutha De Danann arrived at medieval Ireland in dark clouds shrouded in mist led by the great goddess Danu. The Dagda was their father god, and his dark companions included Morrigan, his Phantom Queen; the great 8-foot-tall warrior Lugh, Manannán, warrior god of the sea; the wise druid Brigid, and the young enchanter Aengus. The Tutha De Danann brought with them four great treasures:

The Stone of Fál

The Spear of Lugh

The Sword of Light

The Cauldron of the Dagda.

These treasures are buried throughout Eire. Maps directing you to each of the treasures are found someplace in the great dungeon Carraig Phádraig.

You have gathered in the fields outside the dungeon castle with the goal being to find each of the four maps. However, to succeed you must first liberate the castle from the many traps set by Lucifer who is bitter over his defeat by Saint Patrick.

You have a choice to make as you approach the gate: should you go to the graveyard Scully's Cross, the great Round Tower, or Cormac's Chapel? The choice is yours to make.

## The Path of the Graveyard

As you enter the raised plateau and walk among the many high crosses, you see a giant crow overhead. You realize this must be the Morrigan, Goddess of War in her animal form. Sure enough, the crow lands on top of Scully's Cross and predicts that you will eventually die in battle, but also signals the treasure of Lug's spear can be yours if you defeat the Eóghanachta clan. The spear can be found 50 miles north, but the clan will allow no easy passage there.

## The Path of the Round Tower

As you approach the great Round Tower, you notice the first stair is 8 feet off the ground. You also notice a piece of parchment paper, which you pick up and read. The Latin script written from a monk's hand indicates the Belfy at the top of the tower's narrow stairs has a map with directions to the Sword of Light. As you drop the note, you hear the stampeding hoofs of a marauding Viking raid.

The Path of Cormac's Cathedral

As you enter the cathedral and look toward the sarcophagus that holds the corpse of the great King Cormac MacAirt, his apparition rises and speaks to you.

> You need to find the Spear of Lugh to liberate my soul from purgatory and claim your fortune. I was raised by a she-wolf and fought on behalf of Lugh and the Tuatha De Dannan, but the invading Milesians drove us underground. You must travel north to the 16 Kesh Caves and find where my daughter Grainne is hiding.
>
> She will help you to the place of the Great Spear but beware your travel will be met by the Wrath of Fionn MacCool, whom my daughter betrayed on their wedding day, and his army of Fianna, protected by Satan himself.

When I turn the storytelling over to students, I break them into three groups depending on their choice and they continue each of the three storytelling branches among themselves. The activity builds community, promotes storytelling, and uses both imaginative and descriptive language while also improving listening skills.

In the below example, my student Nick describes his current abilities' levels and those of his Viking opponents in a battle scene following the rules of *Fighting Fantasy* game books but responding to my original scenarios and responses to his initial choice of The Path of the Round Tower described above. The roll of die or dice is referred to by the first number. I provide the opponents, in this case the Vikings, skill and stamina level.

> "My current stamina: 20 (3 and 5 +12), Skill 12 (6+6); Vikings: Stamina 5, Skill 5.
>
> *Attack strength =roll +skill."

…

Nick's battle went three rounds. He ends with this narrative account.

> As I grab the map to the sword of light I glance out at a nearby window and see Vikings putting up a ladder to climb the tower. Without another way down the tower, my only option is to fight the Vikings as I make my way down the [narrow stairs].
>
> ….
>
> My first attack appeared to catch the Vikings by surprise as they barely tried to block the swing of my sword. Despite their

best efforts to block my second and third attacks they were unable to stop my swinging sword. As I predicted, this battle was short, and I emerged victorious. I moved the rest of the way down the tower [stairs] and continued my quest.

The story can then continue with instructor feedback, or you can have students work together and with one student playing the DM and the other(s) responding to the narration. The activity is highly engaging and brings students quickly into a storytelling frame of mind. Some students will play straightforward, while others will play with a humorous bent as seems characteristic of this generation.

Finally, as another option for oral storytelling, you can also, believe it or not, follow up this lesson with a board game. The award-winning *Dixit* is a tabletop storytelling game. Players are dealt cards with images and only images. Play begins like a visual novel. On the players turn, he or she must come up with words for the card, a title, a description; something metaphoric or a little slant. You put the card face down and other players must select a picture card to match your description. Cards are shuffled and laid face up. Players guess the storyteller's original card. It's fast paced, off beat, and requires a storyteller's inspiration.

## TEXT ADVENTURES: SPURRING CREATIVITY AND DEMANDING EXACTITUDE OR GOOD READING MAKES GOOD WRITING

Around the same time that *Dungeons and Dragons* made its way around a sort of underground, evolving cult-like fan base, Will Crowther and Tim Anderson and team were using early computers to create text-based adventure games. Gary Gygax had used the dungeon as the setting. His choice of locale derived from childhood days exploring tunnels beneath the Oak Hill Sanatorium in Chicago. This underground motif proved to be a foundational setting for Cowther's *Colossal Cave Adventure* and the *Zork: Underground Kingdom* trilogy both released in the late 1970s.

I like to introduce these text adventures by talking about the dungeon/cave setting in terms of the underground archetype represented in great epics like Virgil's *The Aeneid* and Dante's *Inferno*, so students understand the power of archetypes as well as the literary antecedents of these text adventures. Usually, I bring up *Zork* on the projector and ask students to give input as I type their commands and move the story forward.

West of House.
    You are standing in an open field west of a white house, with
    a boarded front door.
    There is a small mailbox here.

    >

Students learn something about pre-Windows operating systems as a bonus, but the real value here is the need for students to use exact, very concrete language in giving their input. Students are very engaged in this whole class activity and will often play the game on their own time.

*Zork* has several game elements like collecting items, but its strength remains the interaction between player and setting. A dungeon has many trapdoors and secret rooms making for reversals of fortune, suspense, combat, and achievement.

You can follow up *Zork* by playing or assigning a contemporary-style text adventure like *A Dark Room* (2013).

## CHOOSE YOUR OWN ADVENTURE STORIES: THE FUN OF READING

Computer-based text adventures have their analog in children's Choose Your Own Adventure stories, and both formats feed into later digital-based branching narrative games. Edward Packard made the Choose Your Own Adventures format popular in children's literature beginning with *The Cave of Time* in 1979. After reading a passage young readers reach a decision point. For example, in *The Cave of Time* at the end of Chapter 39, the narration presents the reader with the amazing appearance of "the building of the Great Wall of China." The reader then has two choices for continuing the story:

"If you go up to the wall builders, turn to page 82.

If you return to the crevasses, turn to page 87" (39).

This format encourages young students to read because of their active participation in shaping the story. Although not usually an open ending, a CYA might have 14 possible endings. *A Dark Room* mentioned above extends this idea of rereading or re-playability in a digital format by taking a text adventure format and integrating the cell phone to make text input implicate the compulsive use of smartphones and adding a layer of complexity and meta-commentary to an otherwise innocent form of entertainment.

The nonlinear nature of text adventures and CYA is nothing new. There are many novels that represent nonlinear structures and open endings. Alain Robbe-Grillet's *Dans Le Labyrinth* and John Barth's *Lost in the Fun House* come immediately to mind. Both novels enact the structure they describe and frustrate any sense of plot or closure while also providing compelling and sophisticated narration. The innovation of text adventures and CYA rests more with player choice and participation than with nonlinear storytelling.

As an example, the award-winning game *Depression Quest* uses Twine to create an interactive fiction, a sophisticated form of CYA, where players make choices in a second-person narration about a person suffering from clinical depression. This game presents many possible paths and multiple endings but also embodies the experience of depression making the game an extremely effective way of representing the experience of clinical depression and creating empathy in the player. I play this game in small sections with the class so they can appreciate the impact of their choices on the story. Even more, playing *Depression Quest* students realize the lack of choices a depressed person faces.

> By the time you arrive home and change out of your uncomfortable work clothes the stress is weighing down on you like a heavy, wet wool blanket. Your computer seems to be staring you down from your desk. You want to sit down and work but the mere thought of trying to work sends your stress levels flying; more than anything you feel suddenly and absolutely *exhausted*, and feel a strong desire to hide in bed.
> Do you ...
>
> 1. Order some food, grab a drink and hunker down for a night of work.
> 2. Reluctantly sit down at your desk and try to make yourself do something
> 3. Turn on the TV, telling yourself you just need a quick half hour to unwind from work
> 4. Crawl into bed. You're so stressed and overwhelmed you couldn't possibly accomplish anything anyways.

**You are depressed. Interaction is exhausting, and you are becoming more and more withdrawn**. [Bold text is mine to replace the gray background in the game text.]

> By the time you arrive home and change out of your uncomfortable work clothes the stress is weighing down on you like a heavy, wet wool blanket. Your computer seems to be staring you down from your desk. You want to sit down and work but the mere thought of trying to work sends your stress levels flying; more than anything you feel suddenly and absolutely *exhausted*, and feel a strong desire to simply hide in bed.
>
> Do you...
>
> 1. Order some food, grab a drink, and hunker down for a night of work.
> 2. Reluctantly sit down at your desk and try and make yourself do something
> 3: Turn on the TV, telling yourself you just need a quick half hour to unwind from work
> 4: Crawl into bed. You're so stressed and overwhelmed you couldn't possibly accomplish anything anyways.
>
> You are depressed. Interaction is exhausting, and you are becoming more and more withdrawn.

In the above passage, four choices are seen by the player but the first one is crossed out with a strikethrough. This technique reinforces those choices most of us would see as reasonable but are not seen that way by someone with deep depression. The grayed-out text in different font represents the game's narrative voice. This omniscient narrative voice states common facts of clinical depression. Moreover, *Depression Question* shows how the playful aspect of narrative or jumping around the story can be used for serious subjects without sacrificing engaging play.

## HOPSCOTCH OR THE LUDIC IN LITERATURE

In terms of a readers or players playing around with story, by far the best representation of literature as game remains Argentinian novelist Julio Cortázar's *Rayuela* "Hopscotch" (1963). Published decades ahead of branching narratives, interactive fiction, or choose your own adventure, Cortázar's novel combines a highly experimental game narrative with profound metaphysical musings and complex, multilayered storytelling and characterization. The novel presents two primary reading options. You can read the novel in a traditional linear fashion, in which case the novel ends after chapter 36. This is a very unsatisfactory experience that inevitably compels a reader who may have chosen this traditional route (an unlikely choice in my view), to read option two. The second reading path covers 154 chapters, including the so-called expendable or useless chapters discarded in the first reading. Naturally the discarded or wasted always play a more central role than first expected. Like a good mystery, nothing can be overlooked if you want to find a solution or resolution, but the solution never materializes in the novel, nor does the novel end. In leaving out chapter 55, this second reading method winds up in a kind of infinite loop, like the möbius strip in Barth's Lost *in the Fun House.*

Just like any good game, reading path two comes with a Table of Instructions. The instructions are a literary hopscotch court. Hopscotch is played all over the world and has been for hundreds if not thousands of years. Rules and courts vary to a degree, but the principle of hopping around the court squares and picking up an object tossed into a square is similar. The game like Cortázar's narrative reverses itself. The child reaches one end of the court by landing on two feet and reverses direction going back over the court again. A mobile game, hopscotch can be played just about anywhere you can draw a court. Take out a piece of chalk and the city sidewalk becomes a game.

Cortázar composed the novel in a curious way. When living in Paris he simply jotted down observations. Between 1952 and 1956, he states, "I filled up pieces of paper with moments, memories, sometimes inventions, everything copied down from my daily experiences in the city, in France-in Paris, concretely" (177). In writing *Hopscotch*, he also "...was constantly finding sentences, references, and even newspaper ads that echoed with what I was writing, things that had some connection, and so I cut them out and copied them and collected them" (180). All these jottings and cut outs, everything from police reports to snippets of poems, made their way into the novel and appeared after the first narrative of 36 chapters was complete. Later Cortázar took the chapters—the various collected fragments held together by paper clips, put them on the floor of a large studio where "I started wandering around the chapters, leaving behind little pathways and letting myself by led by lines of force" (181). That's how Cortázar wrote the novel; he "had to give randomness room to play."

The novel is immensely playful, but as Cortázar remarks his writing "plays seriously" (p. 156). Playful, fun, experimental, but also a profound meditation on the human condition. Ludic literature, students will discover, has the potential to combine the festive spirit of Shakespeare's festive comedies with the seriousness of his darkest tragedies.

## Teaching Strategy

Have students collect clips from papers or the Internet over the course of a month and simultaneously ask them to keep a writer's journal jotting down their thoughts, observations, memories, on a daily, or every other day basis, for that same month. One day have a student draw out a hopscotch court and ask a few students to randomly throw down their cut-out fragments on a square. Students hop through the court one at a time each one picking up a fragment. Later the fragments are connected by class discussion, and voila, students have a short story as a game. Students learn the play of fiction, the power of experimentation, the role of chance, and the power of language as game to transform how we think about the world.

## FIGHTING FANTASIES OR THE GAME-NOVEL

Ian Livingstone, Steve Jackson, and John Peake, London roommates and young game entrepreneurs, co-founded Games Workshop in 1975. They brought *Dungeons and Dragons* to Europe under an exclusive licensing deal. With that deal in place, Jackson and Livingstone (Peake dropped out of the venture) were off to the races as we say this side of the Atlantic. Soon thereafter Jackson and Livingstone authored or coauthored a series of game books called *Fighting Fantasy*. The game novels turn text adventures into a dynamic game infusing the style of *D&D* into print-based fiction. The two authored the first *Fighting Fantasy* Gamebook, *The Warlock of Firetop Mountain* in 1982. The series has been a phenomenal success for close to 40 years.

Gamebooks combine the Choose Your Own Adventure format with a *D&D* style creating a hybrid novel that truly achieves the status of interactive fiction as game. First, you begin the novel by completing an Adventure Sheet. The reader or player's character, like a video game avatar, has Skill, Stamina, and Luck as initial conditions. Like with *D&D* a die roll determines the value of each attribute. You start an adventure or campaign in *D&D* lingo with a sword, leather armor, a shield, and a backpack with a magic potion and lantern (the key item, by the way, in *Zork*). I started *Deathtrap Dungeon* with Skill=9, Stamina=5, and Luck=5. Reading the novel and playing the game you must not only make choices that determine the direction of the story, but you encounter and do battle with monsters. You must roll two dice and add the number to the monster's Attack Strength and repeat the procedure for yourself. If you have the higher attack strength, you wound the creature and subtract points from its Stamina.

In other words, the reader makes a choice like in most branching stories, but here the game elements add significant interactivity to the reading experience. The stories are written in numbered paragraphs, not chapters. For instance, reading section 9 of *Deathtrap Dungeon*,

> The Orc's morning star thuds into your arm, knocking your sword to the floor. You must fight them bare handed, reducing your SKILL by 4 for the duration of the combat. Fortunately, the tunnel is too narrow for both Orcs to attack you at once. Fight them one at a time.
>
>   First ORC Skill=7 Stamina= 5
>   Second ORC Skill=6 Stamina=4
>   If you win, turn to **257**.

Instead of just making a choice that determines which page you turn to as in *The Cave of Time*, you now must do battle and find out the results to determine whether you continue reading linearly or jump to another place in the story. I have found that this highly interactive form of storytelling and reading has resulted in students reading more than usual. At a time when students do not read as much as most teachers would like, such experiences are compelling and rewarding.

## Teaching Strategy

One approach to Gamebooks that has worked for me asks students to chart or map their journey through the story. This map visualizes narrative and turns the reading experience into a work of art students find memorable. Below is a picture of my student Connor Dearbeck's journey through *The Warlock of Firetop Mountain* (Figures 5.1 and 5.2).

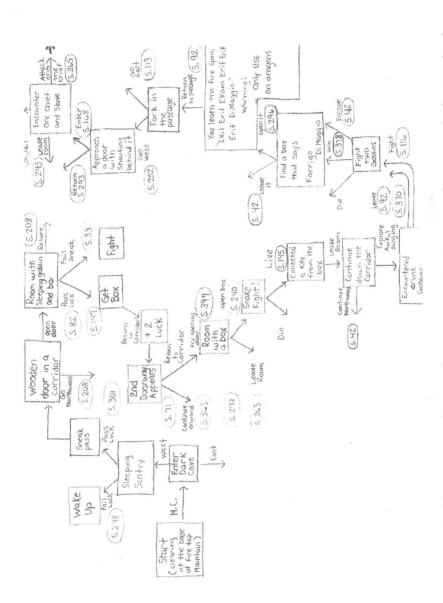

FIGURE 5.1   Conor Dearbeck's journey map from Deathtrap Dungeon. (Map courtesy of Conor Dearbeck. © Used with permission.)

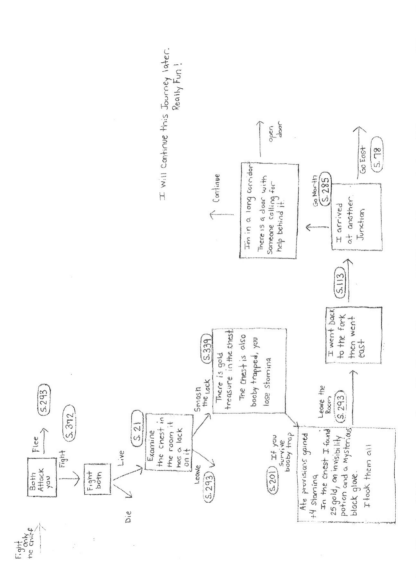

FIGURE 5.2 Conor Dearbeck's journey map from Deathtrap Dungeon 2© Used with permission. (Map courtesy of Conor Dearbeck. © Used with permission.)

## EPISODIC STORYTELLING

In episodic narrative, a game is released in installments, much like Charles Dickens published his long Victorian novels or today how comic books are published on a monthly schedule. In episodic games, an episode releases one at a time to build anticipation. Also, offering the initial episode for free hooks the player into purchasing subsequent episodes. Telltale Games had a breakthrough with *The Walking Dead* in 2012. This game adapted the already successful *Walking Dead* comic books with its built-in episodic storytelling already established by Robert Kirkwood. This series of games also used choice-driven stories to present readers with major ethical decisions that added tension and depth to the stories. *Kentucky Route Zero* kept the old underground narrative of the text adventures' caverns by telling a 5 act story using magic realism inspired by the great Columbia novelist Gabriel Garcia Marquez (one of the characters in the game is farm owner Weaver Marquez), about a road, Route Zero, running underneath Kentucky's caves.

Perhaps, the most compelling episodic game for students, however, would be the *Life is Strange* franchise. This is the game I most often use in class. The school-based setting at Blackwell Academy and the game's youthful characters always seem to grab students' interest and compel their identification with the major characters. The story takes place in fictional Arcadia Bay along the Pacific Northwest coastline. The first episode's protagonist Max Caulfield and her friend Chloe are well-developed multidimensional characters. The game's core dynamic involves searching for a missing student, Amber, as a tornado heads toward town. Decision points in the story contribute to the characters' maturation much like in a traditional bildungsroman or a story of personal development, usually undertaken by an adolescent protagonist.

The primary game mechanic whereby the protagonist Max, named after *Catcher in the Rye's* (J.D. Salinger, 1951) Holden Caulfield, can reverse time, makes every decision particularly powerful. Max's superpower allows her to rethink decisions giving them extra gravity. Moreover, what might prove effective in the short term can have long-term deleterious impact on the characters and their world, so the mechanic makes decision making complex and uncertain. Overall, the story resonates with powerful themes such as teen suicide, sexual orientation, euthanasia, and morality.

Teaching Strategy

I simply ask students to analyze this story or a single episode as they would a traditional short story or novella by identifying themes, symbols, point of view, setting, irony, and characterization. I add to this literary analysis the question, how does the rewinding time mechanic affect your interpretation of the story and the character Max? This rather basic assignment gets at the depth of narrative-driven games and enhances critical reading skills that we might typically teach with a short story. Students will also develop empathy for the characters and develop the reading competencies required to read Fitzgerald, or Hemmingway, or Twain.

## EXPLORATORY STORYTELLING: *WHAT REMAINS OF EDITH FINCH?*

The so-called point-and-click game might best be thought of as an exploratory narrative. Players investigate a location in depth by moving a protagonist around a house, i.e., an aboveground dungeon. Using the mouse to click on objects reveals messages about a room, its past, and inhabitants. Each object becomes a symbol or clue to solving the story's mystery. Here exploration is narration and the story is a rather serendipitous stroll through a building rich in history.

The best example of such storytelling would be *What Remains of Edith Finch?* In this game, you play the eponymous Edith Finch, the last remaining Finch family member, as she explores her ancestral house discovering how all family members have died in mysterious ways. The house is haunted, and the storytelling follows in the tradition of Edgar Allan Poe's horror writing; think of "The Fall of the House of Usher" (1839), one of the greatest short stories in western literature. Each room discloses a separate story woven into the larger narrative where the house, like in Poe's story, becomes the central character.

### Teaching Strategy: *The Museum of Me*

A terrific lesson for this game has been designed by Paul Darvasi, Mathew Farber, and Michelle Bertoli and published by ithrive Games. The game targets social-emotional learning in a brilliant and engaging fashion. I urge all instructors to look at this *Museum of Me* lesson (see Resources below).

## PLAYING THE DETECTIVE STORY: "HERSTORY"

Probably the two greatest stories in the history of western literature are murder mysteries. Oedipus searches for the murderer that brings about a plague and finds himself at the crossroads of destiny. Hamlet meets a ghost on an ominous night compelling him to revenge a murder whose perpetrator is not certain, but whose disclosure in the mousetrap play brings about multiple deaths. Humans seem to love murder mysteries. The genre appeals to both high art and the most compelling pop fiction. Sam Barlow's short game *Herstory* takes up this ancient, ever popular, and fascinating form to tell a murder mystery in a new narrative form.

Is *Herstory* really a game? Is Interactive Fiction a game, or game-like, or just a new form of storytelling? Like narrative, games reach into ancient history. What both have in common is the power to tell a story that entertains and moves people from all walks of life. *The Epic of Gilgamesh*, nearly 3,000 years old, started out as an oral narrative, was then transcribed on clay tablets and from there onward stories went to paper forms to the printing press and now the World Wide Web. For me, Barlow is simply playing with narrative as technology allows, just as Laurence Stern did with *Tristram Shandy* in the 18th century (circa 1759) and all great print-based writers have done as well. The critic Hugh Kenner beautifully described how novelists explored the "book as book." Flaubert, Joyce, and Beckett each in their own way pushed the print medium brought about by the Gutenberg Revolution to the limit. In that sense the novel is a kind of game that uses, subverts, and extends the rules of the medium. Barlow's "game" does the same, only now, fiction has been extended by the digital revolution allowing for a new kind of interactivity between reader and story.

Fiction has always had an implied reader and therefore has an inherent interactivity though not the kind of dynamic, reciprocal interaction we think of with video games or interactive fiction per se. Interestingly, Barlow uses the affordances of film as medium for his story. *Herstory*, also classified as a Full Motion Video game, consists of 271 very short video clips that are scrambled like dispersed pieces of a large puzzle. The game's only character is the suspected killer Hannah Smith played with exquisite nuance by voice actress Viva Siefert. Although the game can be played in the time it takes to watch a feature film, I think of the story as much more television based like a police procedural. Take an episode from any one of Dick Wolf's *Law and Order* series that focuses exclusively on the interrogation scene and you have *Herstory*, sans detectives. We see and hear only Hannah Smith and her account of events regarding her missing husband. Space is totally circumscribed like a Beckett play. The player's action is to search, save and weave together the 271 clips to make sense of the story. In this fashion, the player is very much like the reader of detective stories trying to follow clues to identify the crime's true perpetrator and their reasons for the crime. What gives the game/interactive fiction its twist is the game mechanic. Players search for video clips stored in a database appropriately called L.O.G.I.C. In other words, Barlow uses the affordance of the Internet to propel the action and drive the player/game interaction. The Internet search becomes the detective's new tool. Just as great novelists used footnotes to exploit print, Barlow uses the search engine to exploit the digital platform.

Ultimately, the story's power and innovation come from the question about whether the mystery can be solved? Edgar Allen Poe invented the detective genre with his macabre and brilliant "The Murders on Rue Morgue" (1841). In that story, the "detective" C. August Dupin uses his powers of ratiocination, reasoned thought; a combination of deductive and inductive reasoning to solve the mystery. An interesting aspect of the story is Dupin takes up this mystery for amusement, not for work. He simply likes solving mysteries. It is a game and a fun one. In *Herstory* the player is, like Dupin, an amateur detective in modern times, having to piece together video clips into a cohesive story using the search engine of digital technology and the aptly named database. But can science really solve the mystery? Can Google really deliver us the information we need to solve our various quests? Is Google the road to the truth? The answer is for you the reader and prospective player to find out. The effort is a lesson worth learning.

## Teaching Strategy

Let students ruminate on definitions and genre with the segue being considering whether inclusive definitions are even possible. Is *Herstory* a game or literature, or both, or between the two? Is *Herstory* modern or postmodern? If modern, you will solve the mystery, and if postmodern, you will not. In postmodernism and deconstruction, you put together the puzzle and story with one hand, but the other hand simultaneously scatters the pieces, and fragments the story. Dupin, an amateur detective, plays for fun, but he loves the truth, and thus plays to win. What about you?

## STORIES ON THE GO OR FLORENCE IN LOVE

The rise of tablets and smartphones, which are now ubiquitous among students, has afforded a new kind of storytelling for reading on the go. Touch screens give a material feel back to reading and mobile devices encourage stories told in snippets or bursts, fictional aphorisms. The web, of course, features short paragraphs or chunks followed by Read More…. Most of the writing is poor. Chunks might suit the medium, but they rarely suit good writing. However, several narrative-driven games for mobile devices have emerged to engage players/readers as they lunch, ride the bus, or wait for class. For example, *Brothers: A Tale of Two Sons*. It is a powerful tale of an older and younger brother searching for a cure to save their gravely ill father. The tale has mythic dimensions. Only water from the Tree of Life can save the father. Additionally, the story progresses entirely through play. You manipulate the brothers using dual controls one for each brother. Playing=storytelling. Impressively, the story also moves through symbols, actions, and gestures with spoken language (the in-game language is quite foreign to players) at a minimum.

*To the Moon* (2013), another brilliant narrative-driven game for mobile devices, uses science fiction tropes to reconstruct the memories of a dying man whose final wish is to reach the moon. Implanted memories allow the man to fulfill his wish if only in his mind, but does that matter? If you think you have traveled to the moon, do you have to travel there? What is the truth? Is happiness the highest value? The mini episodes are perfect for any literature class and the story of highest quality.

The small narrative game *Florence* by Mountains, a small Australian studio represents an excellent opportunity to teach interactive narrative as well as engage in vital social-emotional learning. The game is short, broken into Six Acts, and these acts are further broken into chapters, 20 in all. The story is communicated entirely through vision and touch. Most chapters or scenes are only 1–2 minutes in length. This visual storytelling suits today's students. The ease with which you can read a scene and return to the larger narrative later is perfect for students to read at home and discuss through an asynchronous forum or a Zoom session.

The story's protagonist, Florence, is a 25-year-old Chinese-Australian woman who meets and falls in and out of love with an Indian man. The interracial relationship provides a larger arena for discussing the impact of culture on interpersonal relationships as well as the prejudices and biases that such relationships expose. What impresses me about this story is how the game's mechanics perfectly move the narrative. Most interactive narratives require the player to make choices along a branching narrative where different choices, whether of action or dialogue, push the story in different directions. Not so with *Florence*. The story is linear, and the narrative progresses by players touching the phone's screen and completing various puzzles. As noted in a review published in *Wired* touch plays a critical role in storytelling, linking the player to Florence through tactile storytelling, ideal for the smartphone platform.

> The touch play here serves two purposes. It keeps the player engaged in the story, yes. But it also centers touch itself, bringing the body, the movement of the player's fingers and hands, into the experience, connecting touch with the game's emotional tenor. With your own hands, you make this story happen. You open boxes and help Florence's boyfriend unpack when he moves in. You brush Florence's teeth. You share food. With gestures and taps, you interact with the world the way Florence does, with your own two hands (Muncy, 2018).

Each chapter is a mini game with slightly different mechanics. For example, in the chapter "Memories," you meet a 7-year-old Florence working on art. How the player maneuvers objects with his or her finger on the screen will make a painting. Your creativity parallels Florence's creativity. However, the painting returns later in the story to play an important thematic role. Many of these mini games are simple and the chapters mundane. When Florence wakes and brushes her teeth, you simply move the brush back and forth on the screen with your finger. The lead designer Ken Wong, acclaimed designer of the casual game, *Monument Valley*, explains how these simple actions capture the essence of what the story conveys:

> Brushing teeth represents the mundanity of everyday life. In comics they would call it a "slice of life", something based on real human lives and real human experiences. It's not intended to be difficult, the idea is that anybody can get through this and have a nice experience. Later in the game when Krish is in Florence's life, tooth brushing symbolises that they have fallen into a routine.

Key moments worth exploring in class occur early on. For instance, an authority figure appears, whether a teacher or parent (you could read either as applicable), and squashes Florence's creative spirit. School goes from artistic exploration to dead routine, from free expression to rote

FIGURE 5.3 Authority figure scolding Florence as a child. (Image courtesy Annapurna Interactive. © Used with Permission.)

regurgitation. This is a teaching point. Ask students to recall when they had their creative urges thwarted and how this affected them? (Figure 5.3).

In the scene "Music", Florence hears notes and her body levitates as she follows the notes, much like an animal might follow a smell, to its source. The source ends up being a cellist in a public park (Figure 5.4).

Soon a bike accident will bring Florence face to face with Krish, the Indian cellist, and thus begins their relationship. Young love provides another theme to explore. *Romeo and Juliet* is often taught in 9th grade,

FIGURE 5.4 Florence levitating to the sound of a violin. (Image courtesy Annapurna Interactive©. Used with Permission.)

and the great thing about good stories is you can read them at many levels of education with different degrees of sophistication. Shakespeare can be read, performed, and studied in middle school, high school, college, and doctoral seminars.

However, the deeper theme of *Florence* does not concern interracial relationships so much as gender inequality. Simon Parker from *The Guardian* provides this insight:

> As in *La La Land*, this is a story in which a woman stifles her creative yearnings in order to support those of the man with whom she is romantically involved. Florence encourages Krish to enroll in a music course, literally pushing him to the college's front door. The painting set that he buys her as a thank you, meanwhile, sits idle on her desk, buried under a stack of accounting (Florence's mother told her daughter when she was a child to set down the paints and focus on more bankable subjects, so shares culpability). The subtle differences in the way in which Florence and Krish support one another's dreams is telling.

Exploring gender inequality early on with students is extremely important. Dating violence and gender harassment starts early, as early as dating occurs, and all students need to be made aware of gender expectations and roles, some invisible to young people, and how asymmetrical power situations can damage one's self-esteem and growth. No better description of this sad gender unbalance exists than Virginia Woolf's brilliant explanation of how women have served as men's distorting mirror for centuries, "Women have served all these centuries as looking-glasses possessing the magic and delicious power of reflecting the figure of man at twice its natural size" (*A Room of One's Own*, 1929). This famous quote can serve as a provocative discussion prompt where students can provide historical, literary, and personal examples.

In addition to the themes and discussion topics of ethnic identity, interracial relationships, and the power dynamics of a patriarchal culture that overtly and covertly discriminates against females and minority genders, there are three aspects of the game that promote excellent active learning activities.

*Florence*'s storytelling power resides in its use of metaphor and symbol. In a narrative without words, metaphor and symbolic language become a priority. It is an excellent opportunity for students to understand and use metaphor as a communicative tool. For instance, how do you teach the need to compromise when two different parties need to come together? A relationship is itself a metaphor for how different parties need to cooperate. Chinese-Australian and Indian can also be thought of as Republican and Democrat, or the United States and China. In Chapter Ten, "Moving In," Krish moves into Florence's flat (apartment). Two separate spaces must now become one shared space. How do you make this happen? The chapter does this by having the player unpack Krish's belongings from a box and place them on a shelf. Of course, the space is already filled with Florence's belongings, so which of Krish's belongings, often symbols of his culture, will be displayed and which remain in the box? This mini placement or sorting type game embodies the challenge of cooperation. Have students bring in a box of their important items, make pairs, and the two students must place x number of items, say 5 of the 10, they have onto a common space.

Another key learning opportunity occurs in Chapter 8, "Explorations." Krish and Florence explore the city, maybe Sidney or Melbourne, and take pictures of memorable activities. The player touches spots on a city map. A picture materializes just like in the old Polaroid instamatic days.

Students might not know much about Polaroid; therefore, this presents a great opportunity for scientific extension activities and learning about a great American scientist Dr. Edwin Land (1909–1991), the founder of Polaroid (see extension activities below) and inventor of the Polaroid Land Model 95 camera in 1948. However, students are all too familiar with instant pictures taken by their ubiquitous smartphones and posted to Instagram, the same idea but a different technology. Unfortunately, the smartphone's camera has facilitated the obsessive taking of selfies which is symptomatic of a strongly narcissistic aspect of our culture. Counter this trend, by asking students to move around their local neighborhood, city, village, campus, etc., and take pictures of places they consider important and include in the photo someone other than themselves. They can then create a visual story or design a vison board or storytelling map to share with the class. This exercise expands their sense of place as well as connection to others.

Finally, jigsaw-type puzzles feature prominently in *Florence*. Many chapters have the player move pieces around the screen to fit into a puzzle. The puzzles are a perfect metaphor of relationships. At first pieces are tough to fit together, then they fit together seamlessly, and, finally, all too often do not fit together at all. Have students practice their own metaphoric meaning making using *Minecraft* or *LEGO*. These two products require building, and like a relationship that also requires building, the player must fit a variety of pieces together to make a whole structure that survives the challenges brought by the passage of time.

In conclusion, *Florence*'s beautiful integration of story with game mechanics in a series of imagistic snapshots about a relationship's rhythm represents an excellent example of casual game storytelling crafted for a cell phone. The game works well for both high school and college classes in areas such as creative writing, digital storytelling, the Digital Humanities, visual communication, contemporary literature, psychology, interpersonal communication, and the short story. The game can be played effectively paired with a silent movie, *Romeo and Juliet*, the film *Zebrahead* (Drazan, 1992), about a young white male and black female's relationship, Adrian Tomine's graphic novel *Shortcomings* (2007), and similar works.

## LESSON IDEAS

This chapter has lesson ideas/teaching strategies following every section, so here I offer extended ideas on using *Florence* in multiple disciplines including the natural sciences.

### Chemistry/Physics/Art

1 Have students read Land's *Scientific American* article for historical context on instant photo development. You can also draw parallels with Land and one of his modern computer savvy admirers Steve Jobs.

2. Reproduce Land's experiment demonstrating "retinex theory" and "the Land effect" which concerns color theory and perception. This can be expanded into discussions of how Land's ideas have been developed in digital photography and software.

3. Have some fun and ask students to go into the field—i.e., anywhere but the classroom, and find examples showing aspects of Land's theories like color constancy, i.e., the exact same shade of gray can appear as two different shades when adjacent to each other.

### Film

As *Florence* tells a nonverbal story, show students an old silent film that depicts relationships and talk about how silent film's storytelling achieves its effects. D.W. Griffin's *True Heart Susie* (1919) offers an excellent example for parallels with *Florence*. Susie, played by the great Lillian Gish, makes a few unappreciated sacrifices for a man only to end up losing him to a more "fashionable" woman.

### Literature/Graphic Novel

Graphic novels make excellent companion texts to *Florence* because of their emphasis on art as a primary mode of storytelling. Adrian Tomine's *Shortcomings* (Drawn and Quarterly, 2009) would be a superb choice. This story features an Asian American male protagonist, Ben Tanka, and his relationship with a more self-identified Asian American girlfriend, Miko Hayashi. It is a subtle and profound representation of ethnic dynamics in relationships.

## NOTES

1. *The Last of Us* has a zombie apocalypse framework, but the story has a depth of characterization rare for any medium. The cross-country journey of Joel and the young girl Ellie made me think of the post-apocalyptic journey of father and son in Cormac McCarthy's Pulitzer Prize-winning novel *The Road* (2006). Although no writing rises to the level of McCarthy's haunting lyricism, *The Last of Us*'s depiction of the paternal relationship creates a powerful empathetic connection with the player not unlike the relationship between father and son in McCarthy's novel.

2. The best discussion or oral culture remains, what to me is one of the best scholarly books I have ever read, Eric A. Havelock's *Preface to Plato* (Harvard University Press, 1963). Havelock gives a comprehensive account of oral culture and the Homeric state of mind and the transition to rational thought and literate culture after Homer. The book is full of insight into poetry, language, ancient Greek culture, the birth of philosophy, and the lasting cultural consequences of both.

    The folklorist Albert Lord spent years studying the composition of oral narrative in the Balkans. A second edition of his classic book *The Singer of Tales*, edited by Stephen Mitchell and Gregory Nagy (Harvard University Press, 2000), includes DVD recordings of Lord's work and the singers or oral poets, he studied.

## GAMES

*A Dark Room*

Developer and publisher: Doublespeak Games, 2016. Designer: Michel Townsend

An open source, contemporary text adventure with several narrative and game play twists.

*Colossal Cave Adventure*

Developed and designed by Will Crowther. Published: CRL, 1976.

The first interactive fiction text. Crowther's favorite hobby was spelunking. Kentucky, by the way, has the largest system of underground caverns in the country. You can visit this amazing world at Mammoth Cave National Park, https://www.nps.gov/maca/index.htm. It is a UNESCO World Heritage Site.

*Depression Quest*

Developed and published by Quinnspiracy. Designed by Zoë Quinn, 2013.

Serious interactive fiction at its best.

*DixIt*

Designed by Jean-Louis Roubira and published by Libellud, 2008.

An award-winning storytelling-based board game that gives students the flavor of traditional storytelling.

*Dungeons and Dragons*

Developed and designed by Gary Gygax and Dave Arneson, originally published by Tactical Studies Rules, Inc., 1974.

The original and highly influential role-playing fantasy game now has five versions. There are rule books, player handbooks, and many other publications and collectable figurines that go with the game, but the basics require just the dice and a good storyteller.

*Florence*

Developer: Mountains. Publisher: Annapurna Interactive, 2018. Designer: Ken Wong.

A fun, romantic coming-of-age story that tells about the maturation of Florence through clever puzzles and interactive events.

*Herstory*

Developed and published by Sam Barlow, 2015.

An original, highly inventive detective fiction that uses player input and contemporary technology to tell its story.

*Kentucky Route Zero*

Developer: Cardboard Games. Publisher: Annapurna Interactive. Designers: Jake Elliot, Tamas Kemenczy, and Ben Babbit.

A point-and-click adventure in five Acts following the travels of truck driver Conway on his travels along a mysterious underground highway. An inventive story in the tradition of Latin American magic realism.

*The Last of Us*

Developer: Naughty Dog. Publisher: Sony Computer Entertainment. Designer: Jacob Minkoff

An action-adventure game developed for PlayStation. This game has a powerful and compelling narrative that rivals traditional novels in its thematic depth.

*The Legend of Zelda*

Developed and published by Nintendo. Designers: Shigeru Miyamoto and Takashi Tezuka, 1986.

A worldwide franchise of epic proportions this game in many ways serves as a prototype for fantasy adventure storytelling in video games. It is an enormously popular franchise with students.

*Life is Strange 1*

Developed: Dontnod Entertainment. Publisher: Square Enix, 2015.

Published in five installments, this is the best example of episodic interactive narrative in terms of symbolism, characterization, and player choice. As of this writing, there are five games in the franchise.

*Red Dead Redemption 2*

> Developed and published by Rockstar Games. Designer: Imran Sarwar, 2018.

> An open-world adventure with a story worthy of Zane Grey.

*To the Moon*

> Developed and published by Freebird Games, 2011. Designers: Ken Gao and Lannie Sheey III.

> A terrific science fiction narrative about artificial memories, hope, and last wishes. This is an exceptional example of a video game narrative.

*That Dragon Cancer*

> Developer and publisher: Numinous Games, 2016. Designers Ryan Green with Amy Green and Josh Lawson.

> A powerful, emotionally intense video game based on the experience of Ryan and Amy Green as they cope with their son Joel who was diagnosed with cancer as an infant and passed at age 5. This is an example of storytelling that will create empathy in even the most emotionally distant player.

*The Walking Dead*

> Developed and published by Telltale Games, 2012.

> Adapted from the comic series by Robert Kirkman this series uses decision-based storytelling with some exceptionally challenging moral dilemmas to fight your way clear of zombies.

*What Remains of Edith Finch?*

> Developer: Giant Sparrow. Publisher: Annapurna Interactive. Designer: Chris Bell, 2017.

> A terrific storytelling game in the horror/mystery genre worthy of Stephen King and full of player exploration and adventure.

*Zork I or Zork: The Great Underground Empire*

Developers: MIT. Publisher: Infocom, 1980. Designers: Tim Anderson, Marc Blank, Bruce Daniels, and Dave Lebling.

The pioneering text adventure can still be played online. There were three installments, but they were intended as a single epic narrative.

## RESOURCES

Primary Texts

Barth, John. *Lost in the Fun House.* Anchor, Reissue, 1988, originally published in 1968.

A collection of short stories that hovers between a novel and story collection looping back on itself with narration that mimics a Möebius strip.

Cortázar, Julio. *Rayeula* (*Hopscotch*). Alfaguara, 2013, originally published in Spanish in 1963. English translation by Gregory Rabassa, Pantheon Modern Writers, 1967.

Discussed above, *Hopscotch* is a marvel of invention, playfulness, and gameful narration with profound philosophical, primarily existential, and metaphysical themes

Livingstone, Ian, and Jackson, Steve. *Fighting Fantasy* series. Puffin, Wizard Books, Scholastic: 1982------------.

Written in the second person, these highly interactive game books sold in the millions during the 1980s. The first novel *The Warlock of Firestop Mountain* was published in 1982, and Livingston published *The Assassins of Allansia* in 2019. These books are a bridge between print's Choose Your Own Adventures, *Dungeons and Dragons,* and the interactive fantasy of the early personal computer and World Wide Web.

Robbe-Grillet, Alain. *Dans La Labyrinthe.* (*In the Labyrinth*). English Reissue by Grove Press, 2018 published with *Jealousy.* The original French version of the novel was published in 1959 by Éditions de Minuit.

This novel cannot be summarized, but I point out the structure of the novel is like a labyrinth, recursive, twisty, and compelling in ways game-based interactive fiction strives to be.

*Thank You for Playing.* Directed by David Osit and Malika Zouhali-Worrall, 2015. Documentary film.

A moving documentary about Ryan and Amy Green's game *My Dragon Cancer* and its development. The documentary was shown as part of Public Broadcasting System's POV series, which includes classroom activities and guidelines: http://archive.pov.org/thankyouforplaying/.

Tomine, Adrian. *Shortcomings*. Drawn and Quarterly, 2009, originally published, 2007.

A brilliant graphic novel that explores race, ethnic stereotypes, relationships, and culture with the subtlety of Chekhov.

*Zebrahead*. Directed by Anthony Drazan, Triumph Films, 1992.

## Websites/Organizations/Curricula

### Museum of Me

An excellent downloadable curriculum around the game *What Remains of Edith Finch?* written by Paul Darvasi and Mathew Farber for the ithrive Games Foundation. The curriculum includes 11 lessons and addresses Social and Emotional Learning in an English classroom: https://ithrivegames.org/ithrive-curriculum/museum-of-me/.

## Books

Kushner, David, with Shadmi, Koren (Illustrator) *Gary Gygax and the Creation of D&D: Rise of the Dungeon Master*. Nation Books, 2017.

A fun and information biography of Gary Gygax in graphic novel or graphic nonfiction format that can be read in a single setting by students.

Montfort, Nick. *Twisty Little Passages: A Approach to Interactive Fiction*. MIT Press, 2005.

A very good interpretation of how interactive fiction works but would benefit from updating.

Salter, Anastasia. *What Is Your Quest: From Adventure Games to Interactive Fiction*? University of Florida Press, 2014.

A solid overview of interactive fiction from text adventures to future possibilities.

# II

## Games as Transformative Classroom Experiences

# CHAPTER 6

# Using a Game to Counter the Prejudice, Bias, and Discrimination against the Transgender Community

## *If Found and Transformative Storytelling*

### REPRESENTING TRANSGENDER PERSONS DURING A "CULTURE WAR"

Lady Gaga's album *Born This Way* passed its 10th anniversary (May 23, 2021). The album's like-named single has also now passed the 10-year mark (released February 11, 2011). Lady Gaga's anthem to inclusiveness and tolerance with its accompanying music video and Grammy performance showing the imaginary birth of a future, more equitable world appeared to foreshadow a growing, and more positive presence of transgender people in American culture (Lou Reed's pioneering representations

DOI: 10.1201/9781003201465-9

of transgender people many decades ago occurred just as minority groups were becoming a presence, see the below note).[1] Caitlyn Jenner's acceptance speech for the Arthur Ashe Award For Courage on July 16, 2015, at the ESPY Awards had what appeared to be a transformative effect on how many people would begin to see the transgender community as a genuine, fully human, and, finally, welcome in mainstream America.

Streaming and Reality TV media has also helped bring some weight and long-needed attention to the transgender community. "I am Cait" (2015–2016), following the transition of superstar athlete Bruce Jenner to Caitlyn Jenner, and the ongoing Reality TV autobiography of Jazz Jennings in "I am Jazz" (2015–) both displayed the daily reality of transgender women. Chaz Bono appeared on Season 13 of "Dancing with the Stars" (2011), dancing with professional Lacey Schwimmer, and despite plenty of backlash from some viewers, the transgender male celebrity brought a humane perspective for the audience to experience. Fictional portrayals of transgender woman Sophia Burset by Laverne Cox, herself an outspoken transgender woman, in "Orange is the New Black" (2013–2019), and two-time Emmy winner and Golden Globe winner Jeffrey Tambor as transgender woman Maura Pfefferman in "Transparent" (2014–2019) represented a nuanced portrayal of these marginalized citizens. However, even this progressive change in media portraits of the transgender population had a dark current. Mr. Tambor left the show in 2017 after accusations of sexual harassment, including sexual harassment of transgender women, thus undermining his character's portrayal. He was fired from the show in February 2018.

The counternarrative to the slowly emerging progressive representation of transgender people has been the fear mongering, transphobia, and outright discrimination brought to the surface by the election of Donald J. Trump in 2016. For example, President Trump's tweets (2017) denying transgender people the right to serve in the military exemplifies his reactionary, extremist beliefs. The series of tweets ends by saying, "Our military must be focused on decisive and overwhelming victory and cannot be burdened with the tremendous medical costs and disruption that transgender in the military would entail. Thank you." The tweets define potential transgender soldiers who are qualified and willing to serve the country as a burden. Such a statement strips transgender people of their humanity. Thus, a group of people marginalized, criminalized, and stigmatized; victims of a disproportionate number of suicides, homelessness, and poverty find themselves in the crosshairs of public bigotry.

The two narratives about the transgender population and how the country should treat them has wide implication for all minorities. The affirmative, inclusive narrative signaled by Lady Gaga's song, the shows mentioned above, and the Supreme Court's decision in Bostock v. Clayton County Georgia, June 15, 2020, protect the rights of transgender people from discrimination under the Civil Rights Act of 1964, and their decision in the Gavin Grimm case (2021), President Biden's proclamation on the Transgender Day of Visibility (March 31, 20201), and Dr. Rachel Levine's confirmation as Assistant Secretary to Health and Human Services by a vote of 52-48 all affirm equality.[2] In the second narrative, the affirmative response for transgender equality is confronted by the Republican Party and far-right conservative groups who have launched a veritable legal assault on transgender people to restore a purely binary understanding of difference (ACLU, 2021). This assault includes forbidding transgender girls and transgender women from participating in high school or college sports, barriers to the use of gender affirmative bathrooms and other facilities, roadblocks to obtaining proper identity documentation, and even the criminalization of health services (prohibiting doctors from giving youth necessary medical care). In states with republican-controlled legislatures, even those cities that do allow for gender difference will be prevented from enacting municipal laws or regulations that do not align with state law and policy. The Trump-engendered reactionary, anti-democratic movement threatens the transgender community's civil rights in multiple ways. Last year (2021) saw the murder or violent deaths of 17 transgender people, and 2020 witnessed 44 violent fatalities (HRC, 2021).

Ironically, shocking as this reactionary anti-transgender trend is these bills asserting the government's ability to define one's gender are being proposed and enacted by a party that claims to base its philosophy on minimal government interference in the lives of citizens. What could be more intrusive on an individual's privacy than the state telling a person what gender they can live as while moving about in certain public spaces? The Republican Party's shift away from its traditional core values embodied by former Presidents Reagan, George H. Bush, and George W. Bush threatens to turn the party into a cult of personality under an authoritarian leadership that would subvert the foundation of a two-party system upon which a healthy democracy depends. In other words, the stakes are extremely high over the need to protect minority groups.

This young century has already witnessed the rise of the MeToo# and Black Lives Matter movements in response to sexual abuse/sexism/misogyny with respect to the former and racism with respect to the latter. More such organized movements that protect the right of citizens deemed "other" or marginal are needed. In the meanwhile, small and significant changes in promoting better understanding and empathy for the transgender community can be made through works of artistic expression.

Let me return for a moment to Caitlyn Jenner's ESPY speech. She promoted, "the simple idea: accepting people for who they are. Accepting people's differences." Caitlyn goes on to explain how respect generates compassion generates empathy and how empathy creates positive change in people's attitudes and actions, "They [transgender people] deserve your respect. And for that respect comes a more compassionate community, a more empathetic society and a better world for all of us."

More recently, the Canadian actor Elliott Page voiced similar sentiments when coming out (December 1, 2020) on Instagram and through interviews with *Time Magazine* (March 2021) and Oprah Winfrey (April 30, 2021). Such celebrities have an international platform, and considerable national and international influence, but reaching people and encouraging empathy requires continual education and understanding. Games, movies, and literature can all help promote empathy and understanding for marginalized groups of people. In the rest of this essay, I will discuss an exceptional game from Ireland, *If Found* (Dreamfeel, 2020), that can help players in both high school and college, as well as adults, connect with the lived experience of a transgender woman. This connection between those who are different or "other" and those deemed mainstream or acceptable, i.e., the "norm," helps build bridges necessary for genuine equality and the better world referred to by Caitlyn Jenner. Such equality is fundamental to democracy. Art that supports such an inclusive vision should be recognized, encouraged, and promoted.

## KASIO SAYS: TEACHING THE JOURNEY OF DISCOVERY AND ACCEPTANCE THROUGH THE GAME *IF FOUND*

*If Found* (DREAMFEEL, 2020) is an Irish game that explores transgender identity. It is interactive fiction, but one where the interaction does not change the course of the story. There is no branching narrative. Rather, players touch their smartphone's screen (the platform I used to play the game). The mechanic of erasure slowly moves the story from screen to screen, in a very nuanced, emotionally rich fashion.

You play the game as the transgender protagonist Kasio. Her diaries are the game's material. You read her diary, both its words, and the words' visualization—by erasing the screen, dissolving one screen, part by part—to reveal the ongoing story underneath. This sole game mechanic—erasing the screen—resonates with players. Memories vanquish as you explore Kasio's world in a genuinely intimate way. On a smartphone, your touch erases images and scenes as you move your finger back and forth on the screen, which has a powerful effect on your experience of the story. It is like reading a print comic book, where you turn the pages and see the story unfold. In *If Found*, the next scene seems like a new panel of a comic book as you move over the gutter from panel to panel with the image of the previous panel/scene still lingering in your mind and peripheral vision.

The game interweaves two stories. The secondary narrative tells the story of a space explorer Dr. Cassiopeia investigating a black hole, but as the astronaut's name suggests, the protagonists are symbolically linked, both on missions of discovery. Cassiopeia has happened upon a black hole that appears ready to consume the earth; however, she learns through contact with a person on earth called "control," that she can travel through wormholes opened by the black hole to Ireland where she can prevent the apocalypse (sort of like the character 5 in *The Umbrella Academy*).

Kasio's story takes place on the island of Achill, just off the west coast of Ireland's County Mayo. Achill is a beautiful, rugged, very rural island. Kasio has returned from Dublin and her university studies, but her homecoming presents many tribulations. She is disowned by her widowed mother and brother Fergus despite her educational achievements and sincere need for acceptance. Kasio becomes an outsider shamed by her family, full of self-doubt, homeless, and nomadic. She finds temporary residence as a squatter (more common in Ireland and England than the United States, a squatter occupies an abandoned building, house, or apartment) with friend Colum, his boyfriend Jack, and a friend Shans. The trio lives in an abandoned Big House and forms a punk band called the Bandshees. The story represents the day-to-day struggles of a transgender woman trying to find a sense of self and security during the month of December 1993.

Both a universal and a very Irish game, the story retains the Irish dialect, rhythms, and vernacular that many Americans will need to access the game's wonderful glossary to understand. Having lived in Ireland, the language gave the story great texture for me. Understanding the Irish context helps magnify the story's literary depth. First, Achill is a very rural, isolated place which suggests a community of deep conservative values. Such isolated, rather closed communities are exceedingly difficult places for a transgender person to belong. Being transgender in Dublin or New York City is challenging enough but being transgender in say rural North Dakota or on Achill Island amplifies the transgender person's isolation.[2] Also, like much of the Republic of Ireland, Kasio's family is Catholic, and Catholicism plays a critical role in citizens' daily lives. As the story builds toward a family gathering at Christmas, religion and the message of hope grows stronger, but also more tense. Will Kasio find acceptance? Can a transgender woman feel at home when home?

As a not unimportant aside, The Big House in Irish history is not just a big house.[3] It is a mansion, but more specifically an Anglo-Irish Big House, built and occupied by the wealthy, propertied class, Protestants. When these houses were built the Catholic Irish peasants were very much second-class citizens in their own country. The Protestant landowners benefited from the largesse of the British Crown. Irish resentment at the British exploded in County Mayo, where the story of *If Found* is set. In 1798, peasants and the Society of United Irishmen, with some late-stage French assistance, rebelled against the occupying British forces. They did not win, and thousands lost their lives. Still, the spirit of nationalism and the fight for autonomy, to define the Irish as free people living in a free land owes much to this historical moment.

Players do not need to know anything about this Irish history or Ireland to play, enjoy, and learn from the game, but the context I add above provides some additional symbolic meaning for understanding Kasio's transgender situation. If you think of the Big House as dispossessing the Irish from their own home and Kasio and her nomadic "friends" as a dispossessed or homeless gender—homeless in the sense of belonging to a larger, inclusive community—then you have the marginal group among the marginalized people, double outsiders. Hence Kasio's search for a home, a community, and a full sense of identity has deep historical as well as psychological roots.

As mentioned above, *If Found*'s transformative power derives from its slow, intricate detailed depiction of Kasio's quotidian existence. Like a great comic book, the story unfolds through diary pages broken into segments much like a comic page divided into panels. The panel/scene itself dissolves like an aspect-to-aspect transition in comics where each section you erase displays something else, another angle or perspective on the scene. The transitions between scenes feature moment-to-moment transitions, a slow-motion observation of Kasio's inner life reflected through words, sketches, occasional dialogue, and color. Again, like a comic book colorist, the artist's use of color sets both the tone of scenes and evokes the characters' emotions. It is a very tactile or material story. Touching the screen is like turning a comic book page, the digital becoming almost like print. Even character dialogue takes place by touching each character and watching the "speech bubble" appear. The game takes on this physical characteristic in a way that genuinely brings the story out of the digital ether into an authentic, fully realized series of moments in a young transgender woman's life.

In terms of the narrative itself, Kasio struggles with very her tenuous family situation. Her relationship with the Bandshees also has a tenuous, transient quality. Colum and Jack are paired off and Shans ultimately rejects her. A particularly raw scene occurs when Kasio and Shans break into her family's house to steal some necessary survival items and are discovered in the act by Kasio's brother. He stresses the pain Kasio has caused their ma. Kasio ends up alone in the abandoned house burning her diary to survive the cold and feeling on the brink of suicide.

The "straight" world perceives the transgender person as a "freak" (Figure 6.1).

FIGURE 6.1  Kasio as the double outsider. (Image courtesy of Llaura McGee. Used with permission of the Dreamfeel team ©.)

It is a tragic, dehumanizing, and annihilating prejudice. Yet, Kasio moves on. Ultimately, Kasio's relationship with her mother determines the story's falling action. What remains clear to the player is how much Kasio's mother cares for her. She is a traditional Catholic mother, probably devout, living in a very rural, conservative community. Yet, she genuinely struggles to understand her daughter's difference and her struggle, her love moves the story toward reconciliation and acceptance (Figure 6.2).

Irish writing most often has an affirmative trajectory, like the Irish wake: grief mixes with joy, and the end is always a beginning (like James Joyce's *Finnegan's* Wake, 1939). Think of how Joyce's great novel *Ulysses* (1922) ends with Molly's affirmation, however much ambiguous, nonetheless an affirmation. That story is also the story of a double outsider, Leopold Bloom, the wandering Irish Jew. If Bloom is the anti-epic, anti-hero, the everyman, whose triumph is simply returning home, being home, in Dublin, then Kasio-the transgender woman, also embodies that quest for home, where the outsider, the marginal can be at peace with herself. This wonderful game, a profound, interactive story about the player's interaction with the transgender community's daily reality humanizes the transgender experience for players for whom such an existence seems remote and incomprehensible. Students need this humanizing experience, this "encounter" with gender difference before they graduate into a world where difference too often becomes deadly, a real war of the sexes, and the

FIGURE 6.2 Mother and daughter reconciliation. (Image courtesy of Llaura McGee. Used with permission of the Dreamfeel team ©.)

outsider, the one who is perceived as different from the arbitrary norm, the fatal victim of ignorance and hatred.

## NOTES

1. In the great Lou Reed lyric, "Walk on the Wild Side," from his album *Transformer* (RCA Records, 1972), Reed tells the story of five marginalized people, two of whom were transgender women, Holly Woodlawn (1946–2015) and Candy Darling (1944–1974). All five journey toward New York City, where, along with San Francisco, those who are different were welcome (at least in certain neighborhoods and sections). These marginalized people ended up embraced and promoted by Andy Warhol, who was among other things, a kind of Patron Saint for the outcast. Warhol encouraged the "outsiders," creative people discriminated against and scorned by society, to express their unique creativities at his studio, The Factory.
   My subtitle for the section on the game *If Found*, "Kasio Says" plays off another Lou Reed song, "Candy Says" about transgender woman Candy Darling from *The Velvet Underground* (MGM, 1969). Darling's tragic life ended at the young age of 29, a victim of lymphoma.

2. A rare encouraging sign emerged when the U.S. Supreme court refused to hear the case of "Gavin Grimm v. Gloucester County School Board, No. 19-1952 (4th Cir. 2020)." The school district had refused to allow Grimm, a transgender male, born female, to use the boy's bathroom. The school board argued that other students' privacy rights would be violated if Gavin- who identifies as male, used the male bathroom. The court disagreed and upheld the lower court's decision that maintains youth should be allowed to use the bathroom aligned with their gender and rejecting that this claim violated Title IX by discriminating against Gavin. Discrimination is a weak word here because in effect the transgender youth end up being stigmatized, isolated, and humiliated by using an out of the way bathroom separate from all other students. The full case is listed under resources.

3. In correspondence with the game's designer Llaura McGee she mentioned the Big House in the game had some of its design suggested by the famous big house of British land agent Charles Boycott. Boycott, yes, the very man from whose name we get the word and term boycott, moved to Achill Island in 1854 and built the house on 2,000 acres near the village of Doogh. Prior to moving to Achill, Boycott lived on the mainland in Lough Mask, Co. Mayo where the local Irish National Land League helped ostracize him by refusing to do business with Boycott. It is a long and complicated history, but the point being the Irish were fighting back for the land taken, occupied, and exploited by the British. This association of the game with Irish history resonates even more with this background. Kasio being a dispossessed transient occupant with traces of Irish history inscribed on her soul sort if speak.

## LESSON IDEAS

Swimsuits, Society and Self-Discovery: Living with Mirrors

*If Found* can be played in 2 hours and should be assigned as homework between classes. Before assigning such a game or any other potentially controversial work of art the instructor needs to frame the game with a discussion of what transgender means in historical, cultural, and psychological terms. You need to elicit students' thinking about gender. How do they define gender? How is gender different from one's sex? How does one learn about their gender and does this change over time?

In terms of a concrete lesson, an extraordinarily rich theme would be exploring body image. All students will relate to the topic, often in very personal ways. I would start by playing Lou Reed's "Candy Says," and ask students to interpret the lyric the way they would read a poem. The poem told from Candy Darling's perspective includes the line, "Candy says I've come to hate my body...." What a powerful line. What does the world require of one's body and how does that requirement place a particular burden on a transgender person?

Watch the very first episode of "I am Jazz," July 15, 2015, "All About Jazz" where she goes shopping for a bathing suit. Ask students how they feel about watching Jazz thinking about her image and how choosing a swimsuit can be such a major decision. Giving students the opportunity to draw/sketch out responses to the show, or game, can be powerful.

The final episode of *Transparency,* Season 1, "Why Do We Cover Mirrors," September 26, 2014, can provide a tie into the theme of how we see ourselves through reflections and differentiate the outside from the inside of a person. The episode features a funeral and the family members' response to death and mourning. In the Jewish faith, you cover mirrors to prevent feelings of vanity from emerging and detracting one from focusing exclusively on the person being mourned.

Play short excerpts from Elliot Page's interview with Oprah. He talks about an incident when he was ten. He was attending an event at a swimming pool, but he did not have a swimsuit. Consequently, he had to wear male swim trunks. To Him, that moment that we might think of as embarrassing was a moment of joy because he finally could dress as the gender, he felt he was. Jump ahead ten more years, and Elliot talks about his Oscar nomination for the film *Juno* (2007). Elliot was required to attend various red carpet-type events culminating in Oscar night when he was expected to wear a designer evening gown and heels. What we would most likely assume to be a moment of tremendous joy was for him a moment of terror and despair because he was dressed opposite to how he identified. Elliot could not even look at a mirror during this time because he did not want to see himself dressed as a woman.

This brings me to a set of music-based lesson ideas.

## Body Image and Candy Says

Lou Reed's "Candy Says," ends with a powerful refrain (stanzas 2 and 4) where she, channeled by Reed, talks about being older and looking at herself as someone from outside herself speculating on what she would see from a distance.

Ask students to write a short 5-minute in-class paper or illustrate what they will look like in 20 years. You now have material for an immensely powerful class discussion about identity, body image, and culture.

"New York City, the Wild Side and Marginal Groups"

Ask students why the five people Reed catalogs in "Walk on the Wild Side" are traveling to New York City? What makes New York City a desired destination for people ostracized in their home communities? What was New York City and American culture like in the late 1960s and 1970s and what has changed with respect to these marginalized figures?

## Lady Gaga's "Born this Way" Lessons

"The National Anthem and National Identity"

Listen to the song in class and ask students to define an anthem. Mention the National Anthem, what that song means, and why we most often stand and sing as it plays or if one does not stand what does that mean? How does Lady Gaga's song change or expand the meaning of the National Anthem? What is the difference between dancing to a song and singing along with a song?

## Diversity

List the minority groups mentioned in the song and ask students to identify how each of these groups have been marginalized or excluded at different times from the American mainstream society. This would be an opportunity to talk about the anti-Asian hate that arose in America during the COVID-19 pandemic.

## Redefining Oneself

In the lyrics, Gaga draws a distinction between a "finite birth" and an "infinite birth". Explore this difference with the class. The finite birth refers to our birthdate over which we have no control. Ask students how they think the circumstances of their birth might have impacted who they are today, e.g., place of birth, race and ethnicity, anatomical sex, parents, economic standing, historical time. Next explain how an "infinite birth" is both symbolic and literal referring to a person's statement or feeling of being reborn. This birth is under one's control. For example, a gay person who comes out as gay has been reborn in terms of their identity and relationship to society. A religious conversion is another kind of rebirth. In a student's experience even a change of major can be life altering. Maybe your parents or social expectations "determined" your choice of major and in your sophomore year you realized that this choice did not fit you or make you happy, so you make a radical change based on your own terms. I distinctly remember a female engineering major at a major university where I taught changing her major to journalism and transferring to another college. That would be an example of infinite birth. For transgender people the moment of transition could also be thought of as a new birth, but a birth into what they consider to be their true self.

## GAMES

*Dys4ia*

Anna Anthropy designer, originally published by Newgrounds, 2007.

This abstract game can be played in class. It will give students/players a concrete, but metaphoric experience of living the realities of dysphoria and the process of transitioning. There are four levels, each an abstract mini game. As an example, the first three levels are all called "Bullshit": Gender, Medical, and Hormonal, showing the designer's willingness to call out discrimination in all areas. Moving through the game the player encounters abstract representations of obstacles a transgender person faces. For instance, in Gender Bullshit, the player must move a shape through a jagged opening in a yellow brick wall. Inevitably, the player hits the wall. This activity shows how hard "fitting in" is for a transgender person. They are always hitting walls or barriers. However, the wall is yellow brick and ironically, echoes Dorothy's Yellow Brick Road to Oz, but no utopia here. This mini game enacts discrimination in a vivid fashion. The female protagonist is always called a sir. When the player simulates shaving, the rapidly moving razor cuts the image's face thus representing the wound of gender transformation.

*I am Dog(s)*

*A queer little story of discovery, plurality, and therian identity.* Created by SoftAnnaLee. Self-Published, 2021.

A profound, cleverly designed Twine game about transgender identity, non-human affiliations, and self-perception.

*If Found*- Dreamfeel, published by Annapurna Interactive, 2020. Discussed above. *If Found* was co-written by Llaura McGee and Eve Golden-Woods. Founded by game designer Llaura McGee Dreamfeel's team includes in addition to Llaura, Eve Gordon Woods, Liadh Young, Tim Sabo, and Brianna Chew. The studio is based in Dublin, Ireland.

*Saving You, From Yourself*

Created by pcOhidq and self-published, 2018.

A Twine story where you play a therapist and determine patients' transgender identity.

*Tell Me Why-*

Developer: Dontnod Entertainment. Publisher: Xbox Studios, 2020.

An excellent narrative game featuring twins Tyler and Alyson Ronan as they reunite in remote Alaska to investigate the death of their mother. This story-based game has three episodes or chapters. One of the twins, Tyler is a transgender man voiced by a transgender man. The game does an admirable and sensitive job of exploring the perspective of a transgender man in addition to allowing students/players a portrait of Tlingit culture. The Tlingit are indigenous to the Northwest (Alaska and far northwest Canada).

## RESOURCES

Primary Texts

*Becoming Chaz*—Fenton Bailey and Randy Barbato, 2011. Documentary.

An excellent, close-up, and honest documentary about celebrity Chaz Bono's (born Chastity Bono) experiences. Most media attention focuses on transgender women, possibly a reflection on our culture's obsession with the female body. Thankfully, this film gives much-needed attention to transgender men and their experience.

> *I am Cait*—Banim/Murray Productions, *E! Network*, 2015–2016, two seasons.

A Reality TV account of former Olympic Gold Medalist, and celebrity Bruce's Jenner's transition to Caitlyn Jenner. It is a close look at how a famous and wealthy person copes with transitioning into the public spotlight.

> *I am Jazz*—TLC/*The Learning Channel*, 2015-.

A Reality TV show, autobiography of sorts, about teenager Jazz Jennings' transition to a transgender girl. Because Jazz is from an ordinary American family and at an age many students can identify with this show has many valuable talking points for helping students understand a transgender person's thoughts and feelings in an everyday context.

> Lady Gaga, "Born this Way," from *Born This Way* (Innerscope, 2011), 4 minutes and 20 seconds. There are 3 powerful ways to use this song effectively in class (see the Lesson Ideas above).

> *Orange is the New Black-2013–2019, seven Seasons, Netflix*

A nuanced dramatic comedy about a women's prison in upstate New York. Transgender actor Laverne Cox plays a major character Sophia Burset, who is also a transgender woman. Season 1 Episode 3 "Lesbian Request Denied" July 11, 2013, tells the story of Sophia's background and how she ended up an inmate. This would be the best episode to use in a class about gender diversity. The episode is directed by Jodie Foster.

> Reed, Lou. "Candy Says." *The Velvet Underground*. MGM, 1969.

> *Transparent*—Creator Joey Solowoy, 2014–2019, 5 Seasons, *Amazon Studios*

A fine-tuned dramatic comedy with many transgender contributors. The show's creator identifies as non-binary, gender non-conforming and his parent transitioned to transgender. The show focuses on the Pfefferman family and their discovery that the patriarch/father Mort is transgender woman, Maura. The show also has a strong religious component, and many episodes deal with the family and their Jewish faith.

Websites/Organizations

*Human Rights Campaign*—https://www.hrc.org/resources

This organization devotes itself to fighting for equality on behalf of the LBGTQ+ community. The website has numerous resources and support for the community. Support and advice for coming out, and college life are two valuable sections of the website. The organization's report, "Dismantling a Culture of Violence: Understanding Anti-Transgender Violence and Ending the Crisis," Updated December 2020 and available as a free PDF download should be a must-read for students as well as all faculty, counselors, and parents.

https://assets2.hrc.org/files/assets/resources/2018AntiTransViolenceRe portSHORTENED.pdf.

*National Center for Transgender Equality*—https://transequality.org/

An invaluable resource for the promotion of progressive policy change, understanding, and equality for transgender people. They advocate for the transgender community on all issues that impact their lives.

Gavin Grimm v. Gloucester County School Board, No. 19-1952 (4th Cir. 2020). *JUSTIA US* Law, https://law.justia.com/cases/federal/ appellate-courts/ca4/19-1952/19-1952-2020-09-23.html.

This case concerns the use of gender-aligned bathrooms in public schools. Issues of privacy and discrimination are weighed in the context of Title IX. The full Supreme Court opinion can be downloaded from the above site.

Book

Mock, Janet. *Redefining Realness: My Path to Womanhood, Identity, Love & So Much More-* (Atria Books, 2014).

A transgender activist and writer/reporter/editor Janet Mock's memoir describes her transition process, which began in her freshman year in college. It is only appropriate for college age students but has tremendous benefits for college students and educators. She talks about many experiences including her surgery in Thailand and her experience as a sex worker, something some transgender people turn to out of desperation.

# CHAPTER 7

# "Smart Bets" Balancing Uncertainty with Clear Thinking

## Annie Duke's Poker Skills for Everyday Life

W E HAVE ALL HEARD those famous grand metaphors, "Life is a Dream," "Life is a Stage," "Life is a Simulation," and "Life is like Poker." We can, perhaps, agree such metaphors have a smidgen of truth, but outside of metaphysics they probably have little merit. Then again, maybe they do. Annie Duke takes a cognitive psychology approach to the "life is like poker" saying and demonstrates how poker can be applied to life in very positive, practical ways. Her book, *Thinking in Bets: Making Smarter Decisions When You Don't Have all the Facts*, offers a treasure trove of applied game strategies to decision making.

Annie Duke should know about poker; she is a World Series of Poker Champion (2014), but more than that, she combines her poker acumen with a solid foundation in cognitive science. Ms. Duke has a degree from Columbia, and completed all her doctoral course work in psychology at Penn. Her strategies are informed by the latest research in cognitive and

DOI: 10.1201/9781003201465-10

neuroscience. Duke integrates this research with her poker expertise to help readers think more clearly (Figure 7.1).

Poker is a pressure cooker for decision making. As Ms. Duke explains, a single hand of poker may only take 2 minutes, but those 2 minutes might require 20 decisions, and quick decisions at that. Moreover, poker decisions have immediate feedback. You either win or lose money based upon the result of your decision making. How does this apply to life? Well, another game, American football, also requires split-second decisions with implications for winning or losing. Duke begins her excellent book discussing Pete Carroll's much-maligned decision to call a pass play in Super Bowl LXIX that resulted in an interception and Seattle's last-minute loss to the New England Patriots. Terrible result, but Duke claims, a solid decision. In fact, the chances of Russell Wilson throwing an interception in that situation was only about 2%. Her very big point is that *good decisions can result in bad outcomes*. That's life. No guarantees in football (Joe Namath aside), poker, or life. Negative reactions to Carroll's decision by the multitude of Monday morning quarterbacks exemplify what Duke calls resulting.[1] Resulting determines the quality of a decision based upon its result, and this thinking necessarily succumbs to hindsight bias. Humans are

FIGURE 7.1 Portrait photograph of Annie Duke. (Photograph used with permission of Annie Duke ©.)

still unable to see the future, so Duke suggests we stop thinking we can make decisions based on the unknown. Hence the subtitle of her work, "when we don't have all the facts."

We rarely have all the facts when making decisions and Duke address hidden information with three invaluable and interrelated points. First, thoroughly research a decision. Duke became a great poker player, partly through research. She read and studied books by experts (e.g., Doyle Brunson's *Super System: A Course in Poker Power*), talked with experts (like her brother Howard, a master poker player), and observed the best (such as her friend Erik Seidel). Knowing as much as possible surrounding a decision optimizes the decision-making progress. Second, think in terms of probability. A poker player applies math to each situation. You do not know which cards your opponent's hold, but you can know the probability of various combinations based upon your cards and the cards on the table. Third, reframe your thinking from absolutes of black and white to degrees of certainty. The false dilemma of black and white so often used by politicians in their faulty argumentation needs to be rendered as shades of gray. For example, instead of thinking that a decision must be right of wrong, think about a decision having say a 72% chance of a successful outcome (70). Such probabilistic thinking, which is evidence based, helps calibrate one's decisions and improve the likelihood of a positive outcome.

On this last point, Duke stresses an element present in game-based thinking. In game-based thinking, failure is always reframed as an opportunity, a productive failure or failing forward, not a setback, and never a final determination about one's thinking or performance. Duke makes this same point when vociferously arguing against the word wrong (31). She admonishes us not to say things like "I knew it" because we don't know the outcome in advance. For just this reason, I dislike multiple choice tests which demand a correct answer and incorrect answers as if problems and questions can be rendered in such absolute terms. Rather, as Duke suggests, don't be afraid to admit, "I'm unsure," because that statement provides a more accurate representation of the world and forecloses on black and white thinking or essentializing (29).

In thinking about decisions as degrees of accuracy, we are also admitting the potential role of luck or chance, involved in many decisions. In chess, there is no luck, but in poker, like most games, and most of life, chance has a place. You can be a master poker player and still lose to an average player who pulls great cards, against the odds. We cannot rule out luck, but we can prepare for its possibility. I like to think of luck as beating overwhelming odds such as winning a multimillion-dollar Lottery jackpot or a pitcher with a 0.110 batting average hitting a game-winning homerun against a top reliever. Maybe even me, winning a hand of poker against Annie Duke. That's luck, and you can never rule out that unpredictable outcome, but in the long run or big picture, probabilities win out. In ten hands against Annie Duke, I will lose 9. You won't win the huge jackpot twice, and that pitcher will make an out the next nine at bats (that's why his average is 0.110). Again, calibrate decisions based on probabilities of a good outcome.

Let me focus now on how Annie Duke uses the betting process, at the core of poker, as the key to good decision making. For Duke, thinking in bets helps examine whether an outcome results from skill or luck (112). Let's begin with Ms. Duke's definition of a bet as a decision about an uncertain future (3). What the bet does to the decision is activate our prefrontal cortex, if you will, and trigger us to vet a decision based upon evidence (65) not just belief (often a form of wishful thinking, not logical thinking). "By treating decisions as bets, poker players explicitly recognize that they are deciding on alternate futures, even with benefits and risks" (43).

Bets force us to vet our decisions more closely precisely because bets demand accountability. If you lose the bet, you lose money. Most of us do not want to lose money so when we place a bet, we want the chances of success to be high, certainly over 50%. If we bet on low probability, say 5%, we should be able to afford the risk, or at least fully realize the odds of success, defined as winning the bet, are low. Duke nicely describes this betting as vetting,

> The more we realize that we are betting on our beliefs (with happiness, attention, health, money, time or some other limited resource), the more likely we are to temper our statements, getting closer to the truth as we acknowledge the risk inherent in what we believe (66).

Sounds a little like life as *Jeopardy!* means risk, but, of course, in that game, you don't bet your own money. That would really be jeopardy!!! Last semester while conducting a class-wide challenge about superheroes, I stopped midway and asked if anyone thought all their identifications had been correct thus far (thought is belief). One student raised his hand and confidently asserted he believed he had all the correct identifications (he was an excellent student). "Would you bet on that?" I asked (just playing of course to make a point). He now hesitated, the confidence waning a bit. "Yes, I think so." "Would you bet $100 on your answers?" "I would bet $2" was his response. The certainty disappeared in the face of a bet because the bet forced accountability and close examination of how certain he was of the answers. As I said, he is a smart student because he would have lost that bet. Another student, with a lower average succeeded in winning the challenge.

The bet forces accountability and modifies belief. In other words, a bet mediates feedback about a decision.

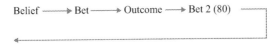

Duke cites plenty of excellent research in neuroscience that shows how frequently most of us shortcut deliberation in favor of quick decisions with little evidence to substantiate their merit. Our tendency is to seek confirmation of already established beliefs reinforcing a limited perspective (i.e., confirmation bias). The clear polarization of Congress illustrates this closed, inflexible approach to decision making. For Duke, the introduction of the betting mechanic disrupts this closed circuit of self-deception.

A belief can suffer from many shortcomings. Perhaps, we think we *must* get some good cards this time as if we can control chance. Maybe we think an advertisement about a product is based on vetted, peer-reviewed research when it's just promotional blather. A bet makes us accountable for the belief and its foundation. If the belief lacks evidence, the bet will most often result in a poor outcome and we lose money, but this accountability gives us valuable feedback that encourages or prompts us to reexamine our belief and what it's based on. This examination, in turn, will make our next bet more deliberate and increase the probability of a good outcome.

One of Duke's favorite sources is Samuel Arbesman's *The Half Life of Facts: Why Everything We Know Has an Expiration Date*. Arbesman historicizes facts to show how often today's facts become tomorrow's fictions. We cannot predict where science and technology will lead us, but research indicates many cherished beliefs will go by the wayside (you know the earth is flat truth of yore or addiction is a moral failing). Duke's point, in following Arbesman, stresses the value of considering alternate explanations, entertaining an open approach to future possibilities, acknowledging uncertainty, and calibrating our decisions.

In a follow-up book called *How to Decide; Simple Tools for Making Better Choices*, Duke has produced a practical handbook to guide people through the decision-making process based on her research in cognitive science and the further application of poker-based skills. Three specific points Duke makes deserve some teasing out. First, is the central role chance must play in decision making. As I have discussed several times in this book luck, chance, or randomness plays a significant role in most games. Randomness maintains an element of surprise, frustrates certainty, and makes the game suspenseful and dramatic. Results are never definite otherwise why play the game? The same in everyday decision making. We never know in advance what the result of our decision will be. Even a high degree of obtaining our desired result does not guarantee that result because the 5% of uncertainty is pure randomness over which we exert no control.

If you acknowledge uncertainty as a fact, refuse the cognitive tendency to align your decision with the result based on hindsight, give up the illusion of total control you think you have over a situation, then you will become a better decision maker. Duke uses a wide array of charts, matrices, graphs, and tables to make her point and help readers make better decisions in the face of uncertainty. She refers to her decision model as "The Three Ps: Preferences, Payoffs, and Probability" (68–99). Addressing uncertainty requires identifying a range of possible outcomes for every decision and then weighting those outcomes based on their desirability, which, in turn, should be based on your value system (something discussed in the next chapter). Once you have weighed each possible outcome you determine the probability of each outcome. Probabilistic thinking is critical to good poker playing and to life in general. Third, you close the gap between certainty, which requires total knowledge of a situation, and complete randomness or a toss of the coin. You close the probability gap by obtaining knowledge over the situation, and you obtain knowledge by diligent research and truly listening to other perspectives. To truly listen, you must quarantine your perspective (225) so others can voice their perspective honestly and without prejudice. This is difficult to do. My partner does a great job with honesty, and this results in arguments because most people, myself often included, do not want to hear a disconfirmation of their opinion.

Improving your knowledge about a situation requires research. Students need to learn this lesson. Too often today students turn to the

Internet for research solely out of convenience but spending a day in the junkyard might only yield one piece that suits your needs. Research takes effort and time. There are no shortcuts. The same with skill development. Practice, practice, practice. Yes, turn on the TV to watch a PGA Tour golf tournament and admire Rory McElroy hitting a 350-yard drive down the left center of the fairway. We admire the talent, but what we don't see and, therefore, often forget is the endless hours of practice professional golfers put into their profession. The great result of that drive did not come just because of natural talent. Students need to understand the value and necessity of effort in obtaining good results.

## WE ARE NOT AS SMART AS WE THINK

A word here about Big Data. Thanks to immense computer processing speeds, we now have tremendous amounts of data that can be crunched down with great precision in determining the probability of different events or decision outcomes. The data is scientific, but that does not eliminate chance. Decisions must be executed based on data and that execution can be confounded by chance elements. Take for an example our national past time, the game of baseball. Let's say N.Y. Yankee star Aaron Judge is batting in the bottom of the 9th inning with his team behind Boston 2–4. There are 2 outs and 2 runners on base. Judge is a tremendous home run hitter, and a home run wins the game, but a single is a more likely outcome than a home run and a single reduces the deficit from 2 runs to 1 run and extends the game. Both managers, all coaches, the batter, and the pitcher all have data broken down into minute details that they have absorbed prior to the game. The pitcher knows that Judge often swings and misses sliders thrown down and out of the strike zone. He also knows a fast ball down in the zone has high probability of being hit for a single, double, or homerun (he will know exact percentages). Judge will have the same precise data about the pitcher. How often does the pitcher throw a slider pitch in this situation? Exact matches of data sets are not easy. Let's say the pitcher decides to throw that slider low and outside because there is an 80% chance Judge will swing and miss at that pitch. Perhaps Judge knows that pitcher will throw that pitch 90% of the time in this situation so he does not swing. From both perspectives chance plays a role. Maybe he throws the pitch for a perfect strike and nicks the corner. Game over, Boston wins. Maybe the pitch slips, he misses the intended target, the ball hangs over the plate, Judge hammers a home run into the upper deck. Game Over, Yankees win. Even the most precise data cannot eliminate chance. The goals, as Duke shows, have to do with maximizing probability by gaining better knowledge, developing an archer's mindset for precision, and making an educated guess. The more educated your guess the more likely you make the right decision.

Finally, a very big caveat. If we reduce chance and improve our knowledge, we still often make poor decisions. Ironically, the probability that humans will make decisions based on probability is not very probable. Our thinking remains clouded by biases, a failure to listen to others, and a wild exaggeration about how smart we think we are. The work of Nobel Prize-winning psychologist Daniel Kahneman (see resources below) goes to great lengths to show and describe the flaws in human judgment. He is worth listening to.

In her consulting work Duke writes about what she calls prediction markets. In this business model a group tests decisions through bets. The bet tests a group's confidence in an executive decision. "People are more willing to offer their opinion when the goal is to win a bet rather than get along with the people in the room" (150). In other words, the bet elicits honesty and honestly challenges groupthink. On a related point, Dukes stresses the value of dissent and skepticism within a group. A homogenous group stagnates. Diversity promotes growth. A bet introduces the possibility of dissent but dissent not as disruption or a leak in the side of a smooth sailing ship, but rather, an interruption of a ship that might be off course if the directions are not as precise as what we believe. Dissent stops a quick unexamined belief or assumed certainty, and allows us time to think through the options, clarify our choice, and genuinely test how certain we are about a decision before putting our cards on the table. The bet does not mean we will be right, but the bet does show we are confident in our decision, and our chances of success are more likely than before the bet is made. If you read *Thinking in Bets*, absorb its research, and apply its strategies, your decisions will improve. Wanna bet?

## NOTE

1. Resulting bears some resemblance to the classic logical fallacy of post hoc ergo propter hoc where people assume something that follows something else must be causal when that often is not the case. B is not always because of A.

## LESSON IDEAS

Duke's book *How to Decide* is a workbook with many examples and exercises to help students make better decisions and I suggest that book for concrete lessons. I also urge faculty to help students identify their core values or driving passion regarding the subject they teach. Likewise, stress over and over the value of effort. Give students plenty of support but do not make things easy!

## RESOURCES

Websites/Organizations

*Alliance for Decision Education*—https://alliancefordecisioneducation.org/

> Cofounded by Annie Duke, this superb non-profit helps students become better decision makers at all levels of education and helps teachers help students be better decision makers. There are many excellent tools and resources associated with this alliance.

*Annie Duke's website*—https://www.annieduke.com/

> Lots of valuable resources, podcasts, a newsletter, and tweets.

Books

Arbesman, Samuel. *The Half-Life of Facts: Why Everything We Know Has an Expiration Date.* (Current, Illustrated edition, 2013.)

> A fun and engaging book that makes the valuable point that facts change. What proved to be a fact during the Renaissance proves to no longer be a fact in The Enlightenment. In other words, technology improves, knowledge evolves and science changes.

Duke, Annie. *How to Decide: Simple Tools for Making Better Choices.* Portfolio/Penguin, 2020.

> An excellent workbook to try out Duke's ideas in many different situations.

Firestein, Stuart. *Ignorance: How It Drives Science.* Oxford University Press, 2012.

> One of my very favorite books to share with students. Life is uncertain, games design for uncertainty, and science, which many people, i.e.,

nonscientists, the media, etc., take as gospel truth, in fact, flourishes because answers are springboards for further questions. If this is your final answer, then you have stopped doing science.

Kahneman, Daniel. *Thinking Fast, and Slow.* Farrar, Straus and Giroux, 2011.

A brilliant, heavily researched book by the Noble Prize-winning Israeli psychologist. He outlines two thinking systems, System 1 and System 2. Everyone should read this book.

# CHAPTER 8

# Chess for Self, School, and Society

## THE GRAND GAME

If there was one game, I would recommend every single student learn to play, chess would be that game. Chess is one of the few entirely skill-based games. It is a game that teaches both character and a range of competencies relevant to school, career, and citizenship. I outlined some of the strategic thinking skills chess teaches in the conclusion of my book *Teaching in the Game-Based Classroom: Practical Strategies for Grades 6–12* (2021). No game teaches strategic thinking better than chess, but chess also requires patience, composure, self-efficacy, emotional intelligence, critical thinking, and problem solving.

Chess also has a global reach, costs next to nothing to play, and can potentially erase social-economic barriers. The rise of Esports through computer-based games has been invaluable in teaching teamwork, thinking skills, and sportsmanship to youth, but I would urge chess as the first step to both club and competition in schools' dedication to non-athletic competitive games. Certainly, Esports tournaments attract large audiences on Twitch, and in person as well, but nothing compares to the drama of the 1972 match between the U.S.'s Bobby Fisher and the U.S.S.R.'s Boris Spassky.[1] This was a symbolic cold war battle between the world's superpowers, and the two Grandest of Grandmasters. The race to space replayed as a chess match.

DOI: 10.1201/9781003201465-11

The excellent New York City Chess in the Schools program (see the Resources below) mission statement states, "Chess in the Schools fosters intellectual and social development of low income youth through chess education." This wide-ranging program should be replicated in other major cities across the country. In this chapter, I will show the value of chess as a school program through a discussion of how chess transformed an impoverished middle school in Brooklyn by discussing the documentary *Brooklyn Castle* (2012). In the second half of the chapter, I will point to a founding father, Ben Franklin's application of chess to life as an exemplar of the values that have been in decline across the country. Chess can help to bring back the importance of ethos to citizenship in public life.[2]

## PREVENTING CHECKMATE: CHESS AS AN ACADEMIC AND SOCIAL INTERVENTION

In the opening episode of HBO's acclaimed series, *The Wire* (2002–2008), the character D'Angelo, who manages the street level drug sales of a West Baltimore housing project, happens upon two of his runners, Wallace and Bodie playing checkers on a chess board. D'Angelo seizes this moment to teach his partners the superiority of chess as a game. This brilliant emblematic scene foreshadows the entire 5-year series. D'Angelo uses chess as a metaphor for the drug game that holds out only checkmate for these young inner city players. D'Angelo holds up the king and stresses the need to protect this vital piece. In the drug game, the king is D'Angelo's uncle Avon Barksdale, the West Baltimore drug lord. When he comes to the pawn, D'Angleo identifies his buddies as these important, but lowly figures—the street soldiers who benefit the powerful pieces but who themselves "get capped quick." Indeed Bodie, Wallace, and D'Angelo, as well, suffer early and violent deaths. Inner city chess becomes the governing metaphor for a no-win game for the inner city youth of *The Wire*. However, chess can also be a metaphor and game for the dignity, growth, and transformation of inner city youth as the documentary films about chess, *Life of a King* (Jake Goldberger, 2013) and *Brooklyn Castle* (Dellamaggiore, 2012) show.

In *Brooklyn Castle*, we see the power of school clubs in transforming students' overall performance and pro-social action. The film follows five students for a year at I.S. 318-Eugenio Marie De Hostos. As the name suggests this middle school is minority populated. It was one of the poorest districts in the entire United States, and yet, this impoverished Brooklyn school has frequently produced the country's best middle school chess team. Justus Williams became the youngest African-American chess champion at age 12. Rochelle Ballantine won a full scholarship to the University of Texas, Dallas. All five kids followed by the filmmakers learn important lasting lessons through chess. The game of chess has helped transform what experts would consider to be an underperforming school to a vibrant learning community where minority students are praised and rewarded for their end-game strategies not their three-point shooting. Sadly, such after-school programs are the ones most easily and quickly cut by high-level administrators.

What makes the chess club work so well at I.S. 318 seems to me a combination of school building leadership, the late principal Fred Rubino and super cheerleader and assistant principal John Calvin; a dedicated and passionate mentor, coach Elizabeth Vicary Spiegel. They were extraordinary models of how to help kids achieve success and believe in themselves within a culture that supports such extracurricular academic pursuits. That culture includes teachers, administrators, support staff, parents, relatives, community. The big pep rallies usually reserved for the high profile sports are here conducted for chess. It would be nice to see the chess results on the local news. That would be a revolutionary step.

## BEN FRANKLIN AND THE GAME OF CHESS

When somebody tells you to "go fly a kite" tell that person to look up Ben Franklin. Play can often lead to dramatic discoveries and Franklin is a shining example of how fun can often have more beneficial results than those so-called "serious" activities. Ben Franklin, a founding father, and American Renaissance man, serves as an inspiration and symbol to many Americans. What about chess appealed to Franklin? In answering this question, we will move toward a better understanding of Franklin, of games, and character.

Franklin was one of America's first chess players. We can trace his play to 1733. He contributed the first formal U.S. essay on chess called "The Morals of Chess" in 1786 for the *Columbian Magazine*. After beginning the essay with a Shakespearean gambit comparing chess to life itself, Franklin settles into a pragmatic approach to the game. He discovers four critical lifelong competencies from playing chess. Each lesson deserves our attention.

1. Foresight: this trait can be thought of as strategic thinking, the need to anticipate the consequences of each action.

2. Circumspection: this refers to the big picture of a situation, the forest not the trees; a trait characteristic of leaders not followers.

3. Caution: when you decide, make that decision carefully, in other words, act rationally not emotionally—a great enlightenment-based value.

4. Perseverance: here Franklin stresses the necessity of "hoping for favorable change," and never giving up (he does not specifically name the fourth value but hope or perseverance are part of his description).

I would be hard-pressed to think of four more valuable traits for today's students, or, for that matter, any person wanting to be successful.

Let's look at these four values more closely.

## Foresight

The ability to recognize and act on trends. Identifying trends allows a person to extrapolate into the future. You must be forward thinking and plan long range. Elon Musk comes to mind. He saw the trends in travel, the depletion of fossil fuels, and the possibilities of electric cars as a solution to the current energy situation. Rather than fight against the inevitable for short-term gain, he embraced the future. Help students think ahead. Where do they want to be in 5 years, in 10 years, and in 20 years? How can they make plans to get where they want to be? What social and technological changes are likely to occur during these time frames? Use Stephen Covey's Habit # 2, "Begin with the End in Mind" as a guiding principle of teaching students' foresight.[3]

## Circumspection

The ability to look at a situation or decision from multiple perspectives, a kind of 360° self-evaluation. In this context, slogans like "America First" make no sense. You cannot simply be self-directed or inward-focused in a global economy. Systems thinking is a form of circumspection. You need to think through your decisions and actions in relationship to others. When Magnus Carlsen looks at a chess board, he sees every possible move with every piece and all possible responses to each move. Systems are dynamic, they evolve and change. Students live in an ecosystem and must balance many factors: family, friends, grades, relationships, health, and emotional well-being. I don't take circumspection as just being unwilling to take risks; Franklin took risks as do chess grandmasters. It's being aware of the big picture, all the factors involved before making a move that matters, i.e., a calculated risk or educated guess as Annie Duke would have it.

## Caution

Similar but not identical to circumspection. As the adage goes, "error on the side of caution," i.e., do not take unnecessary risks. This habit reflects the poker skills talked about in the previous chapter. Adolescent students are often developmentally opposed to caution, hormones are raging, and they are typically impulsive risk takers. Consequently, many adolescents apply another adage, "throw caution to the wind," and the wind can take one to an unexpected place. A good chess player only takes very calculated risks because one mistake and the game will be over. For example, in game six of the 2021 Chess World Championship held in Dubai, between Magnus Carlsen and Ian Nepomniachiti, the Russian made just one mistake, one imprudent move, the game's 136th after 8 hours of play. He lost the game, and it seems his spirit. Carlsen went on the crush him on the way to yet another title defense. Most matches at the championship level end as a stalemate for just such a reason. Use caution when preparing for an exam. Cramming shows a lack of caution. If you have not read two required chapters during the 5-week unit, then studying all night before the exam will be of little help. Running a yellow traffic light shows lack of caution and often results in accidents or tickets. The reward of not being cautious on the other hand is minimal. You might arrive at your destination 30 seconds earlier than if you stopped.

## Perseverance

Success in college and career requires perseverance. The ability to fight through inevitable setbacks, "the slings and arrows of outrageous fortune" as in the Hamlet soliloquy (III i line 59). Tiger Woods has persevered through numerous back surgeries, personal catastrophe, a serious car accident, and still plays golf, and even prepares to return to championship competition. Do not let failure on an exam or a course hold a student back. True success and mastery only come through constant effort, relentless practice, and self-belief. Survivors of trauma personify perseverance.

Franklin also stresses some of the parameter's integral to all games such as the importance of rules and good gamesmanship. Yet, the trait Franklin stresses above all else is a trait sorely lacking today: civility. Nearly every time I get in my car to drive someplace, I am assaulted by the lack of civility shown by other drivers. No doubt Ben would hate today's gloating football player who dances in the end zone or the idea of running up the score against a weak opponent. Finally, he chides zealous spectators and armchair coaches, and, perhaps, by extension, opinionated journalists. If you have something to say Franklin suggests, say that by playing the game yourself!

On a final note, again pointing to civility, old Ben provides an alternative to modernism's winner take all competition and Vince Lombardi's dictum "winning is everything."[4] Losing the game is less important than winning the "esteem," "respect," and "affection" of your opponent. Do not revel in an opponent's mistakes but take the time to teach the lesser opponent how to not make those mistakes in the future. Playing the game teaches just as the game teaches the teacher. Franklin advocated for a win-win outcome.

## Chess as a Philosophy of Life

My colleague Roumen Bezergianov has used chess as a tool for treating the emotional needs of youth in juvenile detention. His work deepens traditional ideas of social emotional health or character education by explaining and applying the philosophical foundations of the game. Chess becomes a philosophy of life or as he writes, a "clarification of values, a personal philosophy of life and spirituality" (4). For example, take the king, the subject of Roumen's first chapter.

The king represents absolute value or what existential philosopher Martin Heidegger calls Being with a capital B. If you lose the king, you lose the game. Consequently, the king must be protected at all costs. He does do not do much. Yes, a king can move in any direction, but only one space at a time. The king's value means you cannot jeopardize his safety by putting him into action. For Bezergianov, the king "symbolizes those crucial things in life that cannot be bought and sold" (8). Thus, the king gets at our core values. These may or may not change over time but asking students to identify those values they will not compromise can be an invaluable exercise. For me, my dog Roderick has incalculable value. For instance, I would not take a job in another country regardless of how good the job might be for me if I could not bring him with me because that would, in essence, not be good for me on a much deeper level than any financial concerns.

Bezergianov makes many references to the Holocaust survivor Viktor Frankl's work as he explains how chess helps one search for meaning. It is an important and overlooked aspect of education. In fact, such meaning can be considered the value of education itself. Students need to find their purpose or passion for education to give them deep meaning. I always ask students why they have chosen the major they have chosen. Too often the response is utilitarian. That's unfortunate. Yet, I have also found students with a driving passion. One engineering major switched to journalism her junior year and transferred to another college. A second engineering major graduated with her degree but went back to school for nursing and has found tremendous satisfaction in the medical field. Engineering can certainly be a passion just like any major, but help students find what about the major they are passionate about.

In a late chapter on the empty spaces of chess Roumen makes a fascinating and provocative observation worth quoting,

> The empty spaces in chess, similar to *being* and the King, point to that state of holistic mindfulness, beholding of the emptiness and the mysterious potential it holds. By embracing emptiness in a way that is relevant and meaningful to you, you have become a witness and a participant of the creative and miraculous action of transforming your life (75).

Chess brings about such a personal transformation and nothing more can be asked of a game.

## NOTES

1. There are many video clips, discussions, and reproductions of actual games between Fisher and Spassky. I like to stress how this game becomes a theater of international affairs and a key U.S. victory in the Cold War. Students benefit from knowing the larger scope of the game and how games can impact society and history. Students can also observe the gamesmanship of games, sports psychology, and the metagame by observing how Fisher broke down Spassky's concentration and focus in a way similar to how Magnus Carlsen does to opponents today. In one sense, you can win the game before you start to play. The match can be read about in detail through the book: *Chess World Championship 1972: Fischer vs. Spassky* by Larry Evans and Ken

Smith, Ishi Press, 2015. Fischer could hardly be considered a patriot despite his great American victory in Iceland. Fischer was an enigmatic genius. If you are interested in exploring his strange but compelling life, I recommend the excellent biography by Frank Brady, *End Game: Bobby Fischer's Remarkable Rise and Fall-From America's Brightest Prodigy to the Edge of Madness*, Crown, 2012.

2. In ancient Greece, particularly in the work of Aristotle, ethos referred to one character, a person's sense of integrity. One's ethos depends on identifying, clarifying, and following your core values.

3. Stephen Covey's Second Habit, "Begin with the End in Mind," stresses the role of the imagination. You cannot build a bridge until you imagine that bridge. The same principle holds for personal decisions and goals, see: https://www.franklincovey.com/habit-2/.

4. The famous quote, "Winning isn't everything, it's the only think," has often been misattributed to legendary Green Bay Packer's coach Vince Lombardi. The quote originated with U.C.L.A.'s football coach Henry Russell Sanders, but Lombardi embraced the quote, repeated it, and make it, like him, legendary. In competition you only have a winner, but I prefer to modify the saying to stress that doing your best and achieving your optimal potential is what matters not winning per se.

## LESSON IDEA

Rather than specify any lesson I would stress teachers advocate for chess clubs and programs in their school or college. I also recommend exploring students' values by way of Franklin's *Autobiography* or Stephen Covey's work. Asking students to write a personal mission statement as Covey suggested can be a powerful and transforming activity.

## RESOURCES

Websites/Organizations

*Chess.com*—https://www.chess.com

> Premiere site for everything chess related. You can solve chess problems, play against a computer, take lessons, find tournaments, and follow the latest news in the chess world.

*Chess in Schools*—https://chessintheschools.org

> A fantastic nonprofit in New York City that focuses on learning through chess. Students learn lifelong skills such as Patience, Critical Thinking, Self-Esteem, Social Skills, Sportsmanship, and Concentration.

*Magnus Carlsen*—https://magnuscarlsen.org/en

> Possibly the greatest chess player in modern history, Norwegian Magnus Carlsen, had been world number one since 2011. The website features four excellent chess-related learning apps: "Magnus Trainer," "Tactics Frenzy," "Knight Runner," and "Play Magnus."

*9 Queens*—https://www.facebook.com/9queens/

> A nonprofit based in Tucson, Arizona, founded by Jennifer Shahade and Jen Hoffman dedicated to empowering disadvantaged students through chess.

Films/Television

*Brooklyn Castle.* Directed by Katie Dellamaggione, Le Castle Film Works, 2012. Documentary Film.

> *Life is King.* Directed by Jake Goldberger, 2014.

> *Life of a King* is a formulaic Hollywood biopic, but the mediocre film brings to life the importance of chess as a game for underprivileged youth in Washington, D.C. Eugene Brown leaves prison after an 18-year sentence for armed robbery with a love of chess. Like most ex-convicts he has a near impossible job finding work and finally, misrepresents his past on a job application to get a position as school janitor. Ultimately, Brown pays the price for not checking the box next to felony, but for a short time he cleans the classrooms and hallways. One day the principal asks Brown to temporarily cover an unruly detention class that has "pushed" its current teacher out the door. Brown quickly commands this class through a combination of street credibility and sheer assertiveness. Surprised at the room's sudden quiet, the principal allows Brown charge of what is essentially a babysitting position, but Brown makes the most of this opportunity to teach the kids his love for chess. Typically, the only legal game films show minority youth playing is basketball, but here Brown uses chess to instill a sense of dignity, discipline, patience, and esteem in these beaten down kids.

> When Brown is reluctantly fired, he perseveres and purchases a foreclosed home which he rehabilitates into the *Big Chair Chess Club*. In time, most of the teens come around to the club and see the value of chess as a game that privileges cognitive skills not athletic skills. Indeed, if public schools spent as much time and energy on chess

clubs as sports teams our schools would reap many benefits. In the end, Brown's success suggests two related realities about much public education. Genuine and deep learning, especially for the poor, happens on the periphery, outside class, or perhaps in detention. If used intelligently such non-academic spaces can serve the most "academic" purposes. Second after-school learning engages students in a way the formal curriculum does not and educators and community leaders need to organize and promote such informal learning spaces.

*Queen's Gambit.* Director: Scott Francis, 2020. Netflix.

An exceptional series following the career of a fictional female chess prodigy Beth Harmon who goes from an orphanage to World Chess Champion.

*Searching for Bobby Fisher.* Director: Steven Zaillian, 1993

Excellent film about a chess prodigy Josh Waitzkin that addresses a question about raising a child with special abilities. The lessons are valuable for today's parents who sometimes obsessively push kids to be stars in an area where they are perceived to be especially talented.

Books

Bezergianov, Roumen. *Character Education through Chess,* 2011.
The book is discussed above in the chapter's final section.

Covey, Stephen R. *The 7 Habits of Highly Effective People: Powerful Lessons in personal change.* Free Press, Revised edition, 2004, originally published in 1990. Far more than a self-help book, Covey's work draws heavily on Benjamin Franklin's practical ideas and value system.

Franklin, Ben. "The Morals of Chess," *The Columbian Magazine,* December 1786. The essay can be found in various places online, including at *American Literature*: https://americanliterature.com/author/benjamin-franklin/essay/the-morals-of-chess. Web.

Shahade, Jennifer. *Play Like a Girl.* Mongoose Press, 2011.
A practical book of strategies and problem solving by a two-time U.S. Women's World Chess Champion. Shahade argues convincingly that aggressive play by women such as Judit Polgar dispels stereotypes of women players and that to play like a woman is to attack.

# CHAPTER 9

# War from the Other Side

## Playing Games to Save Democracy

### *ATTENTAT 1942*: A DOCUMENTARY GAME AS HISTORY AND WARNING

My junior semester abroad ended with an extraordinary group trip to Vienna, Austria. We had been studying the European Union at the famous College d'Europe in Bruges, Belgium. Consequently, what better way to end the semester than the site of the Congress of Vienna? Modern Europe owes much to this historical event. Our motely group overindulged in wine even if we had the privilege of meeting various European diplomats and politicians at the legendary Hofburg Palace. Nothing at our home campuses could compare to such an experience.

Once the week ended, we went our various ways, some back to Brussels and then, on home. Others dreamed of destinations across the continent. As for me, I was spontaneous with an inclination for the offbeat, so I applied for a 10-day visa and took the train across the border into Czechoslovakia. In my oversized backpack, I had two dangerous texts. One, Victor Marchetti's *The CIA and the Cult of Intelligence*, appealing to communists with their anti-American stance. The other, Aleksandr Solzhenitsyn's *The Gulag Archipelago*, contraband that side of the border and thoroughly anti-communist.

DOI: 10.1201/9781003201465-12

I learned more in those 10 days than I ever could reading a history book. Part of what I learned was how important Czechoslovakia, now the Czech Republic, has been in modern history. That acknowledgment brings me to a fabulous game about Czech history and the Holocaust designed by students at Charles University. *Attentat 1942* is a historical documentary style game that mixes archival footage, and photos with interactive comics and live action interviews. The game addresses a key historical moment, the attempted assassination of Nazi Reinhard Heydrich, leader of the German Protectorate of Bohemia and Moravia (Figure 9.1).

In the game you play the grandson of Jindrich Jelínek who was arrested by the Gestapo. In his role you learn about family history, an effective way to humanize the inhumanity of the Nazi occupation. By humanize, I mean dramatize historical events in a personal fashion to generate empathy in the player for the victims of a historical atrocity. For example, interviewing your grandmother about your granddad reminded me of Art Spiegelman's *Maus* (1986–1991) and Art interviewing his father Vladek about Vladek's life in pre-war Poland and then, his being sent to the concentration camps. It is moving and personal story that tells a larger history. In *Attentat 1942*, you are exploring you grandfather's world as

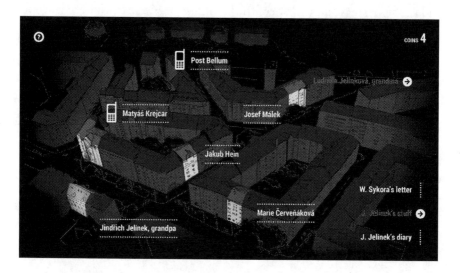

FIGURE 9.1 Interface of *Attentat 1942*. (Image courtesy of Charles Games © Used with permission.)

a historian would be investigating the archive of his life: hidden objects are both personal mementos and historical documents. You uncover a cap from Auschwitz, subversive leaflets, and jazz records, a no for Nazis who associated jazz with American blacks. Thus, the personal merges with the historical, the narrative with the documentary (Figure 9.2).

Mini games are engaging and enlightening. My favorite was a duel of poems between grandma- Ludmila and a Nazi 'suitor' in a restaurant frequented by Nazis. He wants to seduce her, but she distracts or puts him off by reciting poetry in a duel of poems. She survives an abusive situation, and you learn about some great poetry.

The game provides insight into many aspects of the Nazi occupation. The role of the resistance fighters, the place of collaborators, and the power of the radio, especially the subversive nature of listening to BBC broadcasts. The in-game encyclopedia, which can be opened by clicking any new term, person, or place, gives extensive information about all dimensions of the game's world equivalent to a history textbook, but on demand and in the context of the narrative.

As a collaboration between Charles University and the Czech Academy of Sciences, the game has a foundation in professionally researched history. A personal story weaves through archival documents and develops as you interview Czech citizens, played by skilled actors, examine documents, and engage with interactive comics. In an interview with *Gamasutra*

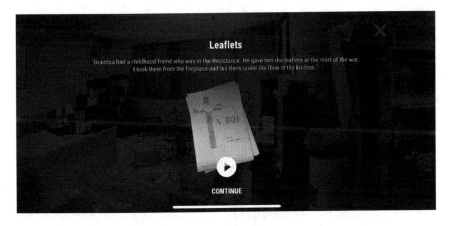

FIGURE 9.2  Leaflets. Resistance documents from the Nazi occupation. (Image courtesy of Charles Games © Used with permission.)

(Couture, 2018), one of the team's members speaks about the how the game's interactive dimensions enhance the player's grasp of history:

> History is oftentimes perceived as a list of important dates and events. Through the interactive interviews in *Attentat 1942*, we connect these overarching narratives with concrete people's lives. The interactivity of the game—the fact that players have to make decisions that matter—immerses players more deeply into the story. The interactive graphic novel segments help players imagine the atmosphere of the times the eyewitnesses are talking about. Overall, the game enhances the understanding of the complex and multifaceted decisions these people had to make.

As mentioned above, everything revolves around the assassination of the Nazi leader Reinhard Heydrich and the Nazi's retaliation for the assassination (he died in the hospital days after the shooting). The game's prelude, video footage of the historical situation on May 27, 1942, presents a rich opening for class discussion to frame a class unit. Is a state sponsored assassination ever legitimate? What better test case then Heydrich who oversaw, "The Final Solution," i.e., the extermination of all Jews.

As an essential question, a unit on the Holocaust could begin with such a question: Should "Operation Anthropoid," the name of the state-sponsored planned assassination of Heydrich, have been followed? Have students take the role of one of the two resistance fighters who carried out the plan, Josef Gabčík, a Slovak, and Jan Kubiš, a Czech, and write out a dramatic monologue about their decision to paratroop into Prague. Follow up, after the activity, and ask students to imagine what Czechoslovakia would have been like during World War II if Heydrich had not been assassinated. How does one event alter the course of history? What if Reverend Martin Luther King had never been assassinated? It is speculation, but a historical thought experiment of gravity and consequence for promoting deep historical understanding.

Nazi reprisals for the attempted assassination were horrific, and nothing showed the extreme brutality and inhumanity of Hitler than the brutal destruction of the entire city of Lidice on June 9, 1942. That Czech city was razed. All men who were captured or tracked down were executed by firing squad. Women and children were deported to concentration camps. A few children were placed with SS officers; 82 children were gassed to death at the Chelmno extermination camp in Poland. This murder factory was the prototype for later, better known extermination camps. You have in these historical scenes the nucleus of essential discussions about the Holocaust, Nazi policy, resistance movements, evil, and World War II in general. In this local Czech history, you also have World History at one of its most intense and life changing moments (Figure 9.3).

This brings me back to my personal journey as a young student. Czechoslovakia survived the Nazi occupation, but at great cost. The war's end brought the country into the Soviet orbit as part of the Eastern Bloc of communist dictatorships. No freedom to speak of. In 1968, a cataclysmic year of upheaval across Europe and the United States, Czechoslovakia flirted with democracy of sorts under the socialist leader Alexander Dubček beginning January 5th. Dubček practiced "socialism with a human face" and lessened censorship of media, travel, and other communist restrictions. His challenge to autocracy did not go well or last long as Soviet tanks rolled into Prague on August 25, 1968 literally putting down their foot on the Czech people. When I walked around Prague that spring

FIGURE 9.3 Houses of Lidice, Czechoslovakia burning, 10 June 1942. (Public domain via WW2 Database, and Sarah Sundin, https://www.sarahsundin.com/today-in-world-war-ii-history-june-10-1942/.)

of 1975, only 7 years after the Soviet invasion, I learned that the average Czech citizen admired Americans, not openly, but they expressed such to me, and they hated the Soviets, again, not openly, but deeply. They sought the everyday freedom we take, but should not take, for granted.

## THE PAST IN THE PRESENT: THE SYNCHRONICITY OF HISTORY

Recall, like in Czechoslovakia, 1968 also saw much upheaval in the United States. The assassination of two dynamic national leaders, one black, one white, who supported peace and integration. April 4th 1968, Reverend Martin Luther King, Jr, was assassinated and a few months later, on June 6, Robert F. Kennedy was assassinated. Over 100 race riots broke out in U.S. cities. The Democratic National Convention in Chicago (August 26–29) experienced rampant violence and chaos. The result of this social chaos eventuated in election of Richard M. Nixon and the extended upheaval his presidency represented. In this kind of social upheaval, extremist leaders emerge. At the time, America witnessed the rise of Alabama Governor George Wallace who ran as a third party candidate. Wallace openly opposed integration, supported Jim Crow laws, and represented a form of white nationalism that prefigured the emergence of Donald J. Trump nearly half a century later.

*Attentat 1942* makes possible important parallels between the rise of totalitarianism in the 1930s and 1940s and more current challenges to democracy. Two examples will bear much fruit in the classroom. First, the grandfather Jelínek's diary. In the point and click exploration of the room this diary turns up. In the 2 March entry reproduced below the grandfather comments on his neighbor Joseph Málek. Málek is one of the figures you interview in the game. He is suspected of being a collaborator. In the cited passage we learn of Málek's distaste for jazz, a dislike shared by many Nazis. We also read about the distortion of truth and the use of media to brainwash the Czechs into accepting the Nazis' version of reality. This misuse or manipulation of the media prefigures the Trump assent to power, when the candidate Trump used Twitter, his celebrity status, Fox News, and other outlets to serve as his political support, and later, help persuade his followers that lies were truth (Figure 9.4).

Let me point to a final example from *Attentat 1942* that foreshadows today's dangerous public discourse. One of the most powerful primary

FIGURE 9.4 Grandfather's Jindrich Jelínková's diary. (Image courtesy of Charles Games © Used with permission.)

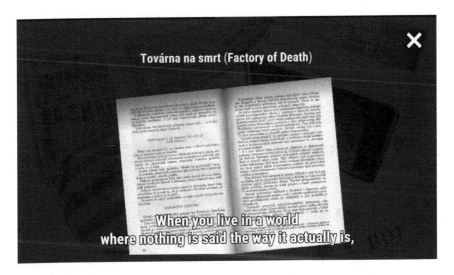

FIGURE 9.5 Factory of Death book 1. (Image courtesy of Charles Games © Used with permission.)

documents unearthed during game play is the Czech text *Továrna na Smrt* ("Factory of Death"). The bold text set off from a reproduction of the primary document speaks tellingly about how a public lie contaminates the entirety of public discourse turning the world upside down (Figures 9.5 and 9.6).

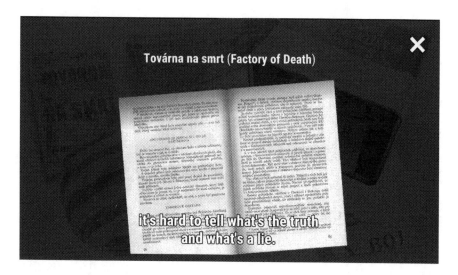

FIGURE 9.6    Factory of Death book 2. (Image courtesy of Charles Games © Used with permission.)

Composed by fellow Czech prisoners, Kulka and Kraus, *The Továrna na Smrt* represents one of the most powerful accounts of Auschwitz that we have. As the final survivors of the camps pass away this kind of primary document becomes more vital than ever as testimony to the horror of the Holocaust. I would argue such texts are imperative for all courses on World War II, Modern European History, World History, and the Holocaust. Eric Kulka survived five different concentration camps and his ghostly presence lingers over this powerful game. The story told by Holocaust survivors cannot be forgotten.

Parallels between the 1930s and 1940s should not be underestimated. Democracies have been undermined. As tense social conditions and media make space for extremist perspectives, and even normalize extremists, then democracy in our country is in peril. *Attentat 1942* provides many lessons for today's students. Lessons on the rise of authoritarianism, the destruction of freedoms, foreign occupation, the tension between resistance and collaboration, the horror of the Holocaust, the danger of media manipulation, and the scapegoating of minorities. In this instance, playing a game is playing through one of the history's darkest moments so that such an atrocity will not repeat itself.

## SHAKESPEARE STILL OUR CONTEMPORARY: THE GAME *THIS WAR OF MINE* AND THE CHALLENGE OF EMPATHY IN A TIME OF INCREASING INTOLERANCE

Great novels, drama, film, dance, fine art, and games provide us with unique experiences. Some experiences push empathy to the limit by allowing us to inhabit reality from the inside. In this kind of artistic encounter, you go to the far end of role playing a person to inhabiting another being something the great Irish actor Daniel Day Lewis did playing Abraham Lincoln. That is what the game *This War of Mine* (2014) asks us to do.

I started college as a Political Science major because I liked politics. Yes, I was young and naïve once. When I met with my assigned advisor sophomore year he asked where I wanted to go to law school. I replied that I had no interest in law school (naïve but smart too). He then suggested I drop Political Science. It would be a waste of time. Why not try an English class? This randomly assigned advisor was a Full Professor of, you guessed it, English. Ironically, he was an expert on John Milton; political thinker if ever there was one. Politics was not a waste of time after all just best understood through the lens of literature. I took a course in "Introduction to Drama."

The professor was small, hunched over constantly fumbling with a pipe (you could smoke in class those days), Slavic looking, speaking in a sputtered but still perfect English with a Polish accent. He talked about Sophocles and tragedy. Turns out, he had lived through something of a Sophoclean tragedy on the stage of Central Europe when the Nazis invaded Poland in 1939. Jan Kott had the cosmopolitan mind of a Man of Letters, multilingual and knowledgeable in many disciplines, but he also lived a dramatic life almost as if inhabiting Shakespeare's histories. I became a Comparative Literature major that semester and my love of literature has never diminished.

Professor Kott fought in the Polish underground, trying to resist the Nazi onslaught, a Shakespearean slaughter of innocents, in their thirst for domination. Kott ran from house to house, sometimes starving, often surviving by an Ariadne's thread, to a hopeful glimmer that would not come to Poland until decades later when he had settled into being a U.S. citizen and Professor of Drama.

I say this as prelude to the game *This War of Mine* because only a Polish sensibility produced by a partitioned country that experienced the horrors of war and the monstrosities of Auschwitz could produce a game of such cruelty and despair. A game one comes back to but also must walk away from. Playing this game requires a strong mind, a stone like heart, and a perseverance not unlike that required to survive a war. Americans have not experienced the horror of war on American soil since Civil War in the 1860s. We have been protected, for the most, part from the theater of cruelty dramatically lived over the last 50 years or more in places like Syria, Ethiopia, Lebanon, and the Ukraine.

In many ways *This War of Mine* echoes the Siege of Sarajevo. You control three civilians trapped in a brutal siege. The three are trying to survive in an abandoned shelter. A clock ticks down the hours. Every day is the same day. You spend the daylight trying to build various items like a bed to rest in, a stove to cook on, a radio to hear news from. At night, you leave the shelter to scavenge various locations, each with their own potential risks and rewards. Every night you risk your life, but you must risk your life to live another day. Your three players have different strengths, one might be fast, another good at bargaining. You must balance the skills and needs of your little collective. At night one will scavenge, another keep watch, and the third try and sleep some. I first played Markos, Pavle and Katia, but lost Markos relatively early.

Physical exhaustion and hunger are constant. Taxing the body necessarily taxes the mind, severely taxes the mind, as your character ruminates, "This will never end." "There's no point anyway." Evan Narcisse, writing for *Kotaku* describes the stress straight on, "*This War of Mine* is the first video game where I've stopped playing because of how depressed it made me feel" (2014). In this sense, the game dramatizes the despair war brings on one's psyche to such an extent the player feels a sense of despair as well. As Zacay observes, "It [the game] remains as brutal and capricious a game as its subject matter" (2014).

Like many games, your characters make decisions, but in *This War of Mine*, players make what Jan Kott called "radical choices." In war, every situation is extreme, and extreme situations demand radical choices. Think about the end of *Hamlet*, every choice is a tragic choice. In *This War of Mine*, you make choices that test whatever ethical integrity you might have left on a daily basis. Maybe a girl gets sexually assaulted as you fail to intervene, or you turn away a starving civilian. In my game play I stole food from an elderly couple begging me to leave them alone.

In game play your characters will experience unsettling emotions such as selfishness, cowardice, coldness, and cruelty along with other despicable behaviors not conceivable in peace time. This brings up the question of empathy, which Narcisse sees erode over the course of the game. Here is a unique challenge for student, player and teacher. If war creates the conditions where players can feel empathy for the civilian victims, then maybe that empathy can bring about changes in our attitude toward war, but can you feel empathy for characters, though victims on the one hand, are also often despicable immoral agents at other times, as the fighting grinds on? No easy answer here. The question returns me to my first college mentor again. Jan Kott did not read Shakespeare as an academic. He had a scholar's brilliant mind, but unlike say, the intellectually revered Harold Bloom who interpreted Shakespeare as an academic often does, a poet whose words need close analysis, Kott, read Shakespeare as a man of the theater. Shakespeare wrote theatre for a popular audience, and not to see his plays as theatre strikes me as very odd and off base. Kott not only read Shakespeare in terms of the stage, but also in terms of the theater of war, World War II as played out across Central Europe. A participant in that war, fighting against the Nazis, Kott could read Shakespeare's histories as the dark meditation they are. In Chapter One of Professor Kott's great *Shakespeare Our Contemporary* (1964), he writes about "The Kings." In this chapter, Kott introduces readers to what he calls the "grand mechanism" of history. The grand mechanism ran through Shakespeare's history plays and through 1930s and 1940s Europe. That's what made Shakespeare, in Kott's perspective, a contemporary in 1964. The grand mechanism turns the "executioner into a victim and the victim into an executioner." As the wheel turns, roles reverse, and there are no victors. Kott fought against the Nazis, part of Poland's People Army, and the underground resistance in Warsaw. Germany eventually lost, but Poland did not win in 1945. Russia's Red Army saved the day, only to delivery Poland to Joseph Stalin, another monster of history. Kott's momentary celebration of the communist party of the mid-1940s ended as a cruel joke with his party renunciation and subsequent departure to the United States.

## TEACHING A NEW KIND OF WARGAME

We can easily see the value of games that teach or build empathy. Empathy helps overcome prejudice and see commonality where previously players only perceived difference. We can fully value a game that raises players' awareness of depression and other players suffering depression to seek treatment. Most of us like games fully of excitement, and fast paced action. These three statements are evident to almost anyone who plays games; therefore, the positive qualities of *This War of Mine* seem ever more elusive to grasp. Why play a game that breaks down empathy you might already possess? Why play a game that produces depression? Why play a game with long stretches of boring repetitive movements? *This War of Mine* does all three, and yet the game has immense value for players and teachers. Evan Narcisse, who stopped playing because the game made him so depressed, nevertheless concludes his review with this startling statement, "It [*This War of Mine*] is the kind of game that could potentially change the way you watch news, treat others or cast a vote in an election." Narcisse is right, let's see why your students need to play this game.

Let's take the three deleterious aspects of game play mentioned above in reverse order: boredom, depression, and empathy. Games are art and what we ask of games should be what we ask of any other art. Samuel Beckett's *En Attendant Godot* (1952) remains one of the most powerful dramas in 20th-century theater. Yet, Beckett stages boredom. Much of Chekhov lacks action as well. We just wait around, but we do that a lot in life, and that's one reason we play games, to "kill" time. A world of reflection can open in these moments. Even war consists of much waiting, more waiting than battlefield action, but that waiting is tense, and fraught with meaning.

Despair? Shakespeare's tragedies are unsparing in their bleak vision of life: Othello strangling his innocent wife, Caesar stabbed to death by his best friend, Lear holding his daughter's lifeless corpse. Watching this kind of brutal drama is not fun, but we watch it. Shakespeare has been staged more often in more languages than any playwright in history. His writing represents the pinnacle of the English language. Do I need say more?

We have empathy for Othello and Lear, they are tragic heroes, but challenging empathy has value. Do all people deserve empathy? Hitler? Stalin? Look back at history, there is a long, long, long list of merciless tyrants not to mention our everyday assortment of child abusers, animal abusers and so on. Challenging empathy brings us into stark confrontation with the dark side of humanity and to deny that is to live in pure fantasy. Not just those we can easily dismiss as evil, but all of us when put in the extremist of situations that demand choices that can easily suspend our moral frameworks. A review in Metro Entertainment about the release of the game's Nintendo Switch Complete Edition observes how the unique mechanic of remorse makes this game's representation of empathy so powerful and transformative.

> This is the only game we can think of where remorse is used as a game mechanic, so even if you're heartless enough not to feel bad about stealing someone else's food the character in the game will

hang their head in shame, drag their feet, and become ever more listless the more horrors they're forced to perform. If left unchecked depression can quickly set in and that can in turn lead to suicide.

In other words, if the game's brutality challenges empathy for characters, the characters' shame at acting without empathy makes you stop and evaluate empathy and the human condition. Professor Kott would call this, in reference to Shakespeare, as example of life imitating art.

## Rethinking War Games

There are wargames and there are games about war. I reserve the problematic term "serious games" for genuine wargames. Wargames are designed for the military for use in actual military combat and strategic planning. They are most often taught in places like the Naval War College. These games help the military plan for actual events, extreme events, where real lives, not avatars, are at risk. Games about war like the enormously popular *Call of Duty* series are for play. They are mostly adolescent power fantasies. First Person Shooters like COD are no doubt lots of fun for millions of players, but these games give a skewed, and, ultimately, superficial perspective on the horrors of war. *This War of Mine* exists somewhere in the middle, but much closer to a genuine wargame than a game about war. War is not glamorous or heroic. Casualties are enormous and inevitable, especially for civilians caught in the crossfire of national, ethnic, or religious conflict. You don't beat *This War of Mine*. You hope to live until a ceasefire. The Siege of Sarajevo, to give a reference point, went from April 5, 1992, until February 29, 1996. That's a very long wait (Figure 9.7).

The Siege of Sarajevo is a good real-world analog for *This War of Mine* because of the civilian catastrophe. The extended siege started with sniper fire on a Muslim wedding. Civilians were targeted throughout the siege, including the over 1,000 children who died (*This War of Mine* also has a version that incudes children). The city's central artery was known as sniper alley. Civilians were routinely shelled by artillery fire to such an extent that NATO took military action (authorized February 9, 1994). In the end, over 8,000 soldiers died fighting over the Bosnian capital, but more to my point, 5, 434 civilians were killed for just being there, living in their home. In terms of empathy, look at the case of Serbian commanders Radko Mladic, "The Butcher of Bosnia" and Dragomir Milosevic (U.N., 2021).[1] Do such heinous monsters merit empathy? Do people who commit crimes against humanity and genocide deserve mercy? (Figure 9.8)

FIGURE 9.7 Character profile. (Image courtesy of 11 bit studios © Used with permission.)

FIGURE 9.8 The ruins of war in *This War of Mine*, final cut. (Image courtesy of 11 bit studios © Used with permission.)

These are big questions, and such historical tragedies need to be discussed and understood by students for there to be any hope of preventing such atrocities in the future. The UN High Commissioner for Human Rights, Michelle Bachelet makes this point in summarizing the International Tribunal's purpose,

I urge Governments and elected and public officials to strive for justice for all victims and survivors of the wars in the former Yugoslavia, to assuage – rather than aggravate – the region's open wounds, and to foster reconciliation and long-lasting peace. Only by honestly addressing the past can a country strive to create an inclusive future and build accountable institutions for all its citizens.

*This War of Mine* also has clear value as an actual wargame. If all military personnel were required to play such a game and to really focus entirely on civilians' experience during armed conflict, then the perception of war might be altered and the willingness to engage ethnic or nationalist differences from a military perspective might be slowed down and efforts at reconciliation extended. Encourage students to play *This War of Mine* and the simplistic power trips unleashed by blockbuster games about war might be shaken up helping students realize war is not a slick, exciting hero's journey but rather a savage journey into the heart of darkness (Figure 9.9).

FIGURE 9.9 Destroyed district of Sarajevo during Siege of Sarajevo. (Hedwig KlawuttkeHedwig Klawuttke (German main account), CC BY-SA 3.0 https://creativecommons.org/licenses/by-sa/3.0, via Wikimedia Commons https://commons.wikimedia.org/wiki/File:Sarajevo_Siege_Part_III.jpg.)

## TEACHING HISTORY DURING A TIME
## OF HISTORICAL DENIAL

Once again, I must trot out the often repeated but rarely listened to dictum from philosopher George Santayana, "Those who forget their history are condemned to repeat it" (1905). The United States has been experiencing a time of dramatic denial. The first step in overcoming a substance use disorder (addiction) is overcoming denial and accepting the reality of your situation. We have a former President who denied the results of a free and democratic election. The Republican Party has by and large gone along with "The Big Lie" and candidates even campaign on a lie before the American public. Censorship of books in public schools continues, and we now have the largely uncritical, uninformed debate over "Critical Race Theory." First, let's dispel with this label. A theory is by definition critical, or it is not a theory. Race theory, like feminist theory, or psychoanalytic theory, or even literary theory, takes a well-thought-out, reasoned, substantively researched perspective on a subject. Feminist theory looks at events through the lens of a feminist and challenges the dominant paradigm of history and culture written from the masculine perspective. Psychoanalytic theory looks at intrapsychic phenomenon, and unconscious psychodynamic factors in the formation of historical actors or artistic and cultural production. Literary theory is an umbrella term for different ways to read and interpret the meaning and value of literature. Similarly, race theory looks specifically at history through the lends of race. Rather than accept textbook history as truth, race theory looks at historical events around issue of race. In the United States, some states now want to whitewash history and even legislate against historical truth as if propaganda is an appropriate way to teach history in an open society. To deny racism or the effects of racism, like the denial of the Holocaust, is to deny history, erase an entire peoples' experience, and perpetuate dangerous, discriminatory, and hateful versions of history that young students might internalize and reproduce. The nightmare of history as James Joyce called it.[2]

In the former Yugoslavia, the Serb Republic's nationalist President Milorad Dodik has banned the teaching of the Massacre[3]. This act is a wholesale denial of history. It serves to extend and empower a racist or ethnic supremist version of reality that discriminates against, devalues and dehumanizes other groups. Yes, there are different historical interpretations of events, but denying reality and pretending there is only one version, the Serbian, or on the other side, the Bosnian, guarantees that ethnic hostility will continue, and that cooperation, harmony and peaceful coexistence will be impossible. This imperialist policy of imposing only one view of the world, the view of the conqueror as Shakespeare writes, "War gives the right to the conquerors to impose any condition they please upon the vanquished." This phony version of history must be challenged and overturned or the future of hostilities around the world will only intensify.

## NOTES

1. Steven Levitsky & Daniel Ziblatt's book *How Democracies Die* (Crown Publishing Group 2018) provides a concise and compelling history of modern autocracies in mid-20th-century Europe and contemporary South America. The Harvard professors show how former president Trump meets all four of their criteria for authoritarian behavior (Table 1, 23–24) and explain how the failure of the Republican Party to serve as gatekeeper preventing his rise to power has created conditions that seriously undermine our democracy, even imperil it (53–71). The book was published before the 2020 election, but Trump's defeat has not dissipated extremism. In fact, the threat to democracy has intensified through voter suppression laws with their thinly veiled racism, and extreme measures taken by some Republican-controlled state legislatures and Republican governors. In terms of the two key aspects of American democracy: mutual respect and forbearance, as of now, mutual respect does not exist. The two parties are polarized in the extreme and see each other as enemies not as respected parties holding different perspectives on a mutual mission to support and sustain democracy. The country seems more divided than any time since the Civil War. Likewise, forbearance continues to be largely inoperative following Trump's defeat. Institutions are weaponized and President Biden's attempts to reach across party lines for bipartisan agreement have largely failed. Extremist points of view like those of Congresswoman Marjorie Taylor Greene go unchecked. Unless there is a shift toward at least some bipartisanship and common ground the darkest of the authors' three scenarios may well take hold (see "Saving Democracy," 204–231). Consequently, any game that gives a historical context to the reality of authoritarianism deserves to be played and discussed with students.

2. In James Joyce's epic novel *Ulysses* (1922), the character Stephen Dedalus claims, "history is a nightmare from which I am trying to awake." He makes the statement in response to a Mr. Deasey's attempt to present history from a single perspective or single voice, one that distorts historical fact and turns history into simplistic propaganda supporting prejudicial, and, usually, imperialistic or oppressive points of view. Without getting

into the complex question of England's occupation of Ireland to which the passage comments, I point out how Chapter Two of Ulysses is an incredible tour de force that displays and subverts an entire range of historical distortions and denials.

3. The Serbians' atrocities have been recorded in many places. On July 11, 1995, Serbs murdered 8,000 Muslims in what has become known as the Srebenica Massacre. Milosevic and Mladic were convicted of various atrocities, the first sentenced to 29 years in prison and the second to life imprisonment. Reading the sections of the actual court transcript (see resources below) can have a strong impact on students.

## GAMES

*Attentat 1942.*

Developed and published by Charles University, The Czech Academy of Sciences, and Charles Games, 2017.

*This War of Mine.*

Developed and published by 11 bit studios, 2014.

*This War of Mine: The Little Ones* brings children into the game world and war zone, a daring but powerful addition.

## LESSON IDEAS

*Attentat 1942*

The design and research team in Czechoslovakia has an entire Teacher's Guide listed under resources that I highly recommend. Two areas worthy of student investigation have pressing relevance to our current situation.

1. "News, Propaganda, Technology, and Dissent"
   In a dictatorship like Czechoslovakia during the Nazi protectorate and then under the Soviet Union news always comes under government control and, consequently, can neither accurately serve the country's citizens nor provide honest information to outsiders. Censorship always limits what gets reported. Nonetheless, people always find ways to get accurate news spread among themselves and to the outside world. For example, even me bringing in a banned

novel by a Soviet dissident in 1975 served to give an alternative perspective on the country's official news or propaganda. During the Nazi occupation, Czech citizens could pass information among themselves through the leaflets Jelínk receives, in the game, from a friend. Additionally, British Broadcasting Company (BBC) news could get through to the people via radio. These forms of underground communication are vital to resisting authoritarianism.

Today, in a democracy there is a wide variety of information available, but much of that information is propaganda masquerading as news. Additionally, social media forms that could serve as alternatives to mainstream broadcasting often exist with no fact checking, hence their accuracy and authority must always be in doubt. How does one provide and obtain accurate information in modern democracy? The misinformation spread by President Trump through Twitter, and, at times, Fox News, has parallels throughout the entire Vietnam War period when the U.S. government consistently lied to the public about the war. The publication of the famous *Pentagon Papers* in 1971 leaked by Dr. Daniel Ellsberg provides a historical case in point.

Break students into teams and ask them to research the situation surrounding the *Pentagon Papers*. Have another group research underground or alternative publications in the United States like *Ramparts* magazine from Berkley California or *The Village Voice* from New York City. Students can report on their research and compare the mainstream version of news with alternative and underground perspectives on the same news.

2. "The Social Role of Editorials"

One of the important challenges during the game concerns your grandfather's neighbor Joseph Málek. Málek was a journalist, and your grandparents suspected him of being a collaborator, which in your interview with him, he refutes. In the game narrative Málek is tasked with writing an editorial that supports the Nazi Protectorate. If he is a collaborator that does not present a problem, but if he opposes the Nazis and wants to keep his job, and perhaps, his life, he must write a more neutral editorial—perhaps one that subtly undermines the occupying regime. The player must fit together paragraphs in a way that satisfies the Nazi censors. Put students in a similar historical situation and ask them to write an original editorial about the situation in Prague or maybe about the destruction of Lidice. You can follow up by asking students to write an editorial for a U.S. paper and then discuss the differences in writing editorials under both forms of government as a class.

3. "Samizdat: Underground Information and Freedom of the Press in Autocracies"

During World War II and since underground information in communist Soviet bloc countries was referred to as Samizdat. Many of these publications were makeshift and spread by hand, which you encounter during the game. Students can research some of this work in archives, but also compare the use of these print based dissident publications with the use of Twitter to spread censored information in contemporary dictatorships, such as Twitter use during the Arab uprisings, e.g., the fall of Egypt's Hosni Mubarak in February 2011. This could be tied into the game specifically through Operation Prospero (1951–1956) in the aftermath of World War II when Allied Forces dropped leaflets and information over Soviet controlled Czechoslovakia through balloons (Lasar, 2010). A group of students could also identify sources of underground information in current dictatorships like Venezuela.

You could even ask students a discussion question like is WikiLeaks a form of Samizdat in the West?

4. Radio "The Forgotten Medium"

Today's students have a very limited experience of radio as a medium, but in the pre-digital world radio's value both as entertainment and news cannot be overestimated. The game makes clear the subversive role the London based BBC played in getting accurate information to Czech citizens. Radio Free Europe, sponsor of the abovementioned Operation Prospero, also played a critical role during the war years and their aftermath. In class, have students listen to archived broadcasts during World War II and then discuss the importance of radio in fighting historical dictatorships.

5. Student Creativity

In groups have students create a simulated dissident campaign using what they consider to be current forms of information about a dictatorship under attack or challenge from popular opposition. Also have students create their own radio broadcast and play the broadcast during class regarding news that would be difficult for citizens in a dictatorship to obtain.

*This War of Mine*

1. "Muslims and Jews: Faith and Hope in War Zone"

     The relationship between Jews and Muslims in Sarajevo is not well known, but their interfaith assistance to each other has been a way to overcome the atrocities of war and prejudice. Reaching way back to the 15th-century, Muslims helped Jews escape Spanish terror. During World War II, Muslims hid Jews from the Nazis and even gave them Muslim names. They also saved the Sarajevo Haggadah, a sacred text. During the 1992 siege, Jews, in turn, saved Muslims, and even provided Muslims refuge in a Jewish cemetery. Ask students to research similar historical examples where groups reached across faith, race, or ethnicity to help others during a period of civil unrest or war. This project gives students a positive message of hope when studying periods of historical despair.

2. "War Stories as Memory and Salvation"

     The site "A Story at Every Corner" (see Resources below) gives voice to the many stories told during a catastrophe. Stories give people hope, provide lessons for the future, and help give voice to the adult realities of large scale conflict. Likewise, studying the transmission of stories from worn torn areas of the world can be invaluable in understanding fighting's aftermath. Perhaps, more the half the surviving population of Sarajevo suffered from PTSD. Another half of the pre-war population left the country, displaced persons, and refugees, many going to countries entirely outside the former Yugoslavia. Ivanna Macek's chapter on "Memories of Sarajevo" studies the stories/memories of displaced persons who arrived in Sweden from Sarajevo. Have students read this chapter and talk not only about the role of memory, but also the situation of children of survivors as in Art Spiegelman's relationship to his Holocaust survivor father. Ask students to write a story from the perspective of a character from *This War of Mine* following a cease fire. What are the person's most vivid memories and what does their experience says about survival, siege conditions, and the human spirit?

3. "Crime and Punishment"

Ask students to read a section of the actual verdict of case from the International Crime Tribunal for the former Yugoslavia. I would suggest Section II: Evidence of the Case against Dragomir Milosevic, 12 December 2007, https://www.icty.org/en/case/dragomir_milosevic. This primary document brings the atrocities of this general to students' awareness in a way that will jar their thinking. Discuss the importance of the tribunal and why testimony is so important to justice. You could also hold a mock trial of another historical figure who has committed crimes against humanity. This kind of activity allows rich and memorable exploration of morality and justice.

4. "Rebuilding"

Students make some extraordinary buildings and small cites using Minecraft, so give them a map of Sarajevo before the siege and one of the city in ruins following the ceasefire. Ask them to rebuild Sarajevo. This project not only challenges city planning, and architecture but history and culture. How do you restore Byzantine architecture in the 21st century? What are the effects of war on the very buildings of history?

5. Have students listen to Ngozi Adichie's Ted Talk "The danger of a single voice" and debate the merits of leaving out parts of history or presenting historical events from a textbook perspective in secondary education. You can make the debate international since denial and the use of history to teaching only favorable realities that erase a nation's dark spots has been used in many countries, democracies, and dictatorships alike. This exercise would be especially valuable in Schools of Education.

## RESOURCES

Websites/Organizations/Curriculum

*The Anti-Defamation League*- https://www.adl.org/sites/default/files/documents/assets/pdf/education-outreach/guidelines-for-teaching-about-the-holocaust.pdf

Dedicated to fighting anti-Semitism and all forms of hate speech and action the ADL publishes, "Guidelines for Teaching About the Holocaust," which should be a preliminary step in preparing lessons for any teacher.

*Attentat 1942 Teacher's Guide*—by Shawn Glybor, November 15, 2019.

This excellent teacher's guide comes with an educational license to the game. It is the first place to begin your unit and lesson planning.

## AUSCHWITZ-BIRKENAU A MEMORIAL AND MUSEUM

http://auschwitz.org/en/

The museum in based in city of Oświęcim, Poland, and tours begin at the actual historical site of Auschwitz. Obviously, nothing could be as powerful, and overwhelming as visiting the actual site and museum, but the online history and exhibits are also an indispensable educational resource.

*Gaming the Past: historical video games in the classroom and beyond*— https://gamingthepast.net/

An excellent, comprehensive site devoted to games and history. It covers video games, tabletop games, simulations and more. The site is the product of high school history teacher Jeremiah McCall (see his book below). These is a specific discussion of *Attentat 1942* at https:// gamingthepast.net/2017/11/24/attentat-1942-review/

*International Criminal Tribunal for the former Yugoslavia, 1993–2017.*

https://www.icty.org./en

An important international tribunal based in The Hague, Netherlands. This site provides rich primary documentation on war crimes, witnessing, justice, accountability, and humanitarian law.

*Holocaust and Human Behavior, Facing History*

https://www.facinghistory.org/sites/default/files/publications/
Holocaust_Human_Behavior_revised_edition.pdf.

This publication from the Facing History organization is an extraordinary, indispensable, and comprehensive guide to exploring racism, anti-Semitism, biases, prejudice, morality, history, and justice.

*PBS Learning Media*

https://ny.pbslearningmedia.org/collection/teaching-the-holocaust/

Public Broadcasting Service's lessons on teaching the Holocaust, especially through art.

*Radio Free Europe/Radio Liberty*

https://www.rferl.org

Tracks human rights and freedom of the press in countries that practice censorship. As of today, 23 countries are followed.

*Reporters San Frontíere (RSP)*

https://rsf.org/

The best guide to international reporting on freedom. You can view translations on the site.

*Story at every corner*

https://storyateverycorner.com/

A personal website of a globetrotting couple that gives voice to stories of all kinds, but the blog pertaining to the Siege of Sarajevo is particularly powerful, https://storyateverycorner.com/sarajevo-under-siege/.

*United States Holocaust Memorial Museum*

https://www.ushmm.org

Based in Washington, D.C., this museum demands a personal visit if you are ever in the U.S. capital. The online site has a section called "Teach" that provides guidelines, tools, poster sets, research, and other critical information about the Holocaust, how to teach, why to teach, and how to handle Holocaust deniers.

## Books/Articles/Essays/Talks

Adichie, Ngozi. "The danger of a single story." *Ted Talk*, 7 October 2007.

A terrific talk from a Nigerian novelist discussing the importance of diversity in literature, culture, and history.

Giovanni, Janine di. "From Sarajevo to Aleppo: Lessons on Surviving a Siege." *The Atlantic*, 12 October 2016, https://amp.theatlantic.com/amp/article/503843/.

Havel, Václav. "The Power of the Powerless", https://web.archive.org/web/20120107141633/http://www.vaclavhavel.cz/showtrans.php?cat=clanky&val=72_aj_clanky.html&typ=HTML

Václav Havel's essay, written in 1978, describes conditions of living under Soviet domination. Havel was the first president of the Czech Republic following the dissolution of the Soviet empire and his essays are a must read for understanding Eastern Europe since the end of World War II. Free version of the essay is available online.

Kulka, Erick and Kraus, Ota. *The Death Factory/ Tovarna na Smrt.* Translated by Stephen Jolly. Pergamon Press, 1966, originally published in Czech by Praha Cĭn, 1946.

A powerful primary document; eyewitness account of life in Auschwitz.

Levitzky, Steven and Ziblatt, Daniel. *How Democracies Die* (Crown Publishing Group, 2018).

An excellent book on the collapse of democracy in modern times with a warning about the threat to American democracy posed by the rise of right wing extremism surfacing under former President Trump.

There is "A Reader's Guide to Levitzky and Ziblatt's *How Democracies Die,*" printed at the back of the book, (Penguin Random House LLC, 2019). Additionally, online can be found "How Democracies Die Teacher's Guide," (Penguin

Random House), https://www.penguinrandomhouse.com/books/562246/how-democracies-die-by-steven-levitsky-and-daniel-ziblatt/9781524762940/teachers-guide/.

This guide incudes classroom exercises, discussion questions, resources, etc.

Macek, Ivvana. "Transmission and Transformation: Memories of the Siege of Sarajevo," in Dowdall, A. and Horne, J. (eds.). *Civilians Under Siege from Sarajevo to Troy,* pp. 15–35. https://doi.or/10.1057/978-1-137-58532-5_2, 2018.

A study of migrants, refugees, and others from Sarajevo who ended up in Sweden. The author discusses and analyzes their stories and memories of a traumatic event.

McCall, Jeremiah. *Gaming the Past: Using Video Games to Teach Secondary History* (Routledge, 2011).

An excellent, eminently practical book on using games in high school history and social studies classes.

Milosz, Czeslaw. *The Captive Mind* Vintage Classics, reissue. 1990. Translated by Susan Mitchell.

Composed in 1953 the Polish Nobel Prize-winning poet's prose masterpiece gives an imaginative and powerful account of dictatorships, the power of brainwashing, and the psychology of collaboration. I studied with one of Milosz's contemporaries, the Polish drama critic Jan Kott, and *The Captive Mind* brilliantly captures the appeal of authoritarianism while also describing the exchange of Nazi domination of Eastern Europe for Soviet domination under Stalin. I can think of no better book for our students to read in these polarized times.

# CHAPTER 10

# The Child as Mother to Man

## A Game for Saving Nature

## RUNNING WITH HOPE

Encourage your kids, your students to play *Alba: A Wildlife Adventure*. Play the game yourself and with your kids or grandkids. Perhaps, just as important, encourage your local politicians to play the game. That might be a hard sell, but they usually have kids, so that's the way around their probable reluctance to play. Alba is a game about an active young girl exploring nature during a visit to her grandparents. Alba's play runs against the tide of adult development and the oncoming tidal wave of disaster.

In this fun, innocent game, you play the child protagonist Alba as she visits her grandparents on the island of Pina Da Mar for a summer vacation in the luxurious sun. Alba's exuberant positivity and childhood innocence bring magic and hope to players living through a pandemic and other disasters that drain one's positive energy. Reviewer Mark Delaney beautifully captures the game's childhood wonder:

> More than any other game I've played, Alba captures the magical optimism of childhood. Adults can be cynical, weathered by jobs and bills, but for Alba, like for a lot of children, the world is still full of wonder, and she feels big and brave enough to change it for

the better. The most wonderful part of Alba: no one tells her she can't — and so she does (2021).

Alba explores the island with a purpose. Her quest is to locate, identify, and learn about the island's species. Alba has basic assets: a map of the island, a notebook, a cellphone, and a field guide. Only the cellphone represents current technology, but in a beautiful inversion, the cell phone serves to render itself secondary to the adventure. Alba uses the camera to photograph different species that she then identifies and records. You are collecting information and wisdom not coins. Most impressive, the technology of the game itself serves to prompt kids outdoors into nature exploring and playing. Virtual bird watching can never replace hiking nature's trials and the joy of spotting an "indigo bunting" not a pixelated bird.

Little Alba skips around the island. She runs, jumps, and hops like kids on a Saturday afternoon. She is full of joy, enthusiastic and earnest in her explorations. The game's pace is leisurely. You can play slow or fast, but speed contributes nothing. This is the Mediterranean where life is slow, lunches long, and work something you get to when you get to it. No compulsive need to work work work as life passes by. That's one of the game's primary pleasures, the child's timeless pace of exploration and play. Curiosity does not let schedules dictate the day's rhythms.

As you slide your finger across the screen, skipping Alba around the island, she often comes across the outline of a hand. The player touches the hand to clean up all the surrounding litter, most likely from careless and irresponsible adults. In this ongoing mission Alba becomes a kind of one-person cleanup crew. Her goal, admirable and vital on a local level, has a potentially cumulative effect. Many local environments make up the whole earth's ecosystem. I currently live on the very edge of the Albany Pine Bush Preserve, a rare inland pine barren sand dune natural environment home to many rare plants and species.[1] When I walk along the road on its northeastern edge, I see litter everywhere: Big Mac wrappers tossed out of the car by lazy, thoughtless adults, empty soda cans from the local convenience store, convenience today, catastrophe tomorrow, and assorted garbage from nearby Walmart. Alba's actions are a tiny bulwark against this kind of encroaching catastrophe spreading across the globe.

Alba has some specific missions too. As she explores some ruins, her friend Inés, looks over the edge of a small cliff down to the ocean and remarks, "Oh no! Look! There's a stranded dolphin!" Her little cartoon face looks troubled, but thoughtful as she invites Alba to help the dolphin. In a wonderful gesture, Alba asks for help to whoever she comes across. Her innocent sincerity, the genuineness of her plea, works. Everyone wants to help Alba. Here is a big lesson. Be polite, be sincere, stress the seriousness of your purpose, and ask for help. The sight of a dolphin trapped in a net on the beach has disturbing resonance. One of the most beautiful, graceful, and intelligent mammals of the world helplessly wrapped in the net of human neglect. Thankfully, Alba finds a group of adults and kids to help her. Together they save the dolphin (Figure 10.1). Ticking off a To-Do List could not be more rewarding.

Players will find joy in these quests. Alba's in-game success seeps out into your consciousness. The simulated rescue might just move some players to real rescues. As I stress over and over, we need to take responsibility for the condition of our surroundings and if those surroundings are littered with trash, do something about it!

FIGURE 10.1   Dolphin rescue from *Alba: A Wildlife Adventure*. (Image courtesy of Ustwo Games. © Used with Permission.)

## THE LOCAL IS GLOBAL, THE GLOBAL IS LOCAL

As I have commented above, the game is full of marvelous quests or tasks. The biggest quest is Alba's desire to save the Pinar Del Mar's nature conservancy. The game's thematic conflict has archetypal significance. A real estate developer wants to build a big resort hotel that will ruin the conservancy. It's a common story in the United States and elsewhere, and such alarming commonness makes the game's message more urgent. Back to where I reside for the moment. Common story, unique place. The Pyramid Management Group, a primary developer, wants to build around, next to, and, through the Albany Pine Brush Preserve (see photo of protected land in Figures 10.2 and 10.3).[2] They have expressed the desire to build, build, build office space, a Costco, and all the grisly wonders of developers' greed.[3] Let's have some dull corporate gray to contrast with the beautiful orange Orioles and Rose-breasted Grosbeaks flying about. Pyramid is joined by The Cardona Development Group and their nearby construction of a ghastly 24-unit apartment complex on Pine Lane.

FIGURE 10.2 Albany Pine Bush. ("Courtesy of the Albany Pine Bush Preserve Commission" ©.)

In the game, Alba and Inés must gather signatures on a petition to the major to block development. Their action echoes here and across the globe. The country witnesses the unholy alliance of local politicians with greedy corporate executives on a continual basis. Here by the Albany Pine Bush, corporate interest dictates what happens to local cities, towns, and villages. The City of Albany and the Town of Guilderland's Planning Boards routinely approve unneeded development disregarding the natural environment, and any nonhuman species, sacrificing long-term sustainability for short-term political and economic gain. The local politicians offer the tired cliché with fully unintended irony that corporate development produces quality of life (read the politicians' reelection). The name Guilderland like many names in New York State derives from the Dutch language. Gelderland is a province in the Netherlands. "Guilder" of course is the basic monetary unit in the Netherlands. One can accurately characterize Guilderland as Builderland, a space for overdevelopment and suburban sprawl. The word sprawl, by the way, means unnatural, ungraceful. You get the picture. Nothing artistic about it.

FIGURE 10.3 Developers' destruction of the Albany Pine Bush. (Photograph by the author.)

This quality of life local "planners" promote consists of sitting in already congested traffic, taking 45 minutes to drive a mile, risking your life bicycling, or walking your dog, inhaling fossil fuels, the vista of a crowded human mass, and piles of concrete leaving nature a fading memory, lost to corporate greed. Moreover, thanks to the miraculous mall builder of the Northeastern United States, you can eat, drink, sleep, watch movies, build stuffed bears, get your back rubbed, and buy every item a conspicuous consumer could want at the spectacular Crossgates Mall. Rapp Road where I currently reside cuts through the Albany Pine Bush as well as a

FIGURE 10.4 Rapp Road historical district, Albany New York. (Photograph courtesy of by Beth Tedford. © Used with permission). Rapp Road, Albany, New York. An African American Heritage Site. The historical rural road is now a high-traffic thoroughfare for people on their way to the shopping mall. (Photograph courtesy of Beth Tedford. © Used with permission.)

local historical district of African Americans (Figure 10.4).[4] Intended as a country road for residents this one way road has become nothing but a constant thoroughfare for people on their way to the mall. The road connects two drab products of Pyramid Management Corporation. It has no curb, no sidewalks, barely any lighting, and the posted 20 MPH speed limit is frequently disregarded by motorists going at least twice the legal speed limit in a rush to reach their shopping zen heaven. The City of Albany has done nothing to protect the safety of residents, pedestrians (there is a home for disabled adults on the road as well), or animals. Although there is a police station very nearby, in 18 months I have only seen a police vehicle on the road once. Any naturalist will find walking in this natural area both a safety threat and assault on one's senses. This is what local planning boards call quality of life.

Just as city main streets, and village centers with their family stores, small business owners, walking paths, little parks, village commons, and unique offerings were replaced by bland carbon copy chain stores fed by automobiles and surrounded by parking lot moats, now nature itself will be erased by short-sighted greed. The colonization of nature. Destruction masquerading as progress. The corporate and political leaders who sponsor this parody of progress will be dead when the full consequences of their self-interested "planning" takes full effect, so today's little Albas will inherit what will most likely be empty malls. Children will have no wildlife for any adventure.

## PLAYING THE CHILD HERO

Alba is a hero because of her innocence. Her ardent commitment to doing the right thing. That a Swedish teenager has led the fight against climate change should surprise no one. Adults have abdicated their responsibility. Youth must take charge of the future for there to be a future worth looking forward to. We are very near the point of no return with respect to the inexcusable ruination of the environment. Alba succeeds in building a community of action because of her positivity, her goodness, her childishness. Listen to how reviewer Mark Delaney characterizes the game's child as hero:

> The island is laid back, and so are its residents. Perhaps too laid back – despite its chill nature, there's a definite theme running through of responsibility that's been shirked, people being too

complacent, letting the casual rot of laziness set in. Alba is a force for change, a whirlwind of positivity and energy on this sunny, soporific island. She repairs tables, wildlife pictures, bird boxes, tidies up trash – her activity inspires others to act, to challenge their assumptions of responsibility.

*(Shaw, 2021)*

The child Alba acts, while adults too often sit still. That needs to change.

No, this is not a game of impact, at least on the surface. We can enjoy a fun, lighthearted casual game playable in 3 or 4 hours on a mobile device (it is much better played on a mobile device) with a positive and important message. At the same time, the game's message should not be pushed aside, or trivialized. Too many game reviewers totally miss the point when they acknowledge the game's childlike wonder and applaud its message but then dismiss it with an "oh isn't that nice" type of platitude. The message is anything but nice even if it is delivered via a casually pleasant, exciting gameplay. When you play the game, you need to make sure the game becomes a game of impact, a game for change. Don't just put it down, think cute game and move on to *Candy Crush Saga* or *Fortnite*. If Alba the character does not prompt you to action, your own Alba, if you are an adult, will inherit a world without wilderness. For children playing this game, they should live the game and take Alba as a model for making a better world in any little way they can, recycling bottles, cleaning up the local park, helping a hurt animal. Helping others helps yourself and helps everyone.

## RAINBOWS AND BUTTERFLIES: ART AS SAVIOR

Literature has been my life's great passion. When I think of visionaries, I think of artists, not builders. Art imagines a future of possibility just as it depicts a future of desolation. We make the choice as to the future we will have. Art helps us pay attention to what matters, to the beauty of nature, and why we need to preserve it if we are to survive as a species. Games are works of art, and *Alba, A Wildlife Adventure* is a wonderful work of art. However, as a lover of literature, I want to conclude with a nod to two of the greatest writers of the English language, who can also help us appreciate the world Alba wants to save.

One of the rare species found in the Albany Pine Bush just out my back door is the Karner blue butterfly (*Lycaeides melissa samuelis*) (Figure 10.5). It was placed on the Endangered Species list in 1992. This extraordinary species was discovered by the great novelist Vladimir Nabokov, a Russian who wrote English with an unmatched symphonic beauty. Nabokov loved butterflies. He was a passionate lepidopterist. Nabakov had a professional scientist's understanding of butterflies, especially the blues (Johnson and Coates, 2001, Boyd and Pyle, 2000). In 1941, he went on a famous cross-country road trip to collect and study butterflies (some are in the American Museum of Natural History), a road trip that later materialized in his world-famous novel *Lolita*.[5]

Nabakov's curiosity about butterflies emerged while he was a child in Russia about the same age the game Alba depicts its protagonist. In a memoir describing his entomological journey, Nabokov stops to ponder the butterfly's power of mimicry. He finds in the butterfly's mimicry something Darwin's theory of natural selection cannot explain which leads him

FIGURE 10.5  The Karner blue butterfly, an endangered species. (Photograph courtesy of the Albany Pine Bush Preserve Commission ©.)

to a striking conclusion rendered in prose as intricately extraordinary as the butterfly itself,

> when a protective device was carried to a point of mimetic subtlety, exuberance, and luxury far in excess of a predator's power of appreciation. I discovered in nature the nonutilitarian delights that I sought in art. Both were a form of magic; both were a game of intricate enchantment and deception (1948).

Through art and nature, one reaches beauty, spirituality, transcendence, all the antithesis of utility, the desire to manipulate the world into use value.

Nabakov ends the essay evoking the timeless, an experience of eternity, made possible by attention to "rare butterflies and their food." He observes that the experience of the butterfly goes beyond even the ecstatic: "It is like a momentary vacuum into which rushes all that I love, a sense of oneness with sun and stone, a thrill of gratitude to whom it may concern, perhaps to the contrapuntal genius of human fate or to the tender ghosts humoring a lucky mortal." No such oneness can be found in a resort hotel. Not ever.

A century or so before Nabokov's butterflies, the great British romantic poet William Wordsworth discovered a similar oneness with nature as the Industrial Revolution was transforming the English landscape into manufacturing factories eating up nature's bounty for coal to burn in the furnaces of development. I am not sure how many people read poetry today, but more should. Poetry like nature is beautiful, profound, and spiritual. Wordsworth celebrated children and childhood while knowing what the Industrial Revolution and the pursuit of money and mass production would do throughout the countryside he loved See Figure 10.6, where Wordsworth stayed in England's Lake District.. Children like Alba have a curious, open-hearted appreciation for nature, an innocent regard for the interdependence of life. In his brief nine-line lyric, "My Heart Leaps Up," Wordsworth celebrates a rainbow which evokes memories of his childhood. He thinks to himself, how his heart still leaps at the sight of a rainbow, and that he desires this spontaneous feeling to continue into old age for when he stops appreciating the beauty of nature he will die, "And I could wish my days to be/Bound each to each by natural piety."

Wordsworth's reverence for nature is what the game Alba, A Wildlife Adventure evokes through a child's wide eyes. If adults continue to look away from the eyes of children and neglect our ravaging of nature, we will soon

FIGURE 10.6   Dove cottage, The Lake District, England circa 1920. (Abraham, Ashley Perry, Public domain, via Wikimedia Commons https://commons.wikimedia.org/wiki/File:Dove_Cottage_circa_1920.jpg.)

have no wildlife, perhaps no habitable life at all. As Wordsworth famously noted in the above poem, "The child is father to the man," so when we lose the child, we also lose the man, and only humanity's ruins will remain.

## NOTES

1. The Albany Pine Bush Preserve (ihttps://albanypinebush.org/index. php?section=visit-the-pine-bush-preserves) is a Natural Historic Landmark because of its unique ecology consisting of inland pitch pine, scrub oak barrens, and wind-swept sand dunes. The preserve is home to many rare species, but as I mention above, the land has shrunk considerably over the years from human conquest.

2. Pyramid Management Group was formed by the late Robert J. Congel in 1968. It is the largest mall development group in the Northeastern United States. The Crossgates Mall (opened in 1984) is in Albany, New York, the state's capital. It is smack in the middle of the Pine Bush Preserve. The company used subsidiaries and a long-range, highly aggressive, and manipulative plan to buy up precious natural land for development in what has become very overdeveloped, congested space at the expense of existing homeowners, small businesses, and, not least, a natural landmark. It would be interesting to ask students who only know malls, what benefit malls play in society and what they think malls replaced? Malls are a kind of isolated bubble surrounded by an ocean of parked cars they depend upon for their success. Populated by ubiquitous chain stories. There is no sense of place, no identity,

and no genuine community to speak of, but, nonetheless, a convenience for conspicuous consumption and a meeting place for teenagers. The multiplex has concurrently replaced the local movie cinema subdividing space for maximum profit, but only showing the standard blockbuster fare of the day. Again, the multiplex has no character, and there is no sense of place.

3. Save the Pine Bush (https://savethepinebush.org/), a not-for-profit organization started in response and opposition to Pyramid Management Group and its associates. They engage in frequent legal battles with developers and are engaged in one as I write. The organization's motto or tagline is tragically true: "Without Save the Pine Bush, there would be no Pine Bush today." If left to developers, the Pine Bush would not exist today and that appears to be the objective of current corporate action, eliminate nature altogether. Citizen action, like that of little Alba, must continue for any semblance of nature to remain. In this area of New York, we have the chilling lesson of G.E. The great General Electric, which employed much of the region's population when I grew up, dumped 1.3 million PCBs into the majestic Hudson River. Corporations cannot be allowed to operate without regulation for just this reason. The Environmental Protection Agency details the potentially harmful, even fatal consequences of G.E.'s grossly irresponsible behavior on their official site, "Just the Facts-Cleaning Up Hudson River PCBs," https://www3.epa.gov/hudson/just_facts_8_04.htm.

4. Rapp Road, where I currently reside, runs through the Pine Bush Preserve. It is also home to the Rapp Road historical region, a location where African American families settled during the Great Migration North from Mississippi. The small area is placed on the National Register of Historic Places. Many of the homes on both sides of the road were built by these settlers. Thus, aggressive development by Pyramid Management Group threatens not just a natural landmark but a historical one as well. For information, and historical accounts of the area visit the Rapp Road Historical Association: https://rapproad.wordpress.com/about-us/rapp-road-historic-district/.

5. Suzanne Rapp Greene, a curatorial assistant at the American Museum of Natural History, curated Nabokov's famous road trip, "Episode 17: Nabokov's Butterflies 360," American Museum of Natural History, https://www.amnh.org/shelf-life/nabokov-butterflies-360. The trip resulted in many donations to the museum by the famed novelist. Located at 200 Central Park West in New York City, the museum is one place every student should visit. It is a national treasure I still visit every couple of years.

## LESSON IDEA

I urge teachers and professors to implement and encourage some aspects of service learning in their courses. Classrooms must be expanded through games, nature, and community action. Ask students to use their smartphone and walk around their neighborhood or campus neighborhood taking pictures and recording information about all the species they encounter. Students can prepare a simple a guidebook or pamphlet to display in the school or local library.

## GAME

*Alba, A Wildlife Adventure.*

Developed and published by Ustwo Games, 2020.

## RESOURCES

*Defend Them All*

https://www.defendthemall.org/

Dedicated to the protection of animals.

*National Audubon Society*

https://www.audubon.org/

The premier organization devoted to birds and birding. They have an excellent bird guide app, recommend books for kids, and the excellent "Audubon Magazine."

*The Nature Conservancy*

https://www.nature.org/en-us/

A wonderful organization that offers a conservancy newsletter, a partnership with indigenous people, and an excellent section on the website called, "Backyard Birding." They also have many local chapters for students and teachers to contact.

*Sierra Club*

https://www.sierraclub.org/

This nature-driven organization has local chapters and many concrete ways for people to take meaningful action on behalf of the environment.

*World Wildlife Fund*

https://www.worldwildlife.org/

Based in Switzerland, this NGO strives to reduce the human imprint on the environment in every aspect. A vital organization in the effort to slow down the onslaught of overdevelopment.

# CHAPTER 11

# Turning Strangers into Neighbors

*Improving the World through a Game of Gratitude*

## SEARCHING FOR HAPPINESS IN A CYNICAL TIME

New Year's Eve in 2020 witnessed a near empty Times Square in New York City. On a traditional New Year's Eve, a boisterous, joyous crowd of a million celebrants from around the world would be singing, hugging kissing, and blowing gazoos, as the crystal ball dropped signaling a New Year. The pandemic wreaked havoc and brought unfathomable tragedy to so many families. As COVID-19 took over New York, Times Square became, for a period, ghostly, an empty crossroads to a suffering world. In the United States COVID-19 was only part of a larger national struggle. Racial divisions and violence that echoed the race riots of the mid-1960s roared again exposing the citizenry's long-standing, festering wounds. Firmly entrenched partisanship displayed by the two political parties made a mockery of national unity. States seemed as divided as during the confederacy over a century and a half ago. Moreover, the country had a sitting president who stoked divisions, used the "bully pulpit" to literally belittle opponents and mounted an attack on the traditions and institutions of the republic. The social turmoil reached a climax on January 6, 2021, when

DOI: 10.1201/9781003201465-14

the United States Congress experienced an almost unthinkable insurrection. Such ugly circumstances breed cynicism, so how can we individually and collectively pull out of the public health, political and social crises of the last few years?

Let me turn back the clock to 2019, just before the pandemic closed cinemas across the country. One of my favorite movies that year was *A Beautiful Day in the Neighborhood* (Dir. Marielle Heller) starring the inimitable Tom Hanks as Fred Rogers. Fred Rogers, Reverend Rogers, or as best known, Mr. Rogers, exuded warmth and positivity. His show and his presence made any day beautiful. The TV show and its simple puppet stage represented the neighborhood as an extended living room—full of warmth, acceptance, and kindness. Approaching the world through kindness brings positive results. That is what Mr. Roger's approach to life makes possible.

A few years ago, I was a virtual auditor in Yale psychologist Laurie Santos' Massive Open Online Course "The Science of Wellness." Dr. Santos now offers a podcast called "The Happiness Lab" and her Yale course, "The Psychology of the Good Life," is the university's most popular. Not surprisingly, the good life has little to do with lounging on a million-dollar yacht. The good life, what the ancient Greeks called eudaimonia, has much to do with kindness, gratitude, and mindfulness. That so many young students at one of the world's most prestigious universities are enrolling in such a course says something rather unflattering about the state of our society.

Santos' work draws on many people, especially the positive psychology of Martin Seligman (2002). Positive psychology inverts the medical disease model of mental health to stress strengths not weaknesses, i.e., what is right about the person, not what is wrong with the person. Let me give a concrete personal example. In the 1990s when I worked as a community social worker specializing in family systems theory/ counseling, which prefigured much of positive psychology, we strove to re-frame troubled adolescents from being the family scapegoat to being a fully, and often, healthy member of the family and larger community. I vividly recall a one-time session with the family of a boy designated by family court as a juvenile delinquent and placed into residential foster care. The family reinforced the boy's role as a troublemaker whom the system now needed to fix. The parents were divorced, but amicable. They were middle class and highly educated. Both daughters were "healthy": one attended the University of Virginia and ran track, and the other worked and attended a local community college. The entire family, along with the boy's residential social worker and residential care assistant, met in our agency's Long Island office. The first question I raised, "What do you like best about Richard?" (not his real name) left the family speechless. For years they thought of Richard as a problem, the problem. Now they were on the spot and forced to think about him in a more positive way that also forced the family to think about their own role in maintaining the young man as a problem. The family's perspective changed, and things improved. Positive words, thoughts, and actions matter and matter in a big way.

## THE POWER OF KIND WORDS

Games can help bring about such positivity in thought, action, and words. Just recently, the legendary Japanese game designer Shigeru Miyamoto (lead designer of *Donkey Kong*, *Super Mario Brothers*, the Wii controller, *Legend of Zelda*, etc.) interviewed with the *New Yorker's* Simon Parkin (2020). Parkin asks Miyamoto how he would design the world if such a fantastic opportunity arose, and the response is telling: "I wish I could make it so that people were more thoughtful and kinder toward each other." Well, the casual game *Kind Words lo fi chill beats to write to* promotes this wish and helps make it a reality.

*Kind Words* encourages and enables all players to write kind words to strangers. Not random acts of kindness, but deliberate efforts to be nice. When the game opens the screen fills compelling the player to focus on the game, to be present. The game begins with the appearance of a Mail Deer, a magic deer who delivers your letters across the web. These beautiful, graceful animals are perfect messengers. They immediately made me think of Santa Claus's magic reindeer as they transport the jolly figure across the sky so he can bring joy to others. The primary mechanic of the game is writing letters to ambient music conducive to thoughtful writing (hence the game's subtitle). These letters are gifts. The game's action, one of giving. What could be more positive? (Figure 11.1)

There are three basic game actions. One, you write a request and send in it out to an anonymous audience. Two, you look at your inbox and respond to requests for help. Again, the audience is anonymous. Third, you can give thanks for a response by giving a sticker. Stickers, in turn, can be collected to decorate your room a minor but appreciated aspect of the game (based upon my students reports). Anonymity is an important aspect of the letter writing. You do not know who responds to your request and

FIGURE 11.1 The mail deer. (Image courtesy of Ziba Scott. © Uses with permission of Popcannibal.)

you do not know who you are responding to. Such anonymity cuts down on negative letters or trolling because there is no reward and no reaction when some ignorant troll makes a hateful comment. Designer Ziba Scott defines his purpose in designing the game's dynamic, "The flow of conversation goes request, reply, and then a sticker is 'thanks.' No other words. In this way, no troll, no insult ever gets a rise from a victim. No one can ever get that satisfaction of having upset someone if that's what they're trying to do" (2019). The positive norms created by the game's community produce an overwhelmingly positive environment. In essence, the game turns the web's anonymity on its head. So much of the web, especially since the emergence of social media, consists of hate speech, ignorance, bullying, and nasty mean spiritedness, all protected by anonymity. The game uses this anonymity to a positive affect by privileging and reinforcing kindness (Figure 11.2).

A final aspect of the game, which was not present with its initial release, are "paper airplanes." Remember middle school or, in my case, 9th-grade Algebra, where you send paper airplanes around the classroom when bored to death by the class? Here the paper airplanes serve, to echo Sting, as messages in a bottle, little positive snippets from people, often inspiring quotes, that circulate positivity. You can grab one as it floats across your screen and smile.

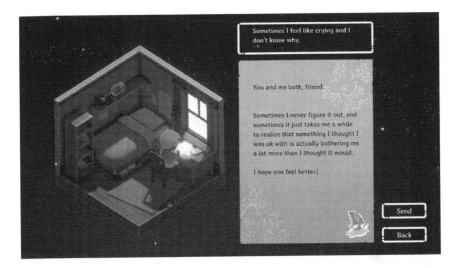

FIGURE 11.2 The kindness of letter writing. (Image courtesy of Ziba Scott. ©
Uses with permission of Popcannibal.)

In one way, the game reminded me of the old "Dear Abbey" newspaper
columns popular when I was young. People around the country would
mail in letters asking Abbey, real name Pauline Phillips, for advice on
various things. She had no professional experience or clinical training,
but most people do not make it to formal therapy, nonetheless, they
need help and that help, like in *Kind Words*, is not hours of therapy,
but simply a caring presence, an active ear that hears the person's concerns in a nonjudgmental way. Yet what distinguishes *Kind Words* from
these advice columns, as one reviewer, remarks, has to be the quantity
of positivity:

> It's not any single message that leaves an impact. It's the sheer
> weight of love and positivity being thrown at you. I'm not going to
> feel any better about myself because some random paper airplane
> told me to love myself, but there is something reassuring about
> such a large community of people all trying so hard to lessen the
> darkness of their peers (2020).

A community of positivity has power to improve lives and environments.
A community of negativity has the power to destroy lives and communities. *Kind Words* moves us toward the former.

One of my students S.G. describes how valuable the giving part of *Kind Words*, i.e., writing a letter, matters:

> A lot of messages that I sent to people; I made sure to let them know how important they are and how everyone around them cares about them deeply. Some players are in worse shape than others, so it is important to speak kindly to people. ...The main objective is to help people, and after just playing for a short period of time, I can feel that I have made a difference in some people's lives by just reaching out and writing a letter to them. Games like these save lives, so it [the game] definitely reached its main purpose, which is to simply help people through their problems."

What more can you ask from a simple little game?

Finally, as mentioned above, January 6, 2021, witnessed one of the worst days in American history. As Congress met to count the ballots of a free election certifying the next president Joseph H. Biden, the presiding president Donald J. Trump spoke before an angry mob of supporters. His words appeared to stir hatred, amplify divisions, and incite, to no small degree, "insurrectionists" storming the Capitol building. For Christians, January 6th or the Twelfth Night is the epiphany, or the day three magi brought gifts for the infant Jesus. Contrasting the hate of a failed insurrection with the power of giving shows, on the one hand, how hateful words do hurt, and on the other hand, how kind words can heal. Play the game and you will see why.

## LESSON IDEAS

1. Encourage students to play the game for a week or two and reflect on their experience. Follow up with an open discussion. Student sharing must be voluntary, but often one share leads to others. Ask students about the kinds of requests they received and how they responded. Ask others how they would respond. No doubt there will be common threads in requests that promote excellent exchanges deepening social emotional learning for the entire class.

2. Have students watch either *It's a Beautiful Day in the Neighborhood* or the documentary *Won't You Be My Neighbor*? (Dir. Morgan Neville, 2019) and write about what a good neighbor entails. How would they

describe their neighborhood and how could their neighborhood be improved? Compare their definition with Robert Frost's famous poem "The Mending Wall" with its famous refrain "Good fences make good neighbors."

3. Read the parable of the Good Samaritan, *Luke* 10:25-37 where Jesus, addressed as teacher, responds to the question, "And who is my neighbor?" with his powerful parable. Debate the responsibility of bystanders. Are there any innocent bystanders?

4. Have students write a lesson plan on kindness for grades K-2. Stress the importance of a positive foundation for a child's healthy growth.

5. Ask students to find examples from their own experience or from history that represent how hate words cause harm and how kind words promote health.

## GAME

*Kind Words* (lo fi chill beats to write to). Developed and published by Popcannibal, 2019.

## RESOURCES

### Primary Sources

*A Beautiful Day in the Neighborhood.* Director: Marcelle Heller, 2019.

A biopic starring Tom Hanks as Fred Rogers.

*Won't You Be My Neighbor.* Director: Morgan Neville, 2018.

Documentary about early childhood educator Fred Rogers.

### Websites/Organizations

*The Happiness Podcast*—http://www.happinesslab.fm

Yale psychologist Laurie Santos' Apple podcast on various ways to achieve the good life including how the ancient Greeks understood happiness and the latest scientific research on which factors lead to happiness. She offers many practical suggestions on living a life of optimism and hope.

*The Positive Psychology Center*—https: //ppc.sas.upenn.edu

> Based at the University of Pennsylvania and featuring many articles, videos, and annotated resources on positive psychology and building resiliency.

## Books

Dalai Lama with Howard Cutler, MD. *The Art of Happiness: A Handbook for Living.* Riverhead Books, 2020.

> Psychiatrist Howard C. Cutler conducts a series of interviews with the Dalai Lama who explains how a change in mindset can change your world. An exceptional example of spiritual thinking from a Buddhist perspective.

Emmons, Robert A. *The Little Book of Gratitude: Create a Life of Happiness and Wellbeing by Giving Thanks.* Gaia Books, 2016.

> Psychologist Robert Emmons is a leader in positive psychology. This practical book has many activities and exercises about giving thanks. It is perfect for bedside reading or for putting in your briefcase or purse for reference throughout the day.

Gilbert, Daniel. *Stumbling on Happiness.* Knopf. 2006.

> A Harvard psychologist provides scientific evidence that shows what we think leads to happiness rarely does. Reading this book will help students step out of the money-driven path of accumulation and reflect on deeper values of family and friendship that COVID-19 has also pushed many people into thinking about.

Sacks, Oliver. *Gratitude.* Knopf, 2015.

> A deeply moving book by the brilliant British neurologist who lived a life of compassion.

Seligman, Martin. *Learned Optimism: How to Change Your Mind and Your Life.* Vintage, Reprint edition 2006, originally published in 1991.

> The "dean" of positive psychology describes how everyone can develop skills for creating and maintaining an optimistic frame of mind.

# III

## Casual Games as Transformative Online Learning Experiences

# CHAPTER 12

# Three Small Games for Big Learning in Math and Physics

T HERE IS NOTHING I treasure more than our pug Roderick. He lives up to the breed's reputation as "a lot of dog in a small space." That is how I would define an ideal casual game. They are small, easy to play, fun, but pack a big punch. Three such games suitable for elementary age school children that college students and their parents can also play and enjoy are *Cut the Rope* (Zepoto Labs, 2010), *Threes!* (Sirvo, 2015), *and Dragon Box Algebra 5+* (Kahout 2012).

These little games take only minutes to learn and can be played in the short bursts ideal for online learning. All three address basic math and physics concepts and principles. However, only one, *Dragon Box*, can be said to have a deliberate educational aim. The other two are entertainment based; nonetheless, they have plenty of learning interwoven through the fun. Collateral learning can be described as learning that takes place because of an activity whose purpose is not primarily educational. We all know collateral damage refers to damage outside a specified target, well the same for collateral learning, but in a positive way.

DOI: 10.1201/9781003201465-16

## CUT THE ROPE: THE PHYSICS OF A CANDY CRUNCHER

This little game has evolved into a small franchise thanks to its near perfect design and an adorable mascot called Om Nom. Like the famous *Sesame Street* cookie monster, this green creature always wants to eat. The game's objective is feeding this little creature by cutting ropes that have delicious pieces of candy dangling from them. You cut the rope by swiping across the touch screen with your finger. Perfect for a smartphone. Sounds easy, right? Well, at the start, but like any good game, the challenges get harder and harder to achieve as you move up levels. More difficult obstacles are placed in your way: spikes, spiders, and more, as well as other objects that can either assist you or inhibit your performance: whoopee cushions that candy that can bounce off, bubbles that lift the candy upward, little guns that blow air on the candy and push it around the screen—sometimes toward Om's waiting mouth and sometimes off the screen to a temporary death.

What do you learn from such a game? Young learners must judge the physics' principles of gravity and motion. They learn this through trial and error making a hypothesis and try it out, but as the levels progress, critical thinking becomes important for optimal success. To collect all 3 stars on each level (after all who wants to be Passable when they can be Excellent?) before you start cutting the rope, you need to plan exactly where to cut and how to use the potential aides available to you. In other words, think before you act! A basic but often unused principle of learning and life. All the while you are playing dexterity is at a premium. You must be precise. Precision in cutting can be applied in many ways in life: cutting food, cutting diamonds (ok students most likely will not do that, but they can learn why precision there is important), cutting wood for building a model ship or bird house, or cutting cloth for designing clothes. All big skills students can take away from this little game.

## THREES! MOTIVATION FOR MATH

Another perfectly designed game that reminds me of the simple, but near intoxicating fun people have playing the paper game *Sudoku*. The game is played on a screen using a 4×4 grid. There are three colors: pink, white, and blue, and, of course, three numbers 1, 2, and 3. It is pattern matching at its best. The players swipe the screen and combine the numbers with the goal always being to create multiples of three or as directions say, "slide blocks to combine factors of three." The higher the numbers you can generate, the higher your score: 3, 6, 12, 24, 48, 96, and so on. Striving to earn high scores generates motivation, both intrinsic and extrinsic. It is not math as we think of math, but it's calculating and thinking of combinations. In our digital age, calculating often escapes many students—ask them to make change when the cash register at McDonald's goes down. You will see what I mean (Figure 12.1).

Any time an element of mathematical thinking can be made fun that is an accomplishment. For me, getting two hits in three times at bat in Little League for a .333 average made mathematical or statistical thinking fun and relevant. That is the collateral learning of *Threes!*

Finally, like with *Cut the Rope*, strategic thinking comes into play. Your tendency is to focus on the two numbers you are trying to combine, but

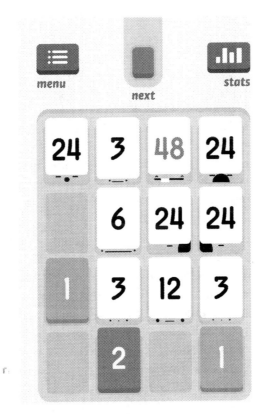

FIGURE 12.1  Thinking in triple. (Image courtesy of Asher Vollmer© Used with permission.)

each time you slide a number the entire grid of blocks moves too. To be a good player, you need to think about the big picture, not just the immediate move. That is a tremendous skill we need more of in school and life.

Let me pause to say a word or two about assessment. Assessment cannot continue to be the testing mania our educational system obsessively administers. Assessment can be fun and meaningful without tests. How long did a student play? That is engagement. Did the students continue when their scores dropped from one game to another? That is persistence. How many levels did the student reach or how many star did he or she collect? That is progress on the one hand, and motivation on the other hand. As mentioned above, you can collect one star and be passable, but still go forward to the next level or collect all three and be great as your move to the next level. My calculated guess is students are more likely to strive for great or excellent in *Threes!* than in ordinary math class and that excitement might transfer onto to high school and beyond.

## *DRAGON BOX ALGEBRA 5+:* STUDENT MATH WARRIORS

Unlike the other two games, *Dragon Box Algebra 5+* was specifically designed to promote learning the principles and procedures of algebra. It has the special virtue of being designed by a former math teacher, Jan-Baptise Huynh, from Vietnam, who formed the game company We Want to Know in his adopted home of Norway where the game was tested.

Playing the game could not be easier or more intuitive. Players try to isolate a box on one side of the screen. You have cards on both sides and the game requires you to balance the cards or equation. Cards have day and night versions, i.e., positive and negative values. The dragon box contains a dragon that develops as the game progresses and the player's skills evolve. Thus the dragon serves an organic purpose.

As the game moves forward the cute monsters transform into letters familiar to algebra—x, b, c, etc. In other words, you learn algebra through play, and you can learn quickly at noticeably young ages, hence the 5+. Dragon Box, owned by Kahoot, also has a more advanced version Algebra 12+ and other math games that can be purchased as Math Packs. The game has won several awards. It has a beautiful aesthetic, easy learning curve, and engaging game play. Students, as young as 3rd grade, appear to be solving algebraic equations rather quickly, but are they really learning algebra at this age? (Figures 12.2–12.4)

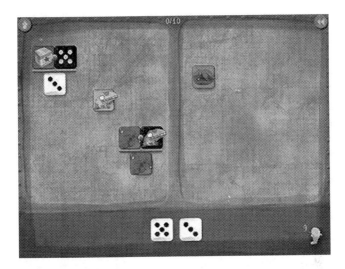

FIGURE 12.2   From dragons to algebraic equations 1. (Image provided by Kahoot DragonBox© Used with permission.)

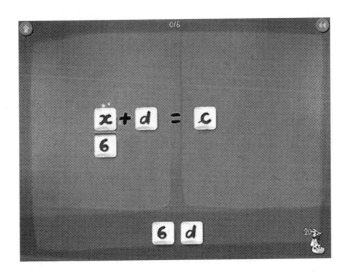

FIGURE 12.3   From dragons to algebraic equations 2. (Image provided by Kahoot DragonBox© Used with permission.)

The reviewer, Brad Fukumoto, for *Ed Surge* raises this learning-based question when pointing to the difference between mastery and fluency. Maybe a nuanced difference, but maybe a big one. Fukumoto also quotes a Carnegie Mellon University study which indicated that learning within

FIGURE 12.4    From dragons to algebraic equations 3. (Image provided by Kahoot DragonBox© Used with permission.)

the game did not transfer out of the game. That is a problem with much of American education. Yes, a student can master the procedures and content for a standardized exam and score high but have learned little as evidenced by performance in subsequent years in the same subject matter. I believe I can teach almost any student to pass the New York State Regents exam in English with little difficulty, but I also believe that many of these students will have inadequate knowledge of both literature and critical reading, as well as insufficient writing skills for success in college. Colleges are full of remedial courses for students who passed exams.

I echo the *Ed Surge* question and suggest we need more research on games in learning. More immediately, I stress that teachers need to be involved in instruction that uses an educational game. In general students will not learn many academic subjects on their own. Games can replace textbooks, but they cannot replace teachers.

## GAMES

*Cut the Rope.*

Designed and published by ZeptoLab UK Limited, 2010.

*Dragon Box Algebra.*

Designed by Jean Baptiste Huyuh with Patrick Marchal, We Want to Know (Norway). Published by DragonBox Kahoot, 2012.

*Threes!*

Developed and published by Siro. Designer: Asher Vollmer, Illustrator: Greg Wohlwend, Composer: Jimmy Hinson.

## LESSON IDEA

Rather than offer specific ideas for grade levels that I do not teach, I make a strong pitch for teachers to find concrete ways for applying the competencies developed in these three games to life problems and curiosities ranging from baseball statistics to the physics of skateboarding.

## RESOURCES

*Common Sense Media*

https://www.commonsensemedia.org/

A reasonably objective site for reviewing games, movies, and other media for students based upon age appropriateness, educational value, and fun. The site is extremely helpful for parents and teachers.

*DragonBox*

https://dragonbox.com/

The site for the *DragonBox Math* games has a helpful blog. There are also extremely useful and printable resources, worksheets, rules, alignment to Common Core Standards, Home School guides, and pedagogical guides for teachers. I also want to point out how the company has a chess game *Magnus Kingdom of Chess* that I highly recommend. Few games are more helpful for students to learn than chess. Even better the team designing the game has partnered with Norway's own Grandmaster Magnus Carlsen, the world chess champion (as of January 2021) and one of the best chess players in history.

*Learning Works for Kids*

https://learningworksforkids.com

A good resource for the use of video games and other digital media to help younger kids learn. The reviewers place a strong emphasis on alternative learners who may have diagnosed learning "disabilities." The organization has practice-oriented playbooks for the video games they recommend. They also offer a wide range of courses called Outschool that are game-based and address the whole child.

# CHAPTER 13

# Playing Small Business Owners

## *Teaching Management, Self-Efficacy, and Authentic Skills through Casual Games*

ANY OF US FONDLY remember our first experience running a business: The Lemonade Stand in front of our house. Small business operators, and tiny entrepreneurs, we were usually helped by our small business owning parents. School did not add much to these early ventures—in my day females took Home Economics, and boys, Shop, entirely stereotypical requirements. Rarely did one take a business course if they were on a so-called academic track. Already we see here numerous educational red flags: gender segregation as well as segregation between academic subjects and vocational subjects. Business does not fit clearly on either side. Even in college, a business major has some split schedule between the classroom academic world and the practical world served by internships and field placements.

Games and simulations can help bridge many of these unhealthy educational divisions, and do so beginning in the elementary grades and continuing into post-graduate professional programs like the infamous MBA. In a game, players can learn critical on-the-job skills in a safe and fun

DOI: 10.1201/9781003201465-17

environment. A child can run a virtual lemonade stand or even a real estate tower. Games can simulate business operations from sole proprietorships to large corporations. Students are more likely to become small business owners. When students are exposed to how these neighborhood businesses drive the day-to-day economy, they are more likely to pursue small business ownership as a career. I suggest that four small, casual games that can be played online in short bursts from elementary school through college and well into adulthood. I still play all four.

## *PAPA'S PIZZERIA TO GO:* MANAGING A NEIGHBORHOOD BUSINESS

Who does not love pizza? In a pandemic, pizza remains the go-to delivery option for food. Regardless of where students live there will most likely be a pizza parlor or pizzeria nearby. The mobile version of the wonderful Flipline Studios (2014) Papa Louie's small business simulation franchise has you playing Roy who must cover the pizzeria while Louie is away (business must be good for Louie). Running a pizzeria is no easy task. Why? Everyone wants pizza. It is all about time management and keeping the constant stream of customers happy. You go through a hectic week managing four stations: "The Order Station," "The Topping Station," "The Baking Station," and "The Cutting Station." Perfect for a smartphone or tablet, you drag toppings onto the pie with your finger, slide the pie into and out of the oven, and cut the pizza with two fingers. You get a satisfaction score and, hopefully, tips (Figure 13.1).

What makes the game a challenge, and fun, revolves around those crazy customers who might want any number of toppings: six banana peppers, and eight pepperonis, cut in six slices. It must be cooked just long enough and served hot on time. These customers are hungry! The more customers,

FIGURE 13.1 The cut station *Papa's Pizzeria to Go.* (Image courtesy of Flipline Studios© Used with permission.)

the more challenging the game. Thankfully for customers, I never worked in a pizzeria. My tips would not fill any child's piggy bank.

The game helps players build important time management skills and cultivate the customer service skills sorely missing from much of today's economy.

## *TINY TOWER:* TEACHING ENTREPRENEURSHIP

In *Tiny Tower* (NimbleBit, 2011), you move up from small business operator to running a more corporate-like business, the eponymous real estate tower. Much like towers in large cities such as New York or Chicago, the "tiny" tower has many floors serving many different purposes. Some floors are residential and some commercial. The commercial floors offer retail, creative, recreational, food, and service options. In the game, your goal is to turn a profit, but that profit depends on keeping workers happy.

Each worker has a skill set you need to hone, and a dream job you would like the bitizen (the characters you play in the game) to have. There are little pop-up quests to perform, but overall, you must collect coins or the in-game currency Bux, which makes play easier, and build floors. However, spending real money is not necessary. Gameplay primarily revolves around taking bitizens up the elevator to their desired floor, managing the workers and building your tower. You can easily play the game in short bursts of time and not lose out on quality in gameplay.

The game simplifies managing a multipurpose skyscraper, so the game can be played in elementary school. Nonetheless, the skills carry along to older students as well. One player impulse will be to build a tower higher and higher which necessarily complicates the game. That tendency can be, and should be, for the most part, resisted. Overbuilding and overdevelopment is a capitalist function that in the long run rarely serves any one well. Likewise, rampant consumerism has deleterious long-term consequences that the game allows to emerge and that will help spur classroom discussion about capitalism's benefits, but also its limitations (Figure 13.2).

For me, the game's value consists in the need to balance happiness or satisfaction with financial stability. Allow students to play the game over a few weeks and then bring their experience into whole class discussion about financial success and consumer or citizen satisfaction. How does building affect the larger community? Should one run up massive profits if tenants are not happy or if the less well off, the non-VIPs, in the game's language, cannot live in your tower? How do students define success? Apply game tasks to concrete thinking about their future. What kind

FIGURE 13.2 My *Tiny Tower*. (Image courtesy of Tiny Tower, NimbleBit LLC©️ Used with permission.)

of building would optimize the future environment they will be living and working in? Use the game as a launch pad for talking about development, community, success, and happiness. There are critical questions rarely thought about on more than a superficial level. The game can also be played alongside the game *Landlord Go* discussed next.

## *LANDLORD GO:* TEACHING REAL ESTATE DEVELOPMENT

From developing and managing a single skyscraper to controlling a portfolio of valuable buildings, *Landlord Go* (Reality Games, 2018) challenges players to build a real estate empire. Students can discover the world former President Donald J. Trump operated in as they buy property in their neighborhood or across the globe. As an augmented reality game (AR) *Landlord to Go* allows students to move about their home locale or the campus region where they attend school and assess property to buy. The game's sophisticated artificial intelligence and GPS feeds real-time data into the game making the player's experience genuinely authentic (*Pocket Gamer*, 2020). In fact, when someone enters a real property that you own in the game world you earn virtual rent! As the developer's advertise, *Landlord Go* is "Monopoly for the Real World." That is the virtue and the vice inherent to the game and its antecedents.

Students will learn about economics, real estate, and monopolies, but monopolies, capitalism, and American society are problematic neighbors, something like frenemies. Let me back up and say that the best way to approach this dynamic AR game begins with a discussion of the Parker Brother's classic board game *Monopoly* (1938). Most students will have played this game with family and friends, and if they have not, urge or even require this game as homework. *Monopoly* asks players to build a monopoly, but a monopoly violates the principles of free market capitalism, crushes competition, while ill serving the public. Yet, monopolies are a dominant force in the United States, now more than ever. Although not strictly speaking monopolies, much of the American economy is strangulated by a few massive corporations in many different industries. Corporations buy up smaller businesses, expand their reach, and stifle real competition. Look at Amazon, Facebook, Hilton or Marriott, Walmart, or Target. Small retail stores are knocked out of business, bookstores have virtually disappeared, and big box chain stores invade all cities, towns, and villages homogenizing once diverse and unique main streets. Students need to learn about the dominating power of huge corporations on the world economy, and *Landlord Go* provides a perfect springboard for critical lessons in American history and economics.

For a start, ask students who owns the local hotels. They will be surprised how many different hotels can be traced back to mega corporations like Hilton and Marriott. Such a concentration of power inevitably supports the wealthy, not the average citizen. After discussion of *Monopoly* move back and have students play the game *Monopoly* was modeled on *The Landlord Game* (self-published). This game designed by Elizabeth "Lizzie" Magie in 1903 presented a dual system of rules. One set stressed the drive toward monopoly and the other a desire for sharing wealth based on the single tax theory of Henry George. A crucial historical lesson on how a woman, an early feminist and design pioneer, has been buried by history and replaced by Charles Darrow who basically stole her game and repackaged it before selling the copyright to Parker Brothers also emerges from this game experience. A man displaces a woman, takes credit for her genius, and profits in money and fame. Even more striking for students will be the fashion in which a game designed to teach equality was co-opted and transformed into a game that teaches inequality. Since the Great Depression American society has grown increasingly unequal. The few grow richer and richer, some more rich than entire countries, most of us tread water, and too many drown. The deepest value of *Landlord to Go* are the historical and economic lessons it provides for discussion and debate.

## *PUNCH CLUB:* TEACHING SELF-EFFICACY AND SPORTS MANAGEMENT

A superb ongoing casual game, *Punch Club* (Lazy Bear Studios, 2016), provides players with an important third-person perspective. You play a kickboxer working his way up the ranks. The third-person point of view allows the player to manage the boxer, but also reflexively learn a good amount of self-management too. The player takes the boxer through legitimate tournaments and less legitimate ones. This is boxer is no Mike Tyson. He is a middle of the road fighter trying to improve. To improve, you need to manage the boxer's training. Training involves lots of exercise and a good diet, but a good diet necessitates money and a so so boxer cannot live by his feet or fists. He needs a job. Nothing comes easy. The game's reflexive nature revolves around the player realizing the immense amount of hard work and effort being a professional athletic requires. Many students dream of becoming Floyd Mayweather or Connor McGregor, but the fantasy that success comes easy needs a reality check, and this game gives students that valuable check.

As a player you cultivate the boxer's three skill areas: strength, agility, and stamina. Generally, only one or two skills can be maximized, and this teaches the need to focus on your strength while keeping some balance in your overall approach to the sport. Mohammed Ali had tremendous agility, George Foreman tremendous strength. Actual fights are controlled by the Artificial Intelligence (AI), but the loss of player control has the virtue of stressing the player's need to prepare for the fight and not just manipulate kicks and punches that characterize most fighting games. Most performance competitions are won during many hours of preparation not the few hours of actual gameplay.

It is an immersive game with a fun story arc. The boxer witnessed his father's (also a kick boxer) murder, and he must track down the killers. It is a replay of the Daredevil origin story—how trauma motivates self-development. Speaking of Daredevil and comics, the game offers a wonderful pastiche of 1980s and 1990s pop culture, including the title's take off on *Fight Club* (Fincher, 1999—film, Palahniuk, 1996—novel). For adults, the nostalgia aspect is fun, and for students, tracking references can be a twist on *Trivial Pursuit*. Asking students to track down references produces a lesson in cultural history.

The game also offers a way to talk with students about sports management, a career area of interest today. The biggest virtue of the game, however, is precisely what many game reviewers dislike about the game such as this review in IGN,

> *Punch Club* became a constant, demoralizing struggle that shattered my enthusiasm. I grew intensely bored, frustrated, and eventually bitter. Enduring the grind gradually got me out of my hole, but after 20 hours -- the vast majority of which spent not fighting -- with plenty more ahead, I'd have sooner started over and played differently from the beginning than finished my first playthrough. I decided to stop playing altogether.
>
> *(Dyer, 2018)*

If you conceive of games as pure fantasy, full of nonstop action, such a complaint makes some sense, but if a game yields any genuine lessons, and this game does, then that lesson is the daily grind. The few exciting hours of a sporting event demand countless hours of preparation. Life is a fight. It is hard work. Escape and fantasy is easy. For pure entertainment, the game might lack some, though not much, but as educational value, the game unexpectedly delivers a real punch!

## LESSON IDEAS FOR AUTHENTIC FIELD-BASED LEARNING

### Papa's Pizzeria to Go

Have students spend half a shift volunteering at a local pizzeria. They can keep a journal observing the minute-by-minute activities. How many pizzas are served? How many are made at one time? What kind of pizzas are ordered and how are they cut? What kind of response do customers offer to workers? How long does a pizza remain in the oven? How long does it take to prepare one? What is the profit on a single pizza? How many pizzas are picked up and how many are delivered? What are the tips like? What happens if someone calls in sick? After a few hours on the job have students write about which skills they have observed that they think would be valuable if they were to open their own small business someday. Although field observations are critical in education schools, I think that they should be stressed and integrated more often into mainstream curricula of both high schools and many college programs.

### Tiny Tower

Just as practicum skills are insufficiently part of high school and college, so too are primary research methods, at least outside the natural sciences. Secondary research from books can be supplanted by teaching primary research methods like interviewing. Have students interview a local real estate developer or property manager. What decisions are made in terms of a building's height and square footage? Why are some retail outlets on some floors and not others? How are decisions made about types of stores or space to rent out? How does rent change based on floor number? What kind of amenities do tenants want? How do you balance worker satisfaction, customer satisfaction, and profit? Next, have students compare their findings with how they operated their Tiny Tower? Which businesses did they operate? Which floor did they place which business on? How often did they move employees around? What was their profit and how many employees were happy?

Finally, ask students to design their own tower using either paper and pencil or an appropriate computer program. How many floors will they build? What rent will they charge? Which businesses will they include and how will space be allocated? What about the aesthetics: color, decorations, carpets, paintings? This exercise presents design thinking at its best. Do not forget to have students think through the relationship of their building to the community. How does the building fit in with the community? Does the building displace some businesses? Do the tenants represent a different economic class than long-term residents? Will the tower's employees be local, or will they be brought in? These discussions and inquiries offer invaluable learning opportunities.

*Landlord Go*

Conduct a contest with students to see who builds the biggest real estate empire. Use this activity as a prelude to a lesson on the history of monopolies in the United States including antitrust laws and President Theodore Roosevelt's policies. Next ask students to identify current examples of government monopoly busting. Discuss why certain companies have not been identified as monopolies. Finally, ask students to conduct some field research in their home communities or a community near campus. Ask them to identify each of the major businesses, who owns them, and where they are located. Students should go back through historical maps, archives, and local historical societies and identify the stores and businesses in the same community 25 and 50 years ago. They can write a historical account of the changes over this time, say from their grandparents' time to their parents' time to today. A last step might be for them to sketch out a community plan for 25 years in the future. What business will be present, who will own them, where will they be located, and what will life be like in their community's future?

*Punch Club*

Ask students to translate what they have learned managing their kickboxer to a field they would like to enter someday, especially a field or hobby where they have autonomy. If they want to be an athlete, a cook, a musician, etc., what must they do to maximize their chances of success? Have students sketch out a monthly schedule with goals, benchmarks for success, daily schedules for working out, practice, studying, and nutrition. How does what you eat effect your stamina and so on? Even if the goal is to be a superior student this exercise has rich lessons to offer.

## RESOURCE

Book

Pilon, Mary. *The Monopolists' Obsession, Fury and the Scandal Behind the World's Favorite Board Game.* Bloomsbury, 2015.

# CHAPTER 14

# Teaching Teamwork with a Public Health Game

G ROUP OR TEAMWORK OFTEN presents a paradox to college and university faculty. Teachers in primary and secondary education have training in group teaching as part of their pre-service education programs necessary for licensure. College faculty rarely have any formal training in teaching groups, but group and teamwork cannot be avoided in the post-graduate world. Regardless of your profession or job, you inevitably must work as part of a team. Sometimes you will have a choice regarding your team members, but often you will not. Consequently, conflict is not uncommon. Even a physician works as part of a critical team during surgery. The reality of life outside school demands that we teach and learn teamwork in school.

Students will arrive in college having done plenty of group work in high school, but surprisingly, often resist such work in a college class. Student resistance combined with faculty unfamiliar with cooperative learning pedagogy makes this vital component of education difficult. Moreover, the lack of standard assessments for teamwork can undermine the entire effort. You cannot ask students to work in a group and then assign tests to individuals. Let's add the newest factor to this quagmire of learning: remote classes. COVID-19 pushed many classes, at least temporarily, online, and teamwork needed to take place among geographically distant students. However, as more businesses move to remote work situations, the need for new employees to be skilled in remote teamwork will be high in a post-pandemic environment.

Game-based learning can facilitate deep group learning in an engaging fashion, both in the traditional classroom and online. For instance, the board game *Pandemic* provides a great opportunity for students to engage in cooperative learning. You cannot win the game, i.e., beat the pandemic, without working together. *Pokemon Go*'s "Raid Battles" require teamwork and *World of Warcraft* has a guild structure where cooperation plays a vital role. The rise of Esports across college campuses and now high schools also stress the importance of team play in games like *League of Legends*, *Overwatch*, *Valorant*, and many others. As with traditional athletic teams, Esports teams require players to take different roles and work as a unit to be successful. Games can be an effective means of teaching the importance of teamwork and prepare for group learning activities in virtually all disciplines.

## *OUTBREAK SQUAD:* FIGHTING EPIDEMICS, A BATTLE FOR PUBLIC HEALTH

Created with a Secondary and Two-Year Postsecondary Agriculture Education Challenge (SPECA) Challenge Grant, National Institute of Food and Agriculture, U.S. Department of Agriculture, a New Mexico State University team designed *Outbreak Squad* to educate students, and parents about food pathogens and serious outbreaks caused by contamination. What could be more relevant during a pandemic than learning to prevent, cope with, and mitigate contagious diseases? You can choose to battle one of several contagious disease outbreaks. Each one is based on an actual historical outbreak. Thus, the game has an authentic basis for any history or social studies class in addition to any class in health, public health, sociology, public policy, and the like. Below is an example from the New Mexico State University webpage on one of the game's outbreaks.

> ***Hammy Burgens***
> **Food Type:**
> Hamburger
> **Pathogen:**
> Shigatoxigenic *E. coli* O157:H7
> **Location:**
> A restaurant chain across four states

**Impact**:

**732** people affected

**178** permanently damaged

**4** deaths

**The real case**

In 1993, a popular fast-food restaurant ran a promotion and discounted their hamburger sales across four states. Unfortunately, the restaurant received meat contaminated with a novel strain of bacteria known as shigatoxigenic *E. coli.* from their suppliers. The restaurant cooked the beef according to federal standards of the time, bringing the internal temperature to 140°F (60°C). However, this temperature was not high enough to kill the bacteria. The guideline has since been raised to 160°F (71.1°C).

**How to prevent or mitigate**

Recalling contaminated products; ensuring that the food is cooked to above 165°F before freezing; following reheating guidelines.

In the game, you play four squad members: The Educator, The Enforcer, The Healthcare Professional, and The Researcher. The game provides information about each role as well as describes career opportunities related to the roles. It is a diverse squad (two women, two men, an African American, and a disabled individual). Each squad member has a set of skills used to combat the outbreak. For example, the Educator can employ Community Outreach, Food Safety Classes, Risk Training, and Food Safety Guidelines. Each skill proves essential to the game and all four members' skills must coalesce, in other words, the team is interdependent, and the squad's success depends upon such interdependence. Students must learn the value of working as part of an interdependent team and the value of communication and balance within a team. In game play each skill has both a cost and a benefit. Food Safety Classes protect the next three high-risk people from infection but costs 2 points.

You begin the level with 10 points. Each moment of the game, each decision provides teachable moments. The player selects which team members and skills to employ within the ten-point limit and then hits Go to fight the attack. Results of the episode are recorded on a disease dashboard at the top of the screen which tallies infected, sick, very sick, and dead in addition to whether the people are low or high risk. The risk category must be thought about when deciding what approach to take each round. You want to use all ten points available, i.e., your resources, but making sure those resources target the disease's spread with precision. This decision making requires careful monitoring of the dynamic dashboard. In other words, the player must show situational awareness of all factors impacting the spread of the disease, manage resources, and implement a balanced team approach. This game introduces students as early as grade five to the value of teamwork and, for older grades and college, can help implement group learning in an authentic public health context transferable to other multidisciplinary problems.

In conclusion, *Project Outbreak* presents a solid game for teaching how teams work in addressing complex, multidimensional problems that demand multiple disciplines and different layers of communication and coordination. Following a day of game play, I would introduce a group activity that addresses a related complex problem in public health, public policy, or a related field and observe how well the teams applied what they learned playing *Outbreak Squad*.

## LESSON IDEAS

1. Use a projector and play through the different rounds of the game with students broken into small groups that reflect the game's four roles. Each team must work together to make decisions about interventions and talk through each decision. The teacher then starts the round, and everyone watches the results before passing on to the next team which needs to reassess the situation based on the results of the previous team's intervention.

2. In a health science, environmental science, consumer science, or public health/public policy class set up a related problem from recent history, maybe the Ebola crisis from the Obama years, the opioid crisis, the HIV crisis, or other problems that have a regional, national, or international scope. The class can determine what kind of professionals are required for addressing the presented problem and then role-play scenarios written by the instructor or an instructional designer in consultation with the subject matter expert. These should be played as small groups with the instructor as outside observer assessing groups using one of the tools provided under Resources.

## GAME

*Outbreak Squad*. Designed and published by New Mexico State University Game Lab, 2019, with funding from the SPECA Challenge Grant, National Institute of Food and Agriculture, U.S. Department of Agriculture.

## RESOURCES

*The Center for Disease Control*

https://www.cdc.gov/outbreaks/index.html

Every science and health professor and teacher should be familiar with the CDC website for its wealth of information, data sources, recommendations, analyses of trends, and official publications. The site has a specific page that gathers information pertaining to both national and international outbreaks of all kinds.

*Eberly Center for Teaching Excellence & Educational Innovation at Carnegie Mellon University*

https://www.cmu.edu/teaching/designteach/design/instructionalstrategies/groupprojects/assess.html

This resource from Carnegie Mellon University has excellent material on how to assess different components of group learning including individuals within a group, the entire group, the group process, and the group product. The site provides many concrete examples of assessment tools that instructors can use in assessing group work.

*New Mexico State University Innovative Media and Extension*

https://innovativemedia.nmsu.edu/

The Learning Games Lab is part of this larger center at the university. The design teams at the development studio include a "user-testing research space, and an exploratory environment for playing and evaluating games and educational tools." Being part of the College of Agriculture, Consumer and Environmental Science, the lab focuses on agriculture. They have many excellent animations, games, apps, and interactive tools.

# CHAPTER 15

# There Is an Imposter *Among Us*

## Teaching Truth in the Time of "The Big Lie"

Many people passed the time during COVID-19 lockdowns and restrictions by playing casual games with a social dimension. *Animal Crossing: New Horizons* certainly represents one such popular game, but no game achieved more rapid success than *Among Us* (Innersloth, 2018). Between mid-2020 and early 2021 virtually every one of my students played the game and many referred to the game as their favorite. A game this popular presents an opportunity for teachers to tap into student-driven interests in a big way, and a way that touches a critical problem in political life: identifying the truth.

*Among Us* is a perfect casual (social deduction) game. It is easy to learn, fast paced, strategic, social, and free. A game can be played in 15 minutes, either online with strangers and/or friends or with friends or classmates over a local network. The game requires between four and ten players and customization allows for many variations on the game's constraints. One person runs the game and players drop into the game as either crew members or imposters on a spaceship. Crew members go about a variety of tasks, some easy, some less easy, necessary to keep the ship moving while

DOI: 10.1201/9781003201465-19

imposters try to sabotage the crew members in all manner of nefarious ways. The imposter seeks to kill crew members one by one, and the crew must ferret out the imposters, i.e., expose the truth before the entire crew is dead. Crew members cannot speak until a body is found, at which time, they hold a meeting and vote. If the vote is unanimous regarding the suspected imposter the suspect is tossed off the ship into oblivion. Team play takes place through the chat feature. The need to vote and reach consensus along with the possibility that the wrong person is "discarded" makes for exciting drama. Emergency meetings can be called at any time. Time duration is set by the game master. Once a player dies, the player becomes a ghost and can aid crew members' work efforts.

For an instructor, there is inherent value in team play and the use of meetings as a vehicle for working with students on team decision making. There is also a deeper potential to explore the nature of truth and fabrication, a distinction so hard to discern in this new century.

Let me suggest some Shakespearean analogues since literature is my field. Is Shakespeare's Iago the ultimate imposter? How does one insinuate oneself among the good to wreak havoc on their cohesiveness? How does one detect the imposter or improviser before it is too late, and you have strangled your innocent wife? World affairs? Is Edward Snowden an imposter or just a traitor? Is Julius Caesar's friend Brutus a friend or an imposter who has masqueraded as a friend? The same with Judas as one of Jesus's disciples. Betrayals speak to insincerity at the deepest level. The trusted confidante is an imposter. How does one tell if one is telling the truth? Is the ghost of Hamlet's father telling the truth? Justice depends on Hamlet's skillful discernment of the truth.

Shakespeare will always be our contemporary, but much as we faculty members would love all students to read the entire corpus of Shakespeare, they are more likely to have played *Among Us*. Consequently, this contemporary game can be a springboard to discuss the nature of impostures, of liars and lying, not just pretty little liars, but big, important liars telling big socially significant lies. We have had a former president of the United States flat out lie to the American public by claiming the 2020 election was stolen from him. Despite absolutely no evidence to support the claim, and a plethora of court cases determining that there was no significant voter fraud and dismissing the president's claims one after the other, still, the now former president persists in what the media has labeled "The Big Lie."

Equally incomprehensible, the attempted insurrection that took place on January 6th at the nation's capital has been whitewashed and denied by many republican members of Congress. These elected national leaders can stand on what an American would be considered hallowed ground and say with a straight face that there was no insurrection all the while news, cameras recorded the invasion of the Capitol live with members of Congress, who now deny the breach, in hiding as marauders ransack the building. Facts clear to the senses are denied.

Even New York, a very blue state cannot claim innocence when it comes to truth-telling. Although former Governor Cuomo displayed genuine leadership in managing the COVID-19 crisis, he also did not tell the truth about the number of COVID-related deaths in the state's nursing homes. That is a big lie. Indeed, how can anyone trust anyone in public leadership when clear and evident facts are simply denied and ignored? If you place your trust in a leader who might turn out to be different than you anticipated, an imposter let us say, you have a genuine national crisis. At this juncture another popular fast-paced game, this time, a board game, can be instructive.

## THE DANGERS OF A SINGLE TRUTH

Like *Among Us*, *Secret Hitler* (2016) is a social deduction game, meaning the goal is ferreting out imposters or calling a player's bluff in poker terminology. Again, like *Among Us*, ten players are ideal. As the game begins you are anonymously assigned to one of two political teams or parties: Liberals or Fascists. The setting is 1930s Germany. The fascists can reveal themselves to each other. One person is Hitler. There is a president with term limits. The new president assumes power rotating clockwise. There is also a chancellor nominated by the president but voted on, ja or nein, by other players. Granted some Jewish groups have legitimately attacked the idea of a game where someone plays Hitler, but the game really focuses entirely on his assent to power not his use of that power to commit the atrocities he ended up committing.[1] Hitler's card shows a reptile in a Nazi uniform.

The person with the Hitler card keeps his eyes closed when fascists reveal themselves, but raises a thumb, so the fascists do know who holds the ultimate card. Liberals are in the dark. Without going into more detail, suffice it to say the game requires a great deal of misinformation, or lying. Fascists, like the imposter from *Among Us*, want to sow chaos. They are entirely Machiavellian. The president receives three policy cards to start round one. The person discards one card and passes the two remaining cards, face down to the chancellor. The chancellor discards one of the two cards and plays the remaining card. Say she passes a fascist policy that gets placed on the board. Now, the fun starts. The advantage of a board game becomes evident. When everyone is close together the conversation becomes heated, frantic, and fun. After all, on one level *Secret Hitler* is a party game.

The conversation vacillates between accusation and self-defense. It is here that lying becomes prominent. Is Jerrod lying? Is Stormy a fascist or a liberal pretending to be fascist? Why did Chancellor Eric enact a fascist policy? You win the game as fascists by naming Hitler chancellor. You accomplish this objective by passing six fascist policies. Liberals, on the other hand, must prevent Hitler from becoming chancellor by passing liberal policies or assassinating him. There are six liberal cards and eleven fascist cards. A Hitler mode, where the possibility of his coming to power becomes imminent extends the game's climax and tension to maximum degree (Boxleiter, 2017). Once the game concludes the instructor can lead a powerful debriefing that can easily transition into the current political situation.

## GAMES AND REALITY, REALITY, AND THE TRUTH

*Among Us* provides a great opportunity to talk about betrayal, the nature of lying and the purpose it serves. *Secret Hitler* ups the ante by hiding not just an imposter, but a potential threat to democracy itself. The design team sent copies of the game to members of Congress, and they also released a Trump expansion pact, so the studio clearly sees the game as commentary on contemporary American politics. In no way does the game establishe an equivalence between 1930s Germany and 2010s America, but the game does suggest parallels between the two eras and points to the very real danger of an authoritarian or quasi-fascist party emerging to challenge American Democracy and the Balance of Powers. Games prompt vital class discussions.

The professor or teaching assistant leading a class debriefing (*Secret Hitler* would only be appropriate to a 12th grade high school class because of its 17+ rating) should remind students that Germany went from a democracy to a dictatorship in only 6 months! Advanced, modern democracies are not at all immune to authoritarian threats. Our democracy requires the two major parties representing alternative perspectives and policies that each party believes serves a free citizenry. If one party no longer represents a perspective on governance, but rather seeks to serve an authoritarian leader who rules or attempts to rule by fiat then democracy as we know it comes under threat. It is not that we would have a one party system like Nazi Germany or Franco's Spain, nonetheless, only one of our two parties would be dedicated to the democratic process.

Donald J. Trump's presidency clearly established an authoritarian style of governance that broke protocols and precedent established by the Office of the President (See Chapter 8 "Trump Against the Guardrails" pp. 176–203 of Levitsky and Ziblatt's *How Democracies Die* (2018) for a full discussion of President Trump's political style). The media was treated as the enemy; if they questioned his policies they were castigated. At the same time, President Trump used social media, especially Twitter and Fox News, to disseminate misinformation or propaganda, a trademark of authoritarian rule. All dissent within the party was squashed. Dissenters, like Mitt Romney, were belittled and isolated. Cabinet members or other high level officials who disagreed with the president were promptly fired rather than listened to. The president hired members of his own family to high level government posts. All these strategies are a form of consolidating power. The slogan "Make America Great Again" echoes fascist slogans from the past, and the narrow definition of who can be considered a true American with its concomitant scapegoating of minorities and fear of a growing nonwhite population all speak to authoritarianism. They are examples of hyper nationalism.

Although President Trump lost the 2020 election he claimed the election was stolen from him. "Stop the Steal" perpetuated "The Big Lie" and has persuaded many in his party to largely accept the lie as truth. States supporting the former president have passed restrictive voting laws and attempted to whitewash and deny the January 6th, 2021 insurrection, another "Big Lie." Consequently, games about imposters, lying, and betrayal can help engage students in the play of truth and lead into discussion of the nature of democracy: its institutions, policies, and dynamics and how none of these can be taken for granted.

## NOTE

1. One of the game's producers, who is Jewish, responds to the question about a game about Hitler in an interview with the *Pittsburgh Jewish Chronicle*.

    "JC: Are you Jewish? If so, did that play any factor in you creating a game about Hitler? Do you have any family members who are Holocaust survivors?

MT: I am Jewish, and I do have family that were survivors. Like most Jews of my generation, I grew up steeped in Jewish history and Holocaust education. I was taught to always be suspicious of authoritarians, to always look out for marginalized groups, and to ask myself Rabbi Hillel's questions: "If not me, who? And if not now, when?"

The rise of authoritarian fascism in America terrifies me, and I don't think it's a coincidence that we see a figure like Donald Trump taking power as the generation that experienced World War II and the Holocaust are passing from living memory. *Secret Hitler* isn't the answer to Trump, but I do think that this is a time when art needs to be fearless about remembering and teaching history."

Tabachanuck, Toby. "Secret Hitler, a game of intrigue and deception, but not for everyone," *Pittsburgh Jewish Chronicle*. December 28, 2016, https://jewishchronicle.timesofisrael.com/secret-hitler-a-game-of-intrigue-and-deception-but-not-for-everyone/.

## LESSON IDEA

*To Tell the Truth:* Identifying the Imposter

One of the most popular television game shows has been *To Tell the Truth*. The show premiered on CBS way back in 1956 with Bud Collyer as host. The show's most recent incarnation on ABC is hosted by comedian Anthony Anderson. The game's premise is simple. You have four celebrity panelists asking questions about three contestants. The host reads a short bio of the mystery guest which is all the information the panel must go by. The objective is to identify which of the three contests is telling the truth about their profession (usually an unusual occupation). The mechanic or rule of this game can be easily adapted to the classroom. Depending on your discipline present a short bio of an important person from your field. This could be an important but lesser-known figure or a figure all students should be aware of. Students then have the challenge of discerning the truth and the three contestant students must learn about the figure they are presenting to fabricate the guest's story in a believable fashion. The game is fast paced; one class period could involve the entire class, and all grade levels are appropriate for such a fun game that teaches a skill in such short supply these days. This game would allow for diversity and uncovering historical people often overlooked by textbooks.

## GAMES

*Among Us*

> Developer and publisher: Innersloth, 2016. Multiplayer (6–10 online or over a local wireless network).

*Secret Hitler*

> Developer and publisher: Goat, Wolf, & Cabbage, LLC. 2016. Board Game for 5–10 players, 10 players are ideal.

*To Tell the Truth*

> Bob Stewart, creator; CBS, NBC, ABC (current), 1956. Television Game Show.

*The Resistance*

> Don Eskridge, creator. 2010. An excellent social deduction board game and the model for *Secret Hitler*. Card Game for 5–10 players. The theme of resistance provides an excellent topic for class discussion on resistance to tyrannical forms of government, especially those of Nazi Germany in Eastern Europe and France.

*Werewolf*

> Dimitry Davidoff, Creator. 1986. This social deduction card game has many variations including *Mafia* and a new variant *Ultimate Werewolf*, Ted Alspach designer, published by Bezier Games, 2008. This version could involve the entire class in a game. Villagers hunt werewolves who feign their innocence with the goal of killing the villagers. A *One Night Ultimate Werewolf* is a faster-paced version of the game. This is the version I play in class. In addition to the intricacies of truth and lying, the game's production of paranoia and mistrust has clear application to contemporary politics and international relationships. The original creator was based in Russia at Moscow State University so there is the paranoia that comes with living in

a totalitarian regime, the nature of international spying, and U.S. paranoia over the origin of COVID-19, the Q-Anon paranoia, the historical paranoia of President Nixon's tenure, and the McCarthy witch-hunts of the 1950s. Finally, the werewolf theme added to the original game from 1986 gives a metaphoric reach to the game: the wolf in sheep's clothing archetype. Who is your real enemy? The enemy within? The entire psychology of the doppelganger plays a major role in the social deduction genre.

# CHAPTER 16

# Teaching Tragedy in Real Time

## *The Syrian Refugee Crisis*

Aمericans know precious little about Syria. Maybe we have intermittently seen some pictures on the national news, but our collective understanding of the country and its national crisis remains as distant as the country's geographic distance from our mainland. If the Syrian refugees are not crossing our border, and few are, then we can, as a country too easily push the tragic plight of these refugees (over 11 million since 2011) into the background of our thoughts.

*Bury me, my Love* seeks to bring awareness of the Syrian refugee crisis to a more global audience, in the first instance Europe, but America as well. This story finds the perfect vehicle in mobile phones to tell a story about people always on the run. As a texting adventure, as opposed to text adventure, the texting feature of cell phones performs the refugee experience.

The story unfolds as a conversation between a Syrian refugee named Nour as she leaves her bombed-out home in Homs and her husband Majd for the safety of Europe. A cell phone works so well because the flow of a text conversation encounters numerous interruptions that a personal conversation does not. The story mimics real-time conversation and the player experiences the time of texting and, consequently, the passage of

DOI: 10.1201/9781003201465-20

**241**

days. Different players will experience different time lags. My journey lasted from March 4 to March 19, or just over 2 weeks. The actual game play might be two hours, but the need to wait for responses turns those two hours into two weeks increasing dramatic tension and suspense. Sometimes Nour must stop conversation to spare her phone's battery, sometimes out of exhaustion, and other times because of a dangerous situation she encounters on her trip across Turkey to Greece and farther. These moments of forced stoppage create a genuinely visceral response in the player/reader. I dislike texting, but I found myself wanting to know if Nour was safe and checked my phone more often than usual to see if Nour was Online, and therefore whether I could resume the conversation in the role of her husband. A novel may end a chapter with suspense, but you flip the page for the next chapter. In this mobile game you cannot move the screen forward until the protagonist is online. Waiting is an integral part of one of the game's mechanics.

The writers, Pierre Corbinair and, to a lesser degree, Florent Maurin, tell the story effectively by representing an authentic conversation between husband and wife.[1] Often the conversation includes teasing and humor that give the couple a strong degree of authenticity. As the player you must chose, at select moments, Majd's response to a situation. Your response has an immediate impact on the story's progress and eventual outcome. In fact, there are 19 possible endings to this story and that variety makes for great re-playability.

The artwork is sparse, but vital to the story. Occasional images inter-rupt the conversation to give a concrete sense of the characters' reality. For instance, a picture of Nour showing off her painted nails gives the reader dramatic relief and makes him or her smile at Nour's silly, but real plea-sure amidst the danger of her journey. Maps provide another important visual anchor to the story. One day Nour reports she has found a map on the internet to help her navigation, but Majd texts the authentic map showing the minefields and imminent danger she faces.

The fiction is modeled to a degree on a nonfiction report by Lucie Souiller that appeared in *Le Monde*, "Le voyage, d'une migrante Syrienne a travers a fils Whats App," about a young Syrian girl named Dana's perilous migration to Germany using a conversation app but now expanded to make Nour's journey more generic for a larger poten-tial audience. The authors juxtapose the humor and affection the mar-ried couple display for each other with the genuine ordeal Nour must overcome to reach safety. In my initial game play, she had to take a boat designed to transport 9 but that ended up carrying 40, resulting in several drownings, a frequent consequence of the Syrian Civil War. She had to deal with thieves, the ever-present danger of potential rapists, extreme hunger, extreme fatigue, and the uncertain intention of armed smugglers (Figure 16.1).

As a player, the fear you feel for Nour while playing her anxious husband is palpable.

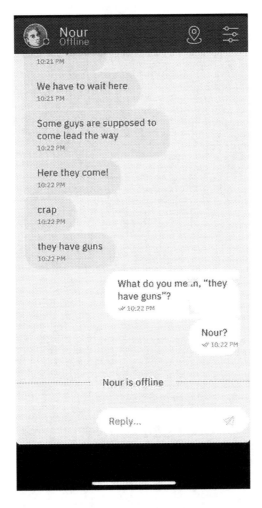

FIGURE 16.1 Nour's text conversation during her perilous journey. (Florent Maurin. Used with permission of The Pixel Hunt ©.)

My path took me from Homs, Syria, by rickety boat to Turkey, across Turkey to the Greek island of Lesbos, and then on to the Greek mainland through Serbia to eventual safety in Croatia (Figure 16.2).

That ending seemed happy, but the story, any player will or should realize, is far from over. What will happen to Nour now? Integration of refugees into other countries is fraught with problems of discrimination, unemployment, poor housing, language barriers, and much more.[2] Furthermore, will Nour ever see her husband again? The game is a kind of middle passage that opens the door to larger questions of migration,

FIGURE 16.2 Map of my journey in the game *Bury me, my Love*. (Florent Maurin. Used with permission of The Pixel Hunt ©.)

dislocation, assimilation, humanitarianism, global responsibility, or, in other words, the REFUGEE CRISIS writ large in capital letters.

## NOTES

1. The lead writer Pierre Corbinais has an excellent blog post about writing this game on *Gamasutra*, "*'Bury me, my Love'*: tips for writing a game that feels real," 2/05/2018.
2. The U. S. government's acceptance of Syrian refugees has been poor. Part of our collective failure has to do with threats, fears, and misconceptions about Muslim countries, in addition to the extra vetting demanded by our post-9/11 climate. For reference see, "The U.S. Has Accepted Only 11 Syrian Refugees This Year," Deborah Amos, NPR/parallels, April 12, 2018, and a brilliant, in-depth feature, "Why Is It So Difficult for Syrian Refuges to Get Into the U.S.," by Eliza Griswold, *The New York Times Magazine*, January 20, 2016.
3. There are many sources for images and stories about Homs, but one possibility is this article in *The Atlantic*, "Syria's City of Homs, Shattered by the War," Alan Taylor, May 14, 2014.

## LESSON IDEAS

1. "Learning between Classes: A Mobile Game as a Journey"

   Teachers and professors are increasingly faced with the dilemma of students' cell phones in the classroom. The phones are virtually sutured to the students' bodies today and they usually present a distraction to student learning and annoyance for the instructor. Nonetheless, they are powerful computers and educators need to find innovative ways to have students use these devices productively. A mobile game like "Bury me, my Love" provides a perfect solution. Students can play the game as they move between classes during a public school day or between days in a college setting. I find the game most useful in a high school and maybe middle school where students spend a long block of time in a school environment every day. Settings can turn off notifications, but I think allowing students to respond as they see fit also has educational value. In this fashion, learning as an ongoing journey can occur as students navigate their day punctuated by Nour's navigation of a much more perilous life-threatening journey. Conversations will spontaneously occur in hallways, the lunchroom, or on the bus, in addition to the classroom, and that can be any classroom, but especially English, and Global

Studies or political science classes. As students experience Nour's day-to-day events on an hour-by-hour basis, they cannot help but develop a more empathetic feeling toward refugees sparking further investigation of the Syrian Civil War.

The game should be presented in a historical context with some up-front learning about the genesis of the civil war. Instructors can use whatever credible sources they feel are most helpful to the class, but I have two strong recommendations. The UNICEF site can be a wealth of learning resources. You can find statistics, firsthand stories, and a humanitarian context for the crisis. UNICEF also drives home the effect of the tragedy on children (#ChildrenofSyria) and that can have a big impact on your students. You can mix in some of the heart-wrenching video clips from CNN or the BBC with newspaper clippings (i.e., links to current stories on the crisis, and topics like: what happens if a border, says Jordan, is closed? How do host countries react to refugees? How does one adjust to a new culture? How does one survive the journey? What happens to the family members left behind? What can be done about the use of chemical weapons? What ethical choices are involved as one leaves home? What is the responsibility of privileged regions like the United States or Europe toward such humanitarian crises?).

2. "The Beauty and the Beast"

Spend a class talking about Homs, Syria.[3] It is the third largest city in the country and the home of the character Nour. The city has a rich heritage stretching back some 8,000 years, and like with Iraq, Americans and American students are largely unaware of this city's extraordinary heritage and how much of what we know as western civilization springs from the cultural fountains of the Middle East. This lesson needs to occur before game play and should include photographs of Homs before and after the start of the civil war. This glorious city has been laid to waste and seeing these dramatic images will give a deep, meaningful, and empathetic context to why Nour must leave Syria, and the sadness she must feel upon her departure.

3. "Searching for Safety"

Help students define and differentiate the often misunderstood designations of refugee, immigrant, migrant, and asylum seekers. How are they different? Is the difference important? Should they be treated differently by potentially host nations? Watch the wonderful 1980s film *El Norte* which tells the moving story of a Guatemalan (native Mayan) brother and sister escaping the terror, discrimination, oppression, and outright murder of their people for the anticipated safety of California. Use the film as content for discussing the journey between countries with oppressed conditions and those with freedom putting an emphasis on governments' responsibility.

## GAME

*Bury me, my Love.* The Pixel Hunt and Figs in cooperation with co-producer ARTE France and published by Playdius Entertainment, 2015.

## RESOURCES

Organizations/Websites/Curriculum Resources

*International Rescue Committee (IRC)*—https://www.rescue.org

> This agency helps people affected by humanitarian crises to survive, recover, and rebuild their lives. In winter 2021, as I write this chapter, nearly half the families in Afghanistan have inadequate food and water. Imagine that!

*Teach Mideast*—https://teachmideast.org/resource_guides/syria-civil-war-and-refugee/

> An educational initiative of the Middle East Policy Council, this site has fantastic resources for studying the Middle East including teaching guides, primary sources, links to documentary films, webinars, lesson plans, and much more. The information on Syria at the above link is exceptional.

*United Nations International Children's Emergency Fund (UNICEF)*—https://www.unicef.org

> Dedicated to helping children around the world. The agency focuses on humanitarian crises such as war, pandemics, child labor, sex trafficking children, homelessness, poverty, natural disasters, and other crises. The annual publication "State of the World's Children" should be a must-read for all agencies and politicians.

*United Nations High Commission for Refugees (UNHCR)*—https://www.unhcr.org

> The UN Refugee Agency based in Geneva, Switzerland, has the mandate to help refugees, forcibly displaced communities, and stateless people.

Primary Texts

*El Norte.* Film. Director: Gregory Nava, 1984.

> A powerful film that follows siblings Enrique and Rosa, children of Mayan descent, who escape a massacre inflicted on their village by the Guatemalan Army in retaliation for the Indians attempting to organize a labor union, and make the journey north through Mexico. Asking students to watch this film will provide a much deeper and personal perspective and context on the immigration issue at the Californian-Mexican border than they will obtain via news or textbooks.

# CHAPTER 17

# Games for College Orientation

## *Social Emotional Learning*

A NXIETY, LIKE DEPRESSION, REPRESENTS a common emotional problem that afflicts people of all ages, genders, races, and ethnicities. It often goes untreated. Also, as with depression, there is an immense difference between everyday anxiety that virtually everyone faces from time to time and the crippling anxiety that afflicts someone with an anxiety disorder. For instance, an introverted or shy person might fear going to a party, attending a social event, or giving a public speech. That is normal anticipatory anxiety. What if I do not know anyone at the party? What if I freeze? What if I forget the words of my speech? What if no one speaks to me and so on are quite typical fear-based scenarios we rehearse in our head. A person with an anxiety disorder will frequently not even get to the point of facing these fears. A former girlfriend of mine, educated, and outgoing, suffered from such an anxiety disorder and, at times, was not able to leave the house for weeks, even to retrieve the mail. This kind of anxiety requires more attention, more public awareness, and more treatment.

College students frequently suffer from anxiety to varying degrees, but they seldom address that anxiety. The COVID-19 pandemic certainly increased the mental health struggles of college students and young people in general. Since every college freshman must take college orientation

DOI: 10.1201/9781003201465-21

and, in some cases, first-year experience courses, these present unique opportunities to discuss critical but often untouched issues like social anxiety, discrimination, and sexual harassment. Games provide one invaluable tool for addressing these issues in an engaging and helpful fashion.

## LIFE IS A MUG OF OATMEAL: *THE AVERAGE EVERYDAY ADVENTURES OF SAMANTHA BROWNE*

The small mobile game *The Average Everyday Adventures of Samantha Browne* (2016) from Lemonsucker Games addresses anxiety disorders in a serious, but very engaging non-threatening fashion. Many game reviewers refer to the game as a visual novel, but unless you are a very avid gamer, that classification is a misnomer. The game plays out in around 15 minutes, so novel does not come close to categorizing the game's purpose which is more like Flash Fiction or a vignette. The game can more properly be considered a short interactive fiction driven by images and animation more than text. The player's choices are limited, but they make a difference in the narrative's direction and the state of the game's hunger meter.

Andrea Ayres (2020) discussed her desire to design a game where every decision registers a slight failure as a strategy to capture the no-win situation of social anxiety. For Samantha Browne that activity is making a mug of oatmeal in the dorm room's common kitchen area. For most students not even something to think about, but for a person suffering from social anxiety such an everyday task can be torturous. Samantha is hungry, but her social anxiety has isolated her in her dorm room for 6 hours. So, at 10:30 in the evening, hoping no one will be in the kitchen, she decides to make the trip down the hall to make a mug of oatmeal (Figure 17.1).

Game play consists of reading text at the bottom of the screen and making decisions in the role of Samantha by clicking on one of two or three choices provided to the player in the center of the screen. Decisions are small, but heavy because you are hungry, and you need to eat! At the same time, the last thing you want as someone with social anxiety is to draw attention to yourself, so even the game's diegetic sound, such as a microwave clock ticking down ("The microwave is so freaking loud," Samantha thinks), beautifully designed by Adrianna Krikl, makes your heart pound in fear!

Reimena Yee's excellent comic book style art engages the player in a colorful adventure while also denoting Samantha's terror. When she

FIGURE 17.1 Samantha Browne in her dorm room. (Andrea Ayers Deets. ©
Used with permission.)

FIGURE 17.2 Samantha experiences vertigo as she begins her journey down the
dorm hallway. (Image courtesy of Andrea Ayers Deets. © Used with permission.)

opens her dorm room door, the art captures Samantha's immediate
anxiety by showing the hallway is an out-of-focus perspective representing Samantha's disorientation in an almost Hitchcockian fashion (i.e., the
film *Vertigo*) (Figure 17.2).

Each decision is measured on an in-game hunger meter that indicates the degree of stress each decision entails. If ineffective decisions are made, they will result in Samantha's anxiety increasing significantly and, soon enough, a Game Over screen. The hunger meter only increases or moves toward higher anxiety levels. It does not lessen until Samantha successfully eats her oatmeal and ends the hunger. In a review of the game for *Rock Paper Shotgun*, John Walker effectively captures how social anxiety amplifies these moments of ordinary anxiety until they become terrorizing. The fear is irrational, but that is why it's a paralyzing disorder.

> You know that moment when you're about to jump off the top diving board? …Or tell the guy or girl that you fancy them? That moment when you realize you're actually going to do it, and your stomach turns, your chest tightens. Imagine someone pressed 'pause' on that moment, and you were stuck there for hours, for days. A moment of awful intensity that's meant to last a couple of seconds somehow not going away, a primitive invasion of fight-or-flight mechanisms at a time when there's nothing to fight, nor anything rational from which to fly.

You can read the game as a version of the hero's journey in a minor key. Samantha leaves the security of home (her dorm room), crosses the threshold (hallway), engages the ordeal, or fights the dragon of fear (the kitchen) and returns home with the prize (a warm mug of oatmeal). The kitchen ordeal is quite engaging. Samantha fears someone will be in the kitchen and her nightmare is confirmed as she opens the door and spots two girls talking at the table. Next, she negotiates a simple electric tea kettle. Such a simple task as figuring out how to "work" an electric kettle (you simply fill with water and heat) particularly hit me as amusing and anxiety provoking. My sophomore year in college I stayed in the dorms over Thanksgiving and my mother sent me an electric kettle to make coffee with. I could not figure out how it made coffee. My befuddlement over the simplest of tasks remains a point of humor decades later. The incident shows how anything new can push one's anxiety level higher, especially using the loud microwave in front of an audience you just know is talking about you!

The game's effectiveness can be measured by one of my student's, an avid gamer, commenting on first playing:

> For instance, the main goal of the game is to go to the communal kitchen and make oatmeal. And yet, a goal this simple

involves many steps that make it hard for the main character to accomplish. It took a lot of thinking and analyzing for Samantha Brown to make oatmeal. This embodies social anxiety as the simple scenario of making oatmeal caused her lots of distress. If the game is an accurate representation of how social anxiety can affect a person, then it made me realize how big of an effect social anxiety has on a person. I don't believe I've had a firm realization of what social anxiety really was. So, this game also helped me realize what social anxiety feels like. As I was playing the game, I failed about twice in total (I let the oatmeal overflow from the mug the first time and I dropped the mug in the hall the second).

This student developed a new awareness and sensitivity to social anxiety and accurately described how what most of us take for granted when completing a routine task can become a monumental mission for someone with severe anxiety.

Talking about Samantha's vertigo when leaving her room and stepping into the hallway, Laura notes,

> …the illusion of the halls [in a dorm] is a true depiction of how it feels to have anxiety and live in a dorm. At times it feels as if you're in an alternative reality and nothing seems the same. Being in a new place, surrounded by strangers, can be difficult for college students.

Another student, Sophia, made a similar observation while noting how social anxiety can result in missing classes,

> Before I played this game, I didn't think social anxiety could be that bad. I always thought that if someone had social anxiety they just didn't want to go out to parties, or talk to strangers. This game showed me that it could be anything that involves even seeing people for a split second or leaving their room at all. I was able to get a better understanding from Samantha's position, which helped me get her to eat her oatmeal and feel comfortable in the community kitchen. For example, if you [the player] selected to say hi to those other girls in the kitchen, they just looked at you and looked away, then Samantha got in her head about it. But if you just did what you had to do, everyone was just minding their own business and not bothering each other. This shows us that we should be nice to everyone because we don't know what people may be dealing with.

Like all interactive fictions, the game has multiple possible endings depending on a player's choices. In one, Samantha burns her hands on the mug and drops it. The mug shatters, spilling oatmeal everywhere and drawing unwanted attention. My first play through ended with Samantha forgetting her dorm room key, being locked out, slumped on the floor in despair. I can imagine myself doing both careless actions, but without suffering the humiliation Samantha feels.

Another of my students, Noah, observed how for a freshman the strangeness of college provokes anxiety,

> Only in college are you thrown by yourself into a place with hundreds or thousands of strangers and are expected to flourish socially. It is hard for people like Samantha to go through the difficult world of college when asking for help can be such a task, even for simple stuff such as in Samantha's case being locked out of their room.

This student had an experience very similar to the character Samantha in a college dining hall when eating alone and feeling overwhelmed. His further observation that asking for help is also difficult for students because of embarrassment or shyness deserves special note.

Of course, Samantha sometimes does successfully make the oatmeal and returns to her room with no hiccups, and a warm satisfied stomach. A hard-won late-night snack. Most of us are not like Samantha Browne, but we all have some Samantha Browne in us.[1]

## THE SWEET AND SOUR WEEK OF AN AFRICAN AMERICAN COLLEGE STUDENT: *SweetXheart*: A GAME FOR CONVERSATIONS ON RACIAL AND SEXUAL HARASSMENT

Catt Small's *SweetXheart* (2020), easily played on a tablet, offers an excellent way to begin talking about class, race, and gender. *SweetXheart* is a short narrative game about a week in the life of Kara, a female African American college student, who attends college in Manhattan and lives in the Bronx.[2] Your goal in playing Kara is simply to get from Monday through Friday successfully, meaning with mental health and sense of self intact. The designer explains this purpose as follows:

> The goal behind *SweetXheart* was to convey what it's like to be someone like me in the United States, a black woman who works

in technology. As you go throughout the day, Kara [the main character] has a lot of different interactions that she experiences and depending on those experiences she either feels more positively or she starts to feel really negative, and at the end of the week the hope is that you can have a positive week which requires five good days. It's really challenging to get five positive days in a row which is honestly quite accurate for me in real life.

Your positive or negative emotional state is measured by a meter in the top left corner of the screen.

After Kara wakes to her smartphone's alarm, and pets her kitten, your first task is to dress Kara for the day. As a male, this act can be weirdly unsettling. Aside from the fact I rarely give any serious consideration to this act you face a kind of masculine bind. College age males might be tempted to dress a female in the kind of sexy, revealing outfits they like to see women wear. However, in a classroom environment males will probably be less forthright and that too becomes a critical point of discussion about gender. For a female, you must negotiate with yourself what to wear and how what you wear will be perceived by all those outside your home. This dilemma is evident in the screenshot below. What might make Kara comfortable might also elicit unintended approaches by males, which will make her uncomfortable. This dress-up or doll-like game mechanic creates these basic, but complex double binds whether you are a male or female player (Figure 17.3).

The urban atmosphere contributes in an important way to the narrative. First, to get to the subway, you must navigate the Bronx streets. Second, living in an outer borough does present you with some particular forms of discrimination. The Bronx is often characterized as New York City's tough borough, and it has been negatively portrayed in most media (Yankee Stadium and the Bronx Zoo aside). The class aspect, subtle and possibly invisible to many players, manifests itself when Kara interacts with her friends Renaud, Iyanna, and Jordan. Kara's first slight comes when she meets her friends in June & Bronco's arcade to play *Dance Extreme*, a version of *Dance Dance Revolution*. Renaud immediately announces, "'I want to go first. Iyanna will you play with me?'" It turns out Kara is never chosen to play first. As a player you need to decide whether you want to make your hurt feelings and discomfort known to your friend, and possibly jeopardizing your friendship. After leaving the arcade you ask your friends if

FIGURE 17.3 What should Kara where? The female double bind. (Image courtesy of Catt Small. © Used with permission.)

they want to grab something to eat and they all turn you down with safe excuses. The excuses make sense "I have food at home," but clearly indicate a subtext of "we really don't want to spend any more time with you."

On the game's final day, you go over to Renaud's house in Queens to discover your other friends are already there. You surmise that they have slept over and enjoyed a night of fun while you were home sleeping. "They did sleep over without you," the game narrates. At the end of this Friday night, they all decided to stay another night while you go back home. "They stay over again. Friday-night-you feel not welcome." Iyanna is white, so the slights against you may be racial or they may be class based. Sorting out the two is not easy, and either way you are the outsider, in an obvious, but subtle way that keeps you on edge, enjoying the friendship, but resenting your secondary status.

Twice in the game Kara must decide who to speak with at college, Jesse, So-yeon or Angelica. I chose So-yeon thinking another minority girl might be receptive, but she appeared only interested in polite, trivial exchanges. Days you are not in class you have other people-oriented choices to make.

Kara interns at Nimble BEE LLC, a tech company. When you finish a project, you need to ask an employee to review it before submitting it to the boss, Mr. Ruiz. After creating a design for a website, I decided to ask the female employee Nita for help. She offered half-baked affirmation but made clear the website needed more work and she would handle it. Your second project, a programming task, meets with outright scorn. It is a tough task, so you ask the programmer Bobby to review it. After all he is a programmer, but his response cruelly shuts you down.

Your time at the School of Fine and Digital Arts is okay, but not exactly what one wants from college. The internship brings the cold shoulder or hostility from employees and patronizing pet names from your boss. You have friendships outside school, but they seem tenuous and leave you feeling left out or secondary—not quite an afterthought, but close enough. Home is good. Your single mom is supportive. On the other hand, dad complains incessantly about mom when you meet him for dinner, so home life is stressful too. The only stress-free interaction is with kitty!

Most taxing of all your interactions belongs to walking to and back from the subway station. When Kara leaves her house for the subway, she is approached by men on the street every single day. This is common for women living in large urban centers like New York or Chicago, but also in a different setting for other women walking to class, sitting in the library, or eating in the dining hall. How a female negotiates these unwanted greetings by strange men presents one of the game's key decision points. The greeting "Good morning sweetheart" or "Beautiful" might just be a polite hello. You do not want to be rude, so say hello. However, the greeting might also be the first step of stranger "hitting on you" or looking to initiate more of an interaction than you want. You do not want to encourage such approaches, another double bind, one most men generally do not face. Journalist Chris Aiken writing for *Black Nerd Problem* makes the same point as me (Figure 17.4),

> ...when the game was over, so was the experience. Then it clicked. Just how much of an advantage I had to be able just to walk away from it all. It's a privilege I had that many women like my wife, Catt, and others don't. They don't get to walk away; this is how they exist in the real world – in a state of discomfort from the way people harass and treat them. These are things that I don't even have to think about dealing with whenever I walk out of the door.

FIGURE 17.4 Kara harassed on the streets of the Bronx. (Image courtesy of Catt Small. © Used with permission.)

The last walk home brings the "Nice tits!" verbal assault, but even such blatant aggression requires thoughtful responses. Earlier in the week Kara's lack of positivity with a random stranger ended up with him throwing a bottle at her. Most of the game presents the player with frequent microaggressions. Confronting anyone might leave you isolated, depressed and angry, but unacknowledged "micro aggressions" can snowball into a major conflagration.[3]

Catt Small published this game amid escalating racial tension and violence that threatens to repeat the violence of the mid-1960s. *SweetXheart* allows for rich classroom conversations around Black Lives Matters as well as MeToo#. A game that helps others experience the subtle daily aggressions against black women begins at the point where change can realistically happen, at the local level, in daily interactions between people who are different from each other. Talk more, understand better, and act differently. This small game helps in a small, but important way, to bring about more positive interpersonal relationships.

## POSTSCRIPT: DIVERSITY ON COLLEGE CAMPUSES, A CONTINUING PROBLEM

Just weeks before I revised this chapter some 300 students at Skidmore College walked out of their classes in protest over what they perceived to be the college administration's woefully inadequate handling of gender violence on campus (this happened on October 21, 2021, as reported in the *Albany Times Union*, see Silberstein in Works Cited). A student was allegedly forced to leave campus for voicing her experience on social media, something she resorted to when Title IX administrators failed to give serious attention to her reporting of harassment (Silberstein, 2021). Skidmore College is just 20 miles north of where I live. The beautiful campus rests in the small, upper-middle-class village of Saratoga Springs famous for its racetrack (horse racing), performing arts center, and mineral springs. Skidmore is a very expensive, competitive, former female-only college that would be considered a place of privilege. Yet much of the female student body apparently felt, at this moment in time, harassed, unsafe, and not listened too.

I am not at all surprised. I have now taught in higher education for three decades and have, at times, observed inadequate responses by college administrations over everything from graduate student housing to incidents of racism. Higher education too often pushes aside systemic problems, which they deal with in a superficial fashion. Here in New York State, problems with sexual harassment in the workplace were dealt with by a state-mandated training on sexually harassment. Offering a brief 1- or 2-hour training that is not repeated or reinforced, and not integrated with day-to-day operations serves only the politicians who want to feel they have done something to address a long-standing unacceptable social reality. Such cursory approaches do little to address systemic problems.

Increasingly on campus and across the globe youth act because of adult negligence. Student advocacy was critical in the 1960s and needs to be so again today. Systemic problems do not just go away and implementing simple mandated training or token policies speeches does not address the root cause of the problems. Orientation is one opportunity to help students advocate for their needs about mental health support, Title IX, housing, and a host of other issues. Students and their families are paying exorbitant tuition fees and residential costs. They should never feel like they are not heard.

## NOTES

1. My own students quoted above offered some practical suggestions for coping with social anxiety based on their experiences. Brynn offered, "… try not to have an 'all or nothing mindset', gradually increase your exposure to social situations, practice deep breathing and meditation exercises, join a support group for social anxiety, and avoid your [directing]attention inward." All excellent suggestions. Laura stated how helping students find "safe zones" in public would help, "introduce them [students struggling with social anxiety] to people in a way and they will feel safe. For example, in the library I used to have a favorite spot but once people took it I felt extremely anxious and worried, but then I found two more in the library so I always know I have a place to go." These astute student observations show how the game helps build peer-to-peer support.

2. Although a game like *SweetXheart* is often classified as a visual novel, a genre made popular in Japan. I find such a classification almost ridiculous. If someone can find me a novel that I can read in 30 minutes, you will be mistaking a short story for a novel, and that is quite a big misclassification.

3. A game or more accurately prototype by students at Rochester Institute of Technology (RIT) called *Gamer Girl: A Harassment Simulator* gets at similar microaggressions of campus life experienced by females. The game follows the sole female in a computer programming class on her daily journey through the harassment masquerading as friendliness perpetrated by male college students. You can play test the game at: http://www.gamergirl.games/game/playtest.

## LESSON IDEAS

As a "serious" casual game, *The Average Everyday Adventures of Samantha Browne* is ideal for all college students to play. It raises awareness of debilitating social anxiety and thus benefits professors, coaches, advisors, and others who work with students throughout their academic careers. It is also a perfect game for online learning modules in distance or blended courses, which benefit from short bursts of instructional material. For students who face more situational or occasional anxiety, the game's short duration allows it to act as a springboard for talking about healthy ways to cope with anxiety (either in person or as an online discussion forum). Test anxiety, anxiety before a big game, anxiety over a campus social event, or the current anxiety swirling around COVID-19 are all examples of situations where faculty, advisors, and counselors, peer or professional, can help students make smart choices and cope successfully with their anxiety. Failure to negotiate anxiety can cause students to make impulsive, ill-advised decisions like going to a crowded party and not wearing a mask during a public health crisis.

In terms of sexual harassment and racial discrimination see my postscript above. Helping students learn to advocate can be immensely empowering for youth.

## RESOURCES

A moment here to remember Dr. Aaron Beck (1921–2021) who died last year at age 100. In terms of dealing with social anxiety, no clinician contributed more to the field than Dr. Beck, generally considered the founder of cognitive behavior therapy.

Websites/Organizations/Centers

*Center for Treatment and Study of Anxiety.* University of Pennsylvania School of Medicine. Penn Psychiatry.

https://www.med.upenn.edu/ctsa/social_anxiety_symptoms.html.

Highly credible and authoritative resources on all aspects of anxiety from a renowned university.

*Anxiety and Depression Society of America*

Resources on helping college students with anxiety: https://adaa.org/ finding-help/helping-others/college-students.

Articles/Chapters/Reports

Abrams, Zara. "Sexual harassment on campus. Advice and resources for psychology students on how best to prevent and respond to misconduct by faculty and others." *American Psychological Association Monitor*, Vol. 49, No. 5. May, 2018. Retrieved from: www.apa.org/monitor/2018/05/ sexual-harassment.

"An Underreported Problem: Campus Sexual Misconduct."

*American Association of University Women***,** https://www.aauw.org/ resources/article/underreported-sexual-misconduct/. N.D. Retrieved 12/ 10/2021.

The fact colleges and universities significantly underreport incidents of sexual harassment has both a shocking effect and a sobering one too.

Underreporting reflects higher education's frequent preoccupation with image at the expense of student well-being.

Green, Adrienne. "The Cost of Balancing Academia and Racism."
*The Atlantic*, 21 January 2016. Retrieved from: https://amp.theatlantic.com/amp/article/424887/. Web.

A stimulating article on the stresses faced by minority students on campus and how the failure to adequately deal with these issues by administrations simply reinforces the discrimination experienced outside the classroom.

Marques, Luana, and LeBlanc, Nicole J.
"Anxiety in college: What we know and how to cope." *Harvard Health blog*, 27 August 2019, https://www.health.harvard.edu/blog/anxiety-in-college-what-we-know-and-how-to-cope-2019052816729.

A short practical guide to helping students adjust to college life. The authors emphasize the importance of the freshman year in a student's transition to college hence my focus on college orientation as a critical moment in the life of a student.

Silberstein, Rachel. "Skidmore vows Title IX changes as students 'out' alleged abusers online." *Times Union*, 20 October 2021. Print.

"Systemic Racism."
*ASHE Higher Education Report*, Vol. 42, Issue 1, pp. 49–71. John Wiley & Sons, Inc.

The Association for the Study of Higher Education conducts extensive research on issues pertaining to higher education and publishes an annual report. The 2020 report addresses the many ramifications and dimensions of systemic racism in higher education.

# IV

## Playing across Boundaries: Interdisciplinary Instruction with Films, Games, and Literature

# CHAPTER 18

# Teaching the *Disclosure* Scene

## *Empathy and Understanding for Transgender People*

### DISCLOSING GENDER FLUIDITY IN A BINARY CULTURE

The documentary *Disclosure* (2020) does an excellent job of reviewing and explaining the negative and stereotypical depictions of transgender people in the media. *Disclosure* is related to, but also quite different than coming out. Both have to do with a private reality being made public, sometimes by choice, and sometimes through the malice of others. *Disclosure* specifically refers to the revelation of a previously hidden sexual identity. Making public a private reality can be a surprise, a disclosed secret whose exposure, usually in a personal encounter or situation, sometimes causes the receiver or confidante of the secret or the audience of the secret's disclosure to have an adverse, even "traumatic" response to the revelation. This often happens as the documentary beautifully shows in both the media and in life. However, *Disclosure* misreads one film, *The Crying Game* (1992), rather badly, though understandably, and this misreading and misrepresentation requires some attention if we want to understand how media can transcend the hateful stereotypes of transgender people it often perpetuates.

DOI: 10.1201/9781003201465-23

## ENDURING STEREOTYPES

First, let me put out there what I take to be three dominate tropes or stereotypes that the media and people, more generally, use to depict transgender people, especially transgender women. One, the transgender person is the butt of a joke. He or she is used for humor, made fun of, and then discarded. The joke is often cruel. Two, the media represents the transgender woman as a pervert, sexual deviant. This representation of the transgender women as pervert can conflate crossdressing with transgender sexuality when they are, in fact, quite different. People cross-dress for many reasons and a sexual fetish can be one reason, but certainly not the only one. Regardless, when presented as a perversion, transgender sexuality necessary becomes entangled with mental illness. If you are turned on dressing in heels and stockings, you must be mad. Think about the classic example of Alfred Hitchcock's *Psycho* (1960). Third, transgender women are depicted as sexual predators. The transgender women in this case, traps men by her outward beauty and allure only to reveal her penis at the moment of seduction. Here the transgender woman is a repetition of the sexist femme fatale archetype where the beautiful siren causes the great male hero to fall from grace: Eve, Delilah, Ishtar, and thousands more. However, there is a curious twist to the transgender woman as seductress. In the classic archetype the heterosexual hero cannot resist the enticements of a hypersexual woman, Mrs. Robinson seducing young Ben in *The Graduate* (1967). How often does a heterosexual man pursue the transgender women for sexual adventure? What does this pursuit signify such about the man's sexual pursuit in such cases? The transgender woman, not the man, is the real victim, but society and the media often reverse this role in a blame the victim mentality.

## *DISCLOSURE* AS HATRED, FEAR OR ACCEPTANCE: *PERSONA 3, ACE VENTURA*, AND *LOLA*

Let me give concrete examples of these negative tropes and how they might be overcome. First, the transgender woman as vulgar joke, but a joke that hides a deeper and more serious misogyny and hate based transgender phobia. In the enormously popular Japanese video game *Persona 3* (Atlus, 2006) there is quest called "Babe Hunt." A group of high school boys decide to play a familiar boy's game. As most of us know, the beach and girls in bikini's often have the effect of over stimulating adolescent males already overactive libidos. In this game, following a suggestion by Junpei, the boys compete to see who can score most of the girls, i.e., the beach babes. In male teen talk, score usually means get the girl in bed, but here I think earning a date, getting a phone number, or even engaging in a decent conversation would be accepted by the male peers to be a "score." The game's premise is sexist. Girls are simply figures to be looked at, lusted for, and hopefully laid. The male hunts and the female coyly and passively waits for the "attack," often a lame pick up line. In the game, the boy who scores the most wins.

There are no winners here. Not unexpectedly, the boys strike out. Their "pickup lines" are silly, and the entire series of beach scenes are very juvenile with juvenile dialogue. However, the hunt's final encounter—the final prey if you will, turns the game on its head. They approach a female referred to as "Beautiful Lady?" No proper name, just an A.I. I assume the designation "lady" means this female is beyond high school age maybe in her mid-twenties. In this scene, the lady, as I said above, turns the table on the boys. She takes the initiative. This reversal of fortune calls the male boasting for what it is: hot air and bluster. The female response to the "beach hunt" might be summarized something like if you got me home little boy you would not know what to do with me. In other words, should the male score he would still lose because he could not satisfy the girl and his deflated ego would end up humiliated. It's all very adolescent, but still telling.

The lady tells the boys they "have no balls," i.e., they are neutered. She offers to show them "a thing or two." Junpei appears to jump at the invitation. Suddenly his pal, Akihiko spots some hair on the lady's chin, and she admits she must have missed a spot. Her identity disclosed, the lady sighs disappointed that she will not have her boy toy. Shocked, Junpei has been had, "SHE's a He!?" Of course, he could have taken the lady to bed or rather she taken him to bed, but in the game's transphobic narrative she is not she, but he, and that masquerade is a turn off for real men and boys too. The entire scene not only turns the transgender woman into an excuse for a practical joke but also represents her as the predator trying to trap innocent males for her "perverse" homosexual pleasure. Two bad tropes in one for this game.

*Ace Ventura: Pet Detective* (Shadyac, 1994) provides perhaps the most egregious misrepresentation of transgender people in contemporary cinema. The film launches comedian Jim Carrey on his meteoric rise to super stardom and the film offers many opportunities for Carrey to show off his slapstick genius. Unfortunately, the silly plot and vitriolic anti-gay writing turns the film into a comedy of horrors.

Ace Ventura (Carrey) has been hired to track down the Miami Dolphin football team's mascot, a dolphin. That is dumber than dumb to echo another Carrey movie. The Miami police chief Lois Einhorn played by Sean Young turns out to be the villain in a stereotypical twist of roles. The mascot has been stolen by a former Dolphin place kicker Ray Finkle who missed an easy field goal costing the Dolphins a championship years ago. Shamed by his failure Finkle goes into hiding and steals the mascot as an act of revenge. When Ventura deduces that Finkle has disguised himself or transitioned into Lois Einhorn, the film delivers its transphobic vitriol.

Ventura forces Lois to strip down to her underwear displaying her male anatomy's most obvious attribute. A disclosure scene for the ages when the male audience of hypermasculine football players and police officers— macho macho men, collectively vomit and/or spit in disgust. They have all been intimate with a woman who turns out to be a man and their realization of what, from their perspective, would be a homoerotic act, causes disgust. The transgender woman becomes an object of disgust. Misogyny masquerading as comedy. It cannot get much worse than that.

However, art also sings a more tolerant song as well. Way back in 1970, around the time of Lou Reed's pioneering "Walk on the Wild Side" lyrics of acceptance the British rock group The Kinks released a now legendary song "Lola." The titular hero "walks like a woman but talked like a man." The song tells of a man's encounter with a transgender woman. The singer knows she is a transgender woman but does not resist her intoxicating spell on him. Unlike the boy from "Beach Hunt" this singer takes up Lola on her offer to "make him a man" goes home with her and presumably enjoys their encounter enough to sing about it with the memorable refrain invoking her name over and over. The song talks about a "mixed up world" where gender is inverted but here the woman's "beard" rather than prompting disgust or anger prompts acceptance. Things may not be what they seem, but what seems normal may not be worth singing about. The wild side or experiencing and accepting the outsider and marginal as fully human should be what really rocks the world rather than fear and hatred.

## SECRETS IN GERUDO TOWN: *THE LEGEND OF ZELDA'S* TRANSPHOBIC MOMENT

*The Legend of Zelda: Breath of the Wild* (Nintendo, 2017) is a beloved game from Nintendo's Zelda franchise. The game has the grandeur and beauty of the best open world adventures. Yes, Anita Sarkeesian has called out the game as sexist, and I can agree with the many avid gamers who feel such a characterization to be slanted, and, perhaps, flat out wrong. Link's feminine qualities and the way he can play with traditionally female costumes have a liberating appeal for players. Nonetheless, the game's transgender scene smacks of transgender discrimination if not outright hatred.

First, let me backup and point out how many of the gamers who defend *Breath of the Wild* against Ms. Sarkissian's criticism make their defense using sexist, vulgar, near misogynistic language. They fail to even see the irony of trying to argue against reading a game as sexist using a defense dripping with sexism. The need for teachers to discuss transphobic and discriminatory aspects of great art becomes evident in such uninformed defenses. We want to graduate students who can criticize an ideological reading of a work of art, but they must make their defense or counter argument in a closely reasoned, logical fashion based on textual evidence informed by historical context and a broad grasp of cultural phenomena. We do not want what I more often read, a biased, personal reading full of stereotypical thinking stripped of context.

Here is the context for the scene I want to discuss. In a quest critical to the game, "Forbidden City Entry," Link approaches the Gates of Gerudo. He needs to get inside the gates, but Gerudo is an all-female enclave akin to Diana Prince/Wonder Woman's Paradise Island. Rumor has it that a man has succeeded in getting past the gates and that man is key to Link's quest. Link finds a source who can help him find this man at the Kara Kara Bazaar atop the General Store. The Bazaar smacks of stereotypical representations of a middle-eastern city, but that's a topic for another day. The woman is wearing traditional Gerudo garb which she will ultimately sell Link as a disguise that enables him entry into the all-female town. Let me pause here for a minute. First, the attire worn by Gerudo women consists of a veil, a top, and a spirwal. This dress style strikes me like what one might expect at a belly dance. Furthermore, the women of Gerudo turn out to be very fond of high heels as if wearing high heels in a dessert makes any sense outside of male fetishizing.

In the game's structure, if Link accuses this woman of being a man, she will dismiss him. Rather, Link must flatter her. The compliment and some currency (600 rupees) will purchase the clothes needed to pass as a woman and get Link inside the gates (a crude metaphor if ever there was one). This informant turns out to be Vilia. She remarks how nice Link looks in his new clothes and Link continues his quest.

Here another sexist trope emerges in addition to the harem style dress, high heels, and girlish giggles. The women of Gerudo are man crazy. They talk about men, think about men, and appear preoccupied with traveling outside town to find a marriage partner. This aspect of the female utopia provides a stark contrast with Diana Prince's Paradise Island or Themyscira where men are barely a thought.

Returning to the quest, Vilia likes Link and invites him to diner. Later, a gust of wind pushes aside her veil to disclose a bread, the mark of masculinity. In Link's eyes the woman is a man in disguise. Vilia; however, presents as a woman. Feminine pronouns are used referring to her and within the game's universe she is clearly a woman. She belongs in Gerudo Town. Consequently, we can infer with full confidence Vilia is a transgender woman, not a male in disguise, but Link denies her self-definition. Whether a penis or a beard, traditional masculine anatomical markers define masculinity in the game's universe irrespective of the character's own self-defined gender identity. Autonomy is stripped away, and gender identity dictated by the state not by the individual. The revelation of male markers underneath the female attire provokes either derisive laughter or disgust. However, unlike *The Crying Game* (see below), *Breath of the Wild* does not elaborate on this brief encounter. There is no frame or evolving relationship. Even if only an isolated moment, the transgender figure remains an objectified freak.

The problematic nature of this scene becomes evident to transgender readers or players of the game. Here is Jennifer Unkle (2017) writing in *Paste*:

> It left me sick to my stomach. Unlike the opportunistic businessman at the town gates who wants in at any cost, this Gerudo didn't seem to have any ulterior motive. Like other transgender women, Vilia was comfortable with her chosen presentation, even shutting Link down if he decided to rudely misgender her. Yet the rest of the world saw her as "the man," the conniving genius that put together her disguise to enter a women-only village as an impostor. It did not matter if she disagreed. The people of Hyrule had decided her identity for her.
>
> …
>
> The game's disdainful stance toward my existence stings even worse when no one else acknowledges it as a problem. Should I let this slide as a small misstep and move on, or address a hurtful joke others ignored and risk looking oversensitive?
>
> When it's my identity on the line, maybe oversensitive is the only way to be.

Eva Herinkova (2021) echoes Unkle's feelings in *Screen Rant,* reinforcing my criticism:

> Regardless of Vilia's "true" in-universe identity, her depiction in *Breath of the Wild* matches harmful stereotypes about transgender women. It encourages players to see them not as real women but as deceptive men, disguising themselves in order to "*infiltrate*" (as the previously mentioned NPC worded it) female-only spaces for some sinister purpose. The game also portrays transgender women as something to laugh at, since Link's compliments about Vilia's appearance are juxtaposed with his apparent belief that she really looks like a man.

Before coming around to the real-world "disclosure scene" let me elaborate on the difference between Link's crossdressing and Vilia's transgender being. A transgender person might cross-dress as a precursor to transitioning, but that becomes an evolution to a new identity. Crossdressing by itself is a temporary behavior where the gender crossdressing remains stable.

As a literary trope, cross dressing has a rich history. Shakespeare used the cross-dress, crossdressing convention of Elizabethan theater where men had to dress as women on stage in an inventive way to explore the deepest significance of gender identity through his female to male cross-dressing Rosalind/Ganymede in *As You Like it* (1596) and Viola/Cesario in *Twelfth Night* (circa 1601). The cross-dressing trope can be empowering or destructive.

In Edmund Spencer's epic *The Faeire Queen* (1590), Britomart appears as a male when she enters combat. A tall, slender woman of classic beauty she defeats enemy knights and proves herself every bit their equal, often superior to, the male warriors she encounters. A servant for Glorianna, allegorical for Queen Elizabeth I, Britomart's very name encodes her fierceness. She is Briton of War. At the tragic end of crossdressing, Euripides' extraordinary Greek drama *The Bacchae* (circa 406 BC) shows King Pentheus dressed as a woman spying on the maenads. In other words, the disguise used to access female privacy is an invasive act of voyeurism. When King Pentheus is revealed, the scene turns nasty, and the Maenads, including the king's mother Agave, tear him to shreds.

## *DRESSED TO KILL:* THE SLASHER AS THERAPIST

The modern disclosure scene as murder site echoes *The Bacchae* reaching a pinnacle in Brian De Palma's film *Dressed to Kill* (1980) a retelling of Alfred Hitchcock's *Psycho* (1960). Here crossdressing merges into transgender identification. The sacred and secret female territory trope—Paradise Island, Gerudo Town, the Maenads' rites, becomes the confidential therapist's office. Following an adulteress encounter with a stranger, the beautiful, sexually frustrated housewife, Kate Miller (Angie Dickinson) ends up having her throat slashed by a tall slender blonde wearing sunglasses. Kate had left her wedding ring at the apartment of her tryst, and when she returns to retrieve it meets her brutal destiny.

The early sequence reeks of sexist misogyny. First, Kate's sexual encounter turns out to be with a stranger who had syphilis. Punishment number one for a female who strays. Murder will be punishment number two for the unfaithful wife. Fortunately, the murder had a witness, another beautiful woman, but this time a high-priced hooker Liz Blake (Nancy Allen). The film now turns into a wild murder mystery worthy of the best Special Victims Unit (SVU) crime story.

The alleged killer appears to be a female patient of Dr. Robert Elliott (Michael Caine) named Bobbi. who Dr. Elliott had treated the victim, Kate Miller. Kate, incidentally, attempted seducing the good doctor but failed. Turns out, Bobbi is a transgender woman who wants sexual reassignment surgery, but Dr. Elliott will not consent to such a procedure. Bobbi is referred to a psychologist Dr. Levy (David Margulies), but not before she also threatens Dr. Elliott, angry over his disapproval of her desire for surgery. In the Hitchcockian twist, true to Euripides' tragic spirit, Bobbi and Dr. Elliott are one in the same. Dr. Elliott murdered Kate while crossdressing as Bobbi. He/she murders Kate in resentment over her attempted seduction of him in the therapy room. Apparently, Dr. Elliott cannot cope with an erection produced by an arousing female presence. Kate is the stereotypical femme fatale, and the victim blamed for the crime.

In the film's convoluted logic spun through the voice of Dr. Levy, Dr. Elliott becomes a closeted transgender woman who wants reassignment surgery; however, the male side of her fights against the full identification with femininity. This logic implies becoming a female is, on some level, disgusting, especially if the transition requires disavowing the penis, sign of power and privilege. Likewise, being turned on by a female seems to carry threatening homoerotic desires that the doctor cannot face. Like with *Breath of the Wild*, *Dressed to Kill* is superior art, and De Palma a masterful director of suspense. Nonetheless, the artistry appears to disclose a misogyny and transphobia with dangerous real world implication, or does it?

## THE PROBLEM WITH TEACHING POLITICAL CORRECTNESS

Politically correct (PC) thinking pervades much of American society, K-12 education, and occasionally higher education as well. When you teach received or accepted "wisdom" you engage in one-dimensional teaching. You teach a subject by reproducing perceived norms, one that is safe, vanilla, and comforting. The status quo as ossified opinion, not a multifaceted reality grounded in serious inquiry. Sometimes teaching PC requires that you not upset a vocal minority (racial, gender, ethnic, geography, religious, etc.), sometimes a long-standing tradition, and sometimes an entrenched political system, local, state, or federal. Unfortunately, if you never upset anyone, you are not asking questions and therefore not seriously teaching, rather you are a vessel for the safe "truth" or the "current" norm at a certain point in social history.

Shakespeare remains the greatest writer in the English language. Nonetheless, Shakespeare's representation of women, at times, demonstrates stereotypical thinking; the shrew Kate who needed to be tamed, and, at other times, especially in sonnets where he refers to a woman's genitals as hell, misogynistic. Shakespeare needs to be criticized for these flaws, but we also need to read Shakespeare's writing in the context of his time and not maintain a ludicrous belief that he should be writing in 1600 as if he was living in 2022. We also need to acknowledge even with flaws his writing remains an extraordinary contribution to culture. Further even with negative representations of women he has many plays with heroic, positive, and admirable female characters such as Rosalind in *As You Like It* or Viola in *Twelfth Night* (both cross-dressers by the way). Shakespeare, like most artists, and most of society, has many dimensions and nuances, so teaching in one dimension benefits no one.

Critics are fond of admiring and praising Brian De Palma's artistry in *Dressed to Kill*. How could you not? The direction is masterful, with split screens, soft focus, endless doubles, and meta commentary. Praise for artistry, however, has been countered with a deluge of criticism directed at the film's alleged misogyny and transphobia. This social criticism strikes me as one dimensional thinking typical of standard politically correct positions. Misogyny, for instance, is an overstatement. A film can represent negative portraits of women without being misogynistic. Let's take *Dressed to Kill's* protagonist Kate Miller as an example.

Is Kate objectified? The camera shows her blurred figure masturbating in the shower with water streaming down. Yes, the camera lingers over her body including her vagina full on, something atypical of "R" rated films and, perhaps, closer to soft core pornography. Is she objectified for male viewers, or could Kate also be represented as a sexual being, autonomous and seeking satisfaction for herself outside the confines of her marital situation? After the shower, Kate engages in very unsatisfying sex with her husband. She is left frustrated. Clearly, she finds him a poor lover. The story criticizes the male not the female.

Kate follows her disappointment by going to the Metropolitan Museum of Art where she engages in a silent flirtation with a total stranger. Kate initiates the scene, a brilliant piece of cinematography with Kate the controlling figure. The extended scene is shot with a steady cam as Kate moves through the museum's spacious, open rooms in an erotic game of cat and mouse with Kate playing the cat. The flirtation leads to a taxi ride where the stranger gives Kate oral sex, and she orgasms in the back seat to the taxi driver's voyeuristic delight. There is no objectification here. Kate goes back to the man's apartment and has more sex. Post coitus, she discovers the man has a venereal disease. Is that punishment for anonymous sex or is her subsequent murder punishment? Is Kate punished by the film's development and design or are the men or both?

These scenes are more nuanced and complex than a simplistic accusation of misogyny suggest. In a fascinating reappraisal of the scene from the perspective of a gay male viewer, Armond White (2015) interprets the scene as a beautiful evocation of gay male sexuality (by proxy) in the 1970s.

> De Palma depicts an urban habit — cruising — that once defined gay life in New York City of sexual alertness and readiness. These prerogatives were liberated by the 1960s- '70s sexual revolution. The scene's combination of lust, apprehension and opportunity idealized cruising as a particular social ritual of desire.

White goes on to argue that the film exceeds stereotypes, "At the core of *Dressed to Kill*, the seductive thrill and thrilling danger of sexual immediacy overwhelm gender stereotypes and facile moralizing." Rather than a hate-fueled objectification of women, the museum scene from this gay male's perspective becomes an empowering embrace of female sexual autonomy.

Students benefit from these counter readings or reading against the grain of mainstream critics. The film can be subject to feminist criticism, but other perspectives as well. For instance, the escort Liz can be read as a negative stereotype of women, but she also becomes a heroic figure who helps Detective Marino (Denis Franz) track down Kate's killer. In the reveal scene, the camera lingers over Liz's body glad in lingerie as she toys with Dr. Elliott, but maybe more than objectification; also, a seductive manipulation of the male duped by his sex drive. Liz risks danger to bring Kate's killer to justice and she also assumes a kind of motherly role toward Kate's teenage son Peter (Keith Gordan).

Likewise, with transphobia. Jessica Crets, a transgender woman writer, views *Dressed to Kill* as indirectly empathic to the transgender community by situating the film's transgender representations in the medical community's unenlightened perspective of the 1970s,

> An argument can be made that Dr. Elliott, who would have been familiar with these gatekeeping guidelines [deciding who is eligible for sex reassignment surgery], would have found it impossible that he could be transgender. Most of his profession would have believed this, which could have caused him to try to squash these desires. In fact, Dr. Elliot represents the psychiatric field's gatekeeping of transgender people for not fitting a very narrow definition, which came from the doctor's own biases over what makes someone a man or a woman.

If the crossdressing psychiatrist represents a transphobic moment, maybe the criticism more deeply concerns the male dominated profession that denied the transgender person's reality in the 1970s, a period of sexual liberation, that did not liberate the transgender community. Moreover, a scene within a scene shows Phil Donahue interviewing a transgender woman—Nancy Hunt—in a more sympathetic fashion that a one-dimensional reading of the film allows.

The actual disclosure scene has nothing to do with genitalia. The film discloses Dr. Elliott's transgender identity when he is shot by a police officer. Elliott as Bobbi falls to the floor and his wig comes off. The horror, and the film plays with multiple genres, resides both in the psychotic or dissociated transgender woman, but also the medical profession's denial of her full transition, a transition that requires the removal of the phallus, something a patriarchal medical profession would not easily tolerate. As Crets concludes, "…there's a compelling metaphor about denying people from being who they are buried under this stylish thriller." Psychiatry dictates you must be either male or female, and, if you are not, you are sent to Bellevue.

You can read the film as misogynistic, but you can also read differently, as White does, "De Palma's horror film premise creates a timeless path to empathy — for women, for transsexuals, for the practice of sexual independence and the fine art of cruising — those gay men have always had to risk." Teach students multiple ways of looking at film and do not just reflect the "accepted" perspective.

## THE SECRET'S OUT AND THE OTHER IS DEAD: SLAUGHTERING SEXUAL DIFFERENCE OR *DRESSED TO KILL* ON THE STREETS OF HARLEM

On a warm summer night, the 13th of August, Islan Nettles and two friends were walking on a Harlem Street not far from where Islan had recently taken a job a H&M. A group of young men were across the street having left one bar and going on their way to another one. A tall slim attractive young black woman, Islan (age 21) caught the eye of one of the men. He and his friends crossed the street to engage the women in conversation. James Dixon seemed drawn to Islan and initiated an unwanted conversation. At 12:20 am most young women in New York City know to keep to themselves. Dixon's flirting was accompanied by his friends' teasing. "That's a Guy." Islan was not keeping a secret. She had transitioned and already come out as a woman as had her two friends, but Mr. Dixon judged only the outward appearance, or as his friends teased, he misjudged. Well, not exactly. Islan was a woman, a transgender woman, but very much a woman to herself, and to her personal world, but to James Dixon, women cannot have dicks and transgender women therefore must secretly be men.

Provoked by the sudden realization Islan was transgender, and humiliated at his friend's mocking, James Dixon, as reported in court records, flew into "a fury." Like one of the Dionysian maenads the recognition that he had "hit" on a transgender woman had fatal results. In a matter of seconds, he threw Islan onto the concrete and bludgeoned her, leaving her limp body on the ground. Five days later she was dead. A transgender woman had been murdered simply for being a transgender woman, for existing!

James Dixon was arrested much later and charged with manslaughter. A murder had been downgraded, and even worse, no hate crime was ever charged. Inexplicably, the actual trial did not start for 2½ years. Of course, the delay has an explanation. The deadly assault of a young, poor black transgender woman apparently did not warrant high priority to the NYPD.

How cruelly ironic that Islan's battered body lie on the street named after the great black abolitionist Frederick Douglas.

Defense lawyers achieved the downgrading of a murder charge to manslaughter using what has popularly been called "the trans panic defense" a version of the equally ludicrous "gay panic defense." This "panic defense" goes back to a celebrated "secret disclosure" on *The Jenny Jones Show*. *The Jenny Jones Show* was a popular daytime talk show similar in some ways to many talk shows on daytime television today. This episode was taped on March 9, 1995, and featured the disclosure of secrets as a theme.

Jonathan Schimtz, a young man from Lake Orion, Michigan, had been invited on the show to meet a secret admirer. He was curious and excited, expecting with some degree of reason the admirer would be a woman. The host Jenny Jones encouraged the secret admirer Scott Amedure to talk about his fantasies regarding Jonathan. This strategy titillates the audience and sets the stage for the big reveal/disclosure. When Jonathan comes out from backstage and learns his secret admirer is a gay man, he politely shakes Scott's hand, but clearly registers surprise, and perhaps shock. Mr. Schimtz emphatically states on the show, "I am definitely heterosexual."

Three days after the taping, Schmitz finds a note from Amedure by his door. He takes money out of the bank and purchases a shot gun. Next, Schimtz takes the note over to Mr. Amedure's mobile home, confronts him about the note, returns to his car, takes out the gun, and shoots Amedure twice in the chest, killing him on the spot. Schimtz then calls 911 and confesses to the murder. When the dispatcher asks him, "Why did you do that?" Schimtz explains, "Because (expletive) picked me on national T.V. and he's a homosexual." No doubt, Schimtz disliked gay men and the exposure on a national show humiliated him.

The "gay panic defense" has its basis in deeply engrained prejudice against homosexuals. Independent of the tragic encounter between Amedure and Schmitz, *The Jenny Jones Show* (the episode never aired) had clear culpability in the crime. Amedure's family sued the show's producers and was initially awarded $25 million. The plaintiff's argued that the show ambushed and lured their client onto the show boost ratings. Of that there can be no doubt, but the verdict was overturned on appeal and no money awarded. A gay man had been murdered, his family now essentially spit on, and the corporate entity never held accountable. Jones maintained the act was entirely individual choice and elided any responsibility. "I never use anyone." The show continued another 8 years.

## THE CRYING GAME AND THE TRANSCENDENCE OF DIFFERENCE

In 1992, Irish film director Neil Jordan released his unconventional art film *The Crying Game*. An initial flop, the film eventually won praise and garnered Jordan an Oscar for best screenplay. As precis, the film tells the story of Fergus, a Northern Irish nationalist and IRA volunteer who holds a black British soldier hostage. No soft hearts in that pairing. The IRA hated the British Army who they saw as an occupying force on Irish soil. Nonetheless, Fergus develops empathy for Jody (note the gender ambiguous name) during the hostage situation. Expectation being Jody will be killed, Jody asks Fergus the favor of going to London, looking up his girlfriend, and letting her know his deep love for her. Indeed, Jody is killed, and Fergus, true to his word, makes his way to London where he looks up Dil, a beautiful slim black woman. They develop a friendship that turns romantic. In the film's big reveal, Dil undresses displaying her penis. Fergus recoils in apparent disgust. Dil remarks, "I'm sorry, I thought you knew." Fergus runs into the bathroom and vomits. He has fallen in love with a transgender woman or, perhaps, a man dressing and acting as a woman, the film does not clarify.

Sadly, even tragically, this scene was repeated, and parodied in many other films and comedy sketches, reducing a complex, nuanced scene of human relationships to a joke. These simplistic parodies represent the revelation that a woman has a penis as a moment of disgust and revulsion. In other words, the transgender woman is an object of ridicule and the worst sexual turn off imaginable. That connotation reinforces the worst dehumanizing beliefs many non-transgender people have toward the transgender community. Even the immensely powerful documentary *Disclosure*, about Hollywood's portrayal of transgender people through the words of many people in the transgender community, single this scene out but misrepresent both the scene and its message. First, the camera moves between both Fergus and Dil. The film captures not just Fergus's visceral disgust but Dil's pain, the moment of self-loathing and doubt about her undressing and honest move toward sexual intimacy. Here the film mirrors and anticipates the 1990s audience's possible disgust or the public revulsion at the naked transgender woman.

But the film does not end with this scene, not by a long shot. Fergus's revulsion is only an immediate, almost automatic response, an involuntary reflex conditioned by social taboos. More important, Fergus loves Dil after the disclosure just as he did before the disclosure as before. Moreover, he is in London only because of a bond he formed with Jody, the enemy. Fergus, the "terrorist" had developed empathy for the soldier, a black soldier too. Fergus crossed two lines during the hostage situation. Boundaries and prejudices broke down. In one telling scene, he must take out the handcuffed Jody's penis so Jodi could urinate. Hardly romantic, but eerily intimate. Perhaps Fergus has emerging feelings about Jody. Maybe Fergus is homosexual or has an emerging homosexual desire toward Jody. Perhaps he sees Jody in Dil. Why not, he had discovered a bond with the oppressor, a positive feeling, an essential humanity underneath the political, nationalist, ideological rigidity.

In one telling scene, Fergus, under the assumed name Jimmy, cuts Dil's long hair and dresses her in Jody's old white cricket uniform to protect Dil from IRA retaliation. A clear sign of affection. Even more, the symbolism reinforces Fergus's deep connection to Jody and betrays any simplistic reading of this film as anti-transgender. On the contrary, the film affirms difference on many levels. Dil, like Jody, is black and the sexual orientation of gender identity dissolves for Fergus through his love for both Jody and Dil. Jordan's film challenges prejudices and barriers to genuine communication, friendship, and community: British vs. Irish, Protestant vs Catholic, Black vs, White, Straight vs, Gay, Male vs. Female, Male vs Transgender.

In the end, the IRA offers Fergus a chance at redemption for not following orders and killing Jody (Jody died by accident, ironically being run over by an armored British army vehicle). Fergus is ordered to assassinate a British Judge, but that never happens. Fergus appears to have had a change of heart vis-a-vis sectarian violence, or maybe he has just seen the value of love as acceptance and hope. Fellow IRA member Jude tracks him down in London intent on killing him for betraying the cause, but she is fatally shot by Dil. In a profound gesture of love, Fergus wipes her prints off the gun, sends her into hiding, and takes the fall for Jude's murder. The film ends with Dil visiting Fergus in prison and asking why he sacrificed himself for her. His response, "it's in my nature." What is Fergus's nature? What a perfect question to ask your class.

## LESSON IDEAS

Chapter 6 provides resources and lesson ideas about working with transgender experiences, communities, individuals, and art. This chapter focuses on a narrow topic about violence against transgender women and the psychodynamics of that violence. These works of art can be studied in a film class, a game studies class, psychology class, sociology class, and more. The primary elements to keep in mind are creating a safe place for discussion, playing scenes in class, and leading very close discussions of what the scenes communicate. You must pay equal attention to the formal qualities of the work and its psychological and interpersonal meaning. To get at social prejudice you need to elicit students' feelings and ideas around gender, and sexual orientation in advance. You also must present alterative readings, such as a gay reading of *Dressed to Kill* discussed above. Challenging prejudice includes and demands dismantling accepted interpretations of art to show the accepted perspective has inherent biases that are hidden by skewed readings. Dramatically different interpretations of the scenes such as hatred against transgender women on the one hand, and more nuanced understandings of a heterosexual male's encounter with transgender woman, on the other hand, will produce heated debate, but the purpose of such a class is precisely getting opinions and prejudices out in the open in a safe environment. Having students watch the Phil Donahue episode where he interviews Nancy Hunt (see resources) would also be an excellent entry way into discussing "disclosure." Archival footage and news reports all contribute to giving the film (*Dressed to Kill*) a historical and social context regarding transgender experiences in the 1970s.

## GAMES

*The Legend of Zelda: Breath of the Wild.* Developed and published by Nintendo, 2017. Action adventure single player game for Nintendo Switch and Wii.

*Persona 3.*

Developed and published by Atlus. A role-playing game for SONY PlayStation

## RESOURCES

Films/Television

*Ace Venture: Pet Detective.* Director: Tom Shadyuc, 1995.

*The Crying Game.*
Director: Neil Jordan, 1992.

*Dressed to Kill.*
Director: Brian De Palma, 1980.

*The Phil Donahue Show.*
"Interview with transsexual Nancy Hunt." 1979, https://www.worldcat.org/title/nancy-hunt/oclc/11458579.

# CHAPTER 19

# Teaching *Over the Top*

## *The Great War through a Game, Painting, Poem, and Superhero Film*

B Y FORTUITOUS CIRCUMSTANCES, A group in my class on "Superheroes and the Millennial" were presenting on Patty Jenkins' path-breaking *Wonder Woman* film (2017). I decided to do some extra reading about the film and came across a guest blog called "Tension and Fear" by historian Mary Gross (2018) about a game addressing the trench warfare aspect World War I. The game *Over the Top* (2007) allowed me to finally root this superhero film in real history and help overcome the popular misconception that superhero films are only escapist in nature. *Wonder Woman*, in turn, offered a lesson on teaching the Great War from an interdisciplinary perspective.

Nothing better crystallizes the horror and absurdity of the Great War than the nasty in the mud experience of combat conducted from the trenches. Literary scholar and war veteran Paul Fussell's classic book *The Great War and Modern Memory* (1975), especially the section on "The Trench Scene" (36–63) in Chapter Two, serves as an excellent introduction or induction to a lesson on World War I. Descriptions of the trenches, the line drawn between the allied and axis powers down France and Belgium, the conditions of living in the trenches with its fixture of fear, insomnia, shell fire, boredom, hunger, and rat infestation are harrowing and will have a strong impact on students (43). Many of Fussell's descriptions about

DOI: 10.1201/9781003201465-24

sunrise and sunset routines, such as "Stand to Arms," will be concretely realized in the art that supplements the lesson.

From this introduction, I play the abovementioned online game *Over the Top* produced by the Canadian War Museum. This short, moving game about Canadian soldiers' experience in the trenches gives students a real eye-opening account of living under extreme conditions. I play the game in class on a projector but also ask students to play on their own and report back with a short blog post or 1-minute paper. The game uses art based on historical photographs and captures the look and feel of the trenches quite well. Game play is simple. It is a form of interactive fiction where the player makes choices at key moments in the narrative and immediately experiences the consequences of those decisions.

Students responded passionately to this short game, and its mixture of mundane daily routines with life or death decisions, as one of my students writes: "In this game I was killed by toxic gas when I realized my mask was cracked and decided not to put it back on" (Zach). Any little flaw in equipment could prove disastrous. Troops moved only feet at a time, and, even then, at great peril. Most students reacted to the sense of hopelessness, the danger of sentry duty, and the endless waiting for the call to attack or the need to defend an attack. Lexi writes, "They [the game] also detailed how rigorous the work and sentry schedules were, allowing you to see into the lives of the soldier around that time. Lastly, it also shows how hard it was to cross no man's land as you have to choose whether to help your fellow soldiers or stay in the trench; I chose to help and ended up dying in the game."

Like Lexi, and most others who play this short game, the end game is death (Figure 19.1).

For college students that stark realization of death while role-playing a soldier, who is nearly the same age as the student, really has a lasting and sobering affect. Do not take anything in life for granted. As for Fussell's larger point, World War I brought an end to the enlightenment idea of progress. Eight million deaths for nothing (21). The philosophy of the absurd articulated by Camu, Kafka, and others begins with the historical absurdity of the Great War.

From the game *Over the Top*, I like to move to an even more authentic experience of World War I represented by Wilfred Owen's great poem "Spring Offensive." A British officer from Shropshire, Owen (1893–1918) died in battle at age 25, only a couple of years older than most of my students. The students' previous experience of playing the game as a soldier

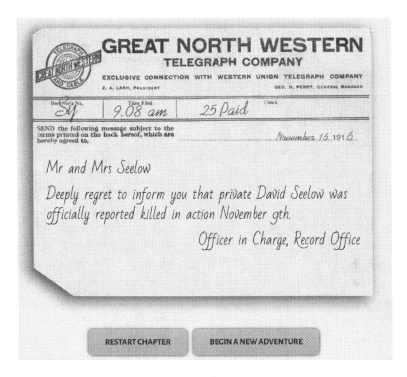

FIGURE 19.1   My death certificate. (Image courtesy of the Candian War Museum. © Used with permission.)

in the trenches gives them a much deeper appreciation of the poem and brings students into a conversation with the value of poetry at a time when poetry's deep voice most needs listening to.

The poem (1917) contrasts the beauty of spring's awakening—the seasonal rebirth, with the imminence of death, as the soldiers wait for the call to go over the top and attack while running straight into a maelstrom of bullets.

> So, soon they topped the hill, and raced together
>     Over an open stretch of herb and heather
>     Exposed. And instantly the whole sky burned
>     With fury against them; and soft sudden cups
>     Opened in thousands for their blood; and the green slopes
>     Chasmed and steepened sheer to infinite space.

You could spend an entire class discussion on the poem in the context of how the students experienced the game *Over the Top*. Perhaps, read letters of Owen about the war or have students write reactions to their initial reading of the poem. How would they [the students] imagine war? Perhaps, have them write a descriptive letter from inside the trenches as they imagine it to family back home.

After encountering the hopelessness expressed in the game and poem, I move to the no man's land scene from Patty Jenkin's film *Wonder Woman* (2017). The shift from game and poem to a movie is a shift to an entirely different perspective on war, not exactly romantic, but certainly hopeful, and purposeful. Diana's mission to serve the allies' cause confronts the horror of war head on when Diana moves among the soldiers in the trenches facing the German threat and their use of lethal gas. I show the *scene* in class and let the students experience the uplifting nature of Diana disclosing her superhero identity as she changes into her warrior costume, and rises, in slow motion, up the ladder from the trenches to lead the troops over the top into no man's land- shown in all its gruesome reality. Wonder Woman uses her bracelets and shield to knock off artillery fire. The superhero, and the superhuman nature of this idealized scene, shows how superhero narrative operates as a modern mythos, a system of belief that favors hope and possibility. It also shows the leadership of women in the most hopeless of situations, and military leadership at that.

In an excellent discussion of *Wonder Woman*'s mythopoesis, George Denson (2017) describes the magic of the no man's land scene:

> The scene in the new *Wonder Woman* film that people are crying over in theaters and raving about afterward happens to be among the most powerfully mythopoetic scenes ever filmed, at the same time it is one of the oldest myths to have been utilized by artists and writers after it had been invented by early military strategists and leaders. And while the scene does have militarist undertones, it is used by director Patty Jenkins in the name of raising the esteem for powerful yet compassionate women as heroes and leaders to a level equal with that of men for having won over a huge and adoring popular audience around the world. …Just the number of little girls and boys who will carry their memory of the magnificently courageous and assertive Diana of Themyscira defying the authority and violence of despotic men is likely to have a century of positive impacts on the future roles of women in politics, both as candidates and voters, as well as on the legislation of laws servicing and protecting women and their rights.

Diana Prince is a warrior, and after discussing this magnificent scene, including the brilliant score, and cinematography (see Guerrasio, 2017), I would also spend some time linking Wonder Woman to the historical "Amazons" by showing the TED-Ed (2018) animation on the historical authenticity of ancient warrior women based on Adrienne Mayor's research. This short lesson brings historical context to the superhero character and shows how the lost history of strong women can be rediscovered through contemporary film making.

Finally, Denson correctly identifies the iconographic proximity of Wonder Woman leading the soldiers into battle with Eugene Delacroix's famous painting, *La Liberté guidant le people* (1839, oil on canvas, Louvre, Paris) (Figure 19.2).

In the painting, a woman carrying the French tricolor in one hand and a musket in the other leads a group of male soldiers over fallen bodies toward victory. Her bare breast echoes the Amazonian warrior mythos. The woman, like Wonder Woman, has allegorical significance. She represents liberty from oppression, and as a woman, a liberation also, on the symbolic plane, from male dominance. Finally, the painting's iconography also foreshadows the famous Statue of Liberty gifted from France to America as a mutual symbol of democracy and a commitment to equality.

FIGURE 19.2 Eugene Delacroix—La liberté guidant le people, Eugene Delacroix, 1830. (Public Domain. The original painting is in the Louvre, Paris, France.)

This constellation of artistic representations of war allows students to experience World War I from a variety of perspectives: both as futility and as the triumph of democracy personified through a strong woman. Unlike a traditional history lecture or reading, art as game, film, poem, and painting will help students see and feel a distant war as something powerful and present.

## GAME

*Over The Top.* Produced by the Canadian War Museum/Musée Canadien De LaGuerre, 2007.

The museum website is an excellent resource for teachers.

## RESOURCES

Primary Texts

*Fiction*

Graves, Robert. *Good-Bye to all That.* Jonathan Cape, 1929.
  A powerful autobiography written with clarity and passion by a British scholar and author.
  Hemmingway, Ernest. *A Farewell to Arms.* Scribner, 1929
  A well-known Hemmingway novel about Frederick Henry and his love for a British nurse during the war, based in part on his youthful experience of war, but with a mature and powerful account of war's horrors.
  McCrae, John. "In Flanders Field".
  A memorable and well-known poem written in 1915. This poem makes the now enduring association of poppies with memories of deceased soldiers. Available online through the *Academy of American Poets*/*Poetry. org*: https://poets.org/poem/flanders-fields.
  Owen, Wilfred. *The Complete Poems and Fragments.* Hogarth Press, 1983.
  One of the most powerful voices from World War I, Owen's poetry provides some of the greatest war poetry of all time. The poem "Soldier's Dream" for instance, written in 1917, expresses his general perspective on war. It was written as he recovered from shell shock. Owen was the authentic voice of the trenches. The famous sonnet "Anthem for Doomed Youth" expresses the deep sorrow of soldiers and describes the funeral

rite of families suffering the inconsolable loss of young patriots. There is much information about the young poet at *The Wilfred Owen Association* website: http://www.wilfredowen.org.uk/.

Remarque, Erich Maria. *All Quiet on the Western Front*. Ballantine Books, Reissue edition 1987; originally published in 1929.

One of the greatest war novels of all time. This novel's told from the German perspective by a 20-year-old soldier Paul Bäumer on the front line. The novel shows the humanity of the soldiers from both sides while exposing the hypocrisy and cold distance of military commanders and the politicians who send kids into war while they rest in the comfort and safety of home far from the cruelty of the trenches.

Rosenberg, Isaac.

"Break of Day in the Trenches." A less well-known poem than the others cited here; nonetheless, a memorable lyric of life in the trenches. The online version can be found at *The Poetry Foundation*: https://www.poetryfoun-dation.org/poetrymagazine/poems/13535/break-of-day-in-the-trenches.

*Film*

*All Quiet on the Western Front*. Director: Lewis Milestone, 1930.

A classic movie adaptation of a classic novel. The film won Oscars for both Best Picture and Best Director. I have watched this film numerous times over the years and the film remains with me to this day.

*1917*. Director Sam Mendes, 2019.

A dramatic, beautifully directed film about a messenger crossing enemy lines to deliver a lifesaving message. Mendes's grandfather served as a runner on the western front. An authentic and moving film.

*Paths of Glory*. Director: Stanley Kubrick, 1957.

A brilliant anti-war film by the legendary director. The film shows the futility of war, but also the tragic reality of how commanders' scapegoat the soldiers on the front line to escape accountability, and literally leave those already putting their lives at risk at another level of risk, pay with your life, and if you survive any problems encountered, they are your fault.

*They Shall Not Grow Old*. Director: Peter Jackson, 2018.

An extraordinary documentary film that lets the soldiers' voice emerge to tell the story of the Great War. The film is immersive, moving, and unforgettable.

*Wonder Woman*. Directed by Patty Jenkins, 2017.

Discussed above. Wonder Woman's first appearance in Sensation Comics placed her in World War I, but she was invented to serve the allies as a symbol of patriotism in World War II, a female counterpart to Captain America.

*Fine Art*

Delacroix, Eugene. *La Liberté guidant le peuple/Liberty Leading the People*, 1830. Painting. Oil on Canvas. On display in Le Louvre, Paris.

Painted as his form of national service, the figure of liberty carrying the tricolor (France's eventual national flag) marks the end of the Enlightenment and the beginning of romanticism, at least on a symbolic plane. The painting's mixture of social classes signals the importance of a republic and the principle of equality.

# CHAPTER 20

# How "Memoirs" about the Iranian Revolution Can Help Change Stereotypical Perceptions of the Muslim as "Other"

## EXPERIENCING ISLAM IN IRELAND: A PERSONAL NOTE BY WAY OF INTRODUCTION

In the Fall of 1979, I was sitting in the living room of my then Irish girlfriend's parents' house in Dublin, Ireland. I had taken a year off from graduate studies at Columbia University to study Anglo-Irish literature, explore Ireland, and, of course, spend time with my favorite colleen. Sinead (all names have been changed for privacy reasons) came from a family of five. Her younger brother lived in London, the eldest sister in Herefordshire, England, married to a British Soldier, and an older brother was married and lived south of Dublin. The second eldest sister lived nearby, and Sinead lived with her parents. At the time I was staying in Sinead's parents' house using her younger

DOI: 10.1201/9781003201465-25

brother's bedroom. I looked forward to meeting Sinead's sister Kathleen for a Christmas Eve dinner. She was bringing her boyfriend with whom she lived, to the dinner. I was a tinge surprised that the sister was living with a man since this was a devout Irish Catholic family, but the real surprise came when Kathleen introduced her boyfriend to me. Farroukh was Muslim, but not an Arab Muslim, that too would have been a big surprise for me, seeing a Catholic woman and a Muslim man together, not a potential powder keg like a Catholic-Protestant match during those years, but certainly an atypical romance. The real surprise turned out to be he was a Muslim from Tehran, Iran. For those younger readers, just a month before our Christmas Eve dinner, on November 4, Iranian nationals, primarily student protesters, occupied the American Embassy in Tehran and took American citizens hostage. They did so out of hatred of the United States' support of the Shah Reza Pahlavi, the deposed Absolute Monarch of Iran from 1953 until that very year of my stay in Ireland, 1979. The Shah had been replaced by the exiled leader Ayatollah Khomeini who referred to the United States as "Satan."

I shook Farroukh's hand as he sat down next to Kathleen. Sinead's father opened the festivities with some Irish fireworks by saying "Do you know David is American?" An invitation to combat if ever there was one. We never fought, but neither did we ever become friends. Rather, we accepted each other out of respect for the sisters, our mutual appreciation of education, and an awareness that our countries' differences did not require personal enmity. Our tolerance grew out of personal contact and respectful exchange. Farroukh's brother, Basir, on the other hand, refused to be in the same room as me. I was American, and, in his eyes, by definition, satanic. The brothers' differing responses to me spoke to a complex Iranian response to the Shah. I genuinely had no real sense of the family's situation vis-à-vis their homeland but relocating to Ireland suggested to me that they may have benefited in some way from the Shah's rule. After all, they were very prosperous, lived in one of the best sections of Dublin, and had relocated to a western country. Farroukh attended the prestigious and private Trinity College. On the other hand, Basir did not attend college, followed strict Muslim rules, and strongly identified with the Ayatollah's fundamentalist principles. The brothers represented divided reactions to Iran's complex relationship with the West.

Most citizens of the United States and Iran obtain their information through a highly biased media's stereotypical reductionism. Given the continued hostilities between America and Iran personal contact between citizens does not happen often. However, another way to establish a rapport and understanding of the other that transcends stereotypes is through storytelling. Video games represent one such powerful storytelling medium. In a review of *1979 Revolution: Black Friday* for *Kill Screen*, Alex Kriss (2016) makes an honest confession about his and by extension many Americans' understandings of Iran—or rather, lack of understanding, and the subsequent benefit the game brought to him,

> The name Ayatollah Khomeini meant more to me as a reference to a joke from *The Simpsons* than as an actual historical figure. As an adult, I became marginally more aware of Iran's contemporary position within Middle East quagmires and U.S. international tensions, but my understanding of its recent history grew no more sophisticated.

Iran sporadically erupts into Americans' consciousness like a nightmare, such as the 1979 hostage crisis (1979–1981), the Iran Contra affair (1985–1987), and most recently the nuclear weapons threat (ongoing to varying degrees of intensity since at least 1981), but our understudying of the country and its history remain as incomprehensible as most nightmares do. For students in The West, Iran, known only through crises points, and then, only through the biased interests of a West that speaks from a position of assumed superiority, appears only a series of static stereotypes: religious fanatics, women covered by veils, the sexes separated (purdah), backwards, and monolithic. As Edward W. Said (1982) remarked, "the West sees Islam as one unchanging thing" (79).

Reducing a complex religion and a complex region to a binary of pro- or anti-American is just as narrow minded and counterproductive as Iran's seeing American only as satanic and decadent. Reductionist and polarized thinking about the other can have nothing but negative outcomes. Intolerance breeds resentment, which produces escalating conflict. Many Americans do not even realize the difference between Iranians and Arabs, let alone the diversity of practices within what we lump under the category Islam. Our willingness as a country to tie ourselves to the Shah under the pretense that he favored modernization and secular rule did nothing but reinforce our unexamined preconceptions that modernization is good and should be every nation's aspiration. Our monolithic thinking inevitable resulted in the result we ended up with a revolution and the establishment of a theocracy.

As teachers and professors, we need to take up the choice proffered by Professor Said, "...to put intellect at the service of power or at the service of criticism, community, and moral sense" (164). For too long the choice has been the former and we continue locked into a confrontational stance toward Iran. We need to move toward the latter option and work in an open minded, multidimensional fashion to better understanding and tolerance of difference. This is where, as Mr. Kriss suggests above, powerful stories about the other, told through the visual mediums of film, graphic novels, or narrative games can be a transformative in helping change biases into greater empathy and increased understanding.

This chapter outlines how art in the form of a video game, graphic memoir and traditional memoir produced by natives from Iran provide an opportunity for students to learn a wider and more tolerant way of looking at Islamic societies. The artists have a complex, divided relationship toward their homeland. Although native Iranians fluent in Farsi, the three also left the country and produced their work from the West, the United States in the case of Nafisi and France in the case of Satrapi. Expatriates represent the reciprocal nature of biases the West as other of Iran, and Iran as other of the West.

## REPRESENTING REVOLUTIONARY IRAN THROUGH A NARRATIVE-DRIVEN ADVENTURE GAME: THE POWER OF ART AS UNDERSTANDING AND EMPATHY

The Islamic Revolution of 1979 turned out to be a world changing event in the same way the Russian Revolution of 1917 had been. Iran was turned upside down. The emergence of an Islamic Republic replacing the Peacock Throne of the Pahlavi dynasty with the faith-based leadership of Ayatollah Khomeini forever changed Iran's relationship to the West. Americans, unlike me, who did not have proximity to an Iranian national, most likely saw the revolution as a rather bizarre event led by religious fanatics screaming "down with America!"[1] As mentioned above, one way to help students more accurately understand the hostility of Iranians toward the United States is by playing the game, *1979 Revolution: Black Friday*.[2]

As a player, you are thrown into the middle of actual history and experience it from the inside as Iranian student/photojournalist Reza Shirazi. As Julie Muncy notes in writing about the game for WIRED (2016),

> 1979's action – the revolution proper, is told through its bookend frames. The game starts post revolution in 1980 with Reza

developing photos of the life changing historical events of 1979. He has become a hardened realist. The game narrative then flashes back to pre-revolution 1978 dramatizing Reza the idealist on the streets of a nation in upheaval.

The revolutionary setting gives the story an immensely captivating and dramatic story arc. As a photojournalist who attempts to keep a journalist's objectivity, Reza struggles to stay on the sidelines, but inevitably ends up being drawn into the revolutionary situation as it grows more intense. Reza records the events of the revolution letting the player witness historical events up close. A brilliant game mechanic lets you move the camera around the screen taking pictures of the revolutionary scene on Black Friday. Black Friday refers to 8 September 1978 when 100 Iranian citizens were shot dead by the Shah's forces in Jaleh Square, Teheran. Historians see that massacre as the tipping point when the Shah's downfall was all but sealed.

As you snap the picture by touch screen or mouse click the photo displays historical facts giving each game event a deeper historical significance. This game mechanic serves to arrest the story as you step out of dramatic, diachronic time and into the contextual or synchronic time of actual history. What you learn as you snap pictures in the street gives context to the narrative. The game plays as a living textbook but filtered through the lens of a protagonist who both documents history and creates it the way a creative nonfiction narrative like Norman Mailer's *Armies of the Night* (1968) did for Vietnam. The in-game photos are juxtaposed with archival photos from the revolutionary period giving the game yet another layer of authenticity.

As creative nonfiction or documentary fiction the cast of characters populating the story are Reza's brother Hossein, cousin Ali, childhood friend Babak, and the de facto group leader Bibi (women by the way played a major role in the Islamic revolution and Bibi dispels Western stereotypes of the Muslim female hidden by chador). As an adaptation of choose your own adventure or branching narratives, the adventure story works off decision trees where player input shapes Reza's character. Unlike more fictional games, this game's historical context makes the decisions authentic and almost always morally ambiguous. Every decision matters, sometimes between life and death. Moreover, your choice of action has a time limit. You have but seconds to make a choice. This time sensitive aspect of decision making gives them urgency and realism. When you are on the street in the middle of unrest whether to throw rocks at security forces must be made immediately, but the consequences are long term. Students most likely will not have been faced with a revolution, but they will have been in tense situations—perhaps even with law enforcement—where decisions are made quickly, and consequences are profound. In this sense the game speaks to young people in a powerful fashion (Figure 20.1).

As Reza you are pulled in one direction by Cousin Ali, a provocateur who advocates the need for violence to dispel the Shah's oppressive forces, and pulled in another direction by your brother Hossein, a SAVAK, one of the Shah's deadly armed security force. This tension distinguishes the game narrative from cinema by forcing the player to make choices, hard choices, even tragic ones. That is the game's essence.

The game over screen gives the player a summary of their game play decisions (Figure 20.2).

This summary would be an excellent artifact for class discussion. In my case, the fact that I took a defiant attitude toward an interrogator but refused to throw rocks during a protest did not surprise me. These

FIGURE 20.1 The ultimate decision from 1979 revolution black Friday. (Image courtesy of Andres Perez-Duarte. Used with permission of InkStories ©.)

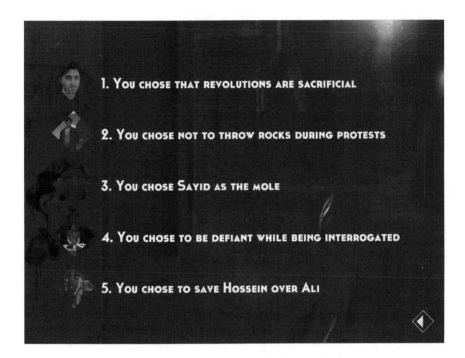

1. You chose that revolutions are sacrificial

2. You chose not to throw rocks during protests

3. You chose Sayid as the mole

4. You chose to be defiant while being interrogated

5. You chose to save Hossein over Ali

FIGURE 20.2  My game over summary. (Image courtesy of Andres Perez-Duarte. Used with permission of InkStories ©.)

actions were congruent with my personality. My decision to choose saving Hossein over Ali proved more unsettling. Yes, I am nonviolent so Ali's propensity for violence was off putting, but Hossein was a member of SAVAK, an extremely violent group. Furthermore, he was a loyalist to the Shah's oppressive regime something alien to how I typically see myself. I am seldom fond of the status quo. It was a quick decision, but; nonetheless, troubling to me. When do you turn your back on family? Any game that pushes you to confront your choices and reassess them has done a great job of educating the player.

## GAME AS HISTORY/HISTORY AS GAME: THE NEBULOUS NATURE OF TRUTH AND CLASSIFICATION

Ordinarily, I find classifying games an imperfect and even ridiculous exercise in futility, but *1979 Revolution*, like its brilliant artistic progenitor *Armies of the Night: History as Novel/The Novel as History* (New Directions, 1968), challenges classification in a profound way that can generate rich class discussion and exploration. Norman Mailer's text justly won the Pulitzer Prize for nonfiction. The text describes the 1967 anti-Vietnam protest march to the Pentagon. The march was a historical fact, and the people described all historical. At the same time, as the book's subtitle tells us, the nonfiction history is a novel narrated in the third person by Mailer, who also participated in the march. The book also won the prestigious National Book Award, but for Art. The text is simultaneously fiction and nonfiction, perhaps, that is true of *1979 Revolution Black Friday* as well. You can teach this ambiguity by letting students play the game *1979 Revolution* and then read one or even two historical accounts of Black Friday from two different newspapers or magazines. Students will discover the events remain the same, but the meaning does not. Maybe the meaning represented by the two accounts differs drastically. Is history true? Historians tell a story of facts, but facts are always mediated by language and perspective. Is 1979 a game as history or history as a game? Spend a class trying to find out and if you do let me know.

## THE VEIL OF TRUTH

Nothing angers or perplexes the West more than the veil. Azar Nafisi's *Reading Lolita in Tehran* (2003) and Marjane Satrapi's graphic memoir *Persepolis* (2003) represent two highly popular nonfiction accounts by Iranian women about the meanings of the veil from Iranian natives who later emigrated to the largely non veil wearing West. They are both relatively privileged women, and their writing reflects the lens of class status. Both experienced the Islamic Revolution. Satrapi left Iran at the emergence of adolescence and Nafisi left to attend college and returned to teach at the University of Teheran where she formed the book club which serves as her memoir's organizing feature. As a comic book or graphic nonfiction, Satrapi's auto-reflections also include a visual narrative making her text somewhat closer to the visually driven video game discussed above.

In talking about how third world women are perceived by the West teachers should keep in mind the caution raised by Chandra Mohanty in her article "Under Western Eyes" (1988). In this article Mohanty argues strongly against the valorization of a Western perspective of third world women and the tendency to represent these "...'Third World Women' as a singular monolithic subject" (61). She vehemently opposes our tendency to view the "third world" from a Western perspective that assumes its position as the center, the norm and defining standard. For Mohanty, the Western perspective, and she means Western women, ends up a totalizing, hegemonic discourse speaking from "privilege and ethnocentric universality" (63–65).

In helping students break the barriers of intolerance, we must help them realize there is no ethnic universalism and no single "third world woman." Rather than assume the Western woman as modern or "the ideal" with her freedom, education, autonomy, and sexuality, and the third world woman as enslaved, uneducated, subservient to the male, and virginal, students need to interrogate and think against the grain of stereotypes to reach a less extreme and hence more tolerant position toward Islamic women.

In this context the veil, at least from the West's point of view, represents what Mohanty sees as the homogenization of the third women and her reduction to a victimhood that requires rescue from the liberated West. Satrapi and Nafisi's memoirs address the veil as both symbol and material reality. Consequently, my comments focus on how the two women represent that veil and its perception by the West. As Professor Said remarks in his book discussed above, the word cover has a dual meaning. Cover as in news coverage or reporting on, and cover as in cover over, place a veil over reality and report only what the Westerner sees. The West only sees the veil not the reality behind the veil. Similarly, Mohanty argues that the veil does not "indicate the universal oppression of women" (75) and that readers must distinguish between the veil as represented in discourse and the veil as material reality worn by Muslim women. In fact, Mohanty shows (75) that under Islamic rule middle class women had a different relationship to the veil than working class women and that veiling oneself for a middle-class women represented solidarity with her "sisters" not victimhood.

## *PERSEPOLIS I:* PLAYING WITH THE VEIL

As with the game *Revolution 1979*, the graphic memoir *Persepolis* and the more traditional memoir *Reading Lolita in Teheran* give us an inside outside perspective on Iran. All three authors are Iranian natives, but they also all left the country and write or film about their homeland and its momentous 1979 revolution from an expatriate's point of view in the United States or France as may be. Moreover, they are adults remembering an earlier time amidst the upheaval of the late 1970s. In this sense the artists have a hybrid perspective that makes for an interesting learning opportunity for students living in a time of strong anti-Islamic sentiment.

*Persepolis* differs from *Reading Lolita* in a few central ways. First, the comic book or graphic memoir form places emphasis on visual narration and gives the memoir a continual dual lens. The panels narrate the story of Marjane growing up while the caption boxes frequently convey the voice of an adult Marjane looking back at her childhood in Iran as an expatriate living in France. As a coming of age story, *Persepolis* both identifies and distances itself from western readers. For most westerners, Iran represents the exotic other or orient as Edward W. Said analyzes in *Orientalism* (1978, see resources). A memoir gives westerners a glimpse behind the veil, a subjective look at life in a Muslim country, which traditional media does not provide. The bildungsroman becomes a kind of voyeuristic experience for westerners. Adolescence is presumed to be a universal experience and Marji experiences the same adolescent struggles that a western child experiences. She wears punk clothes and parties to loud music, puts up a poster of Kim Wilde, smokes her first cigarettes, and searches for western clothes on the black market. Young adults in Europe or the United States can identify with these "universal" experiences of adolescence.

Nonetheless, as Naghibi and O'Malley argue, unlike Nafisi's embrace of liberal western values, Satrapi subverts the identification with "universalism" through "estranging the familiar" (2005). Western adolescents have not lived through a revolution, and they see Muslims only through the distorted lens of western media which represents a privileged position of assumed universality and humanist values. The veil serves as an ideal symbol of estrangement and distance between east and west, but not through the valorization of western liberalism as *Reading Lolita* has been read by some leading scholars.

*Persepolis's* first chapter is "The Veil." The comic book format allows the author to juxtapose pre-veil and post-veil Iran through two separate but linked panels. In 1979, Marji is attending a coed school, learning French, and not wearing a veil (4); another panel, it's 1980 (3), she takes the veil and enters an all-girls school where only Farsi will be spoken. As a child the veil does not signify the oppression of Muslim women just a different situation. The bottom panel of the first page shows the small girls playing with the veil: skipping rope, using the veil as a monster mask, a harness and, in general, a play object. Naghibi and O'Malley call such scenes a slippage of meaning, where the text subverts western values or, at the least, challenges them.

A single panel that begins page 4 perfectly symbolizes Marji's hybrid identities. The caption reads: "I really don't know what to think about the veil. Deep down I was religious, but as a family we were very modern and avant-garde." In the illustration Marji's body is split down the middle, just like the panel itself. The left side has a black background, with white symbols of science and technology, gears, a ruler signifying progress, as in the west's progress and enlightenment (alleged). Marji's body is white, and her hair uncovered. The right half of the panel has a white background with black illustrations of Persian print and ornamentation. Marji's body is in black and her hair covered over. In other words, Marji identifies with both west and east. The veil represents not oppression, but difference.

Perhaps, the best way to help dispel western stereotypes of the veil would be a thought experiment. Ask the females in class how often they have been uncomfortable being around males either of their age or older. How often do they experience unwanted catcalls or stares or uninvited approaches? The day-to-day life of a female student can be very uncomfortable around being objectified, judged solely or predominantly by body image. Next ask them to imagine a day wearing a covering that hid their body where they would not be subject to stares and solicitations. That too will represent a sense of freedom. Hopefully, students will begin to realize that freedom and oppression come in different forms. You can be captive to an imposed covering or captive by uncovering. The veil is polyvalent.

Comparing Nafisi's memoir and Satrapi's graphic memoir makes a certain amount of sense, but they have very different purposes and need to be evaluated in very different terms. Nafisi has been taken to task for allegedly supporting a Western humanist tradition and values as the universal standard while criticizing, certain scholars claim, her native culture.[3] That's a limited reading. First, Satrapi, as a point of contrast, describes and draws her early life history from childhood in Iran through adolescence in Europe. She describes Iran in more detail than Nafisi because her story intersects, as she matures, with the events going on around her. This gives the story a much more middle-eastern feel than Nafisi's memoir. Hillary Chute (2010) reads Satrapi's style as the "…idiom of witness, a manner of testifying that sets a visual language in motion with and against the verbal in order to embody individual and collective experience, to put contingent selves and histories into form" (3). Marji's childhood play necessarily occurs in the context of revolution, the Iran-Iraq War, her extended family's experiences, and so on.

Nafisi's text has no such goal. The book's subtitle is "A Memoir in Books" and that's exactly the case. She tells of her experience inside and outside Iran primary through the lens of a book club reading novels that she loves. Nafisi writes this intellectual memoir as a professor and the books she chooses are hers to choose. They are western masterpieces (see the final section below) that speak to Iran through metaphor. Criticizing the memoir based on its alleged assumption of Western women's freedom as desirable and the Islamic women's "…oppression and backwardness" (Donadey and Ahmed-Ghosh 2008, 629) has its own assumptions.

The veil represents one symbol for understanding Islam and its relationship to the West. Nafisi introduces the veil in her very first chapter through Mahshid and Yassi who "both observed the veil" (12). Nafisi's focuses on Mahshid who she describes as more restrained in her wearing the veil than Yassi, who has a more relaxed attitude. Mahshid wore the scarf before the revolution and for which she was picked on (13). Since her mother was a devout woman her wearing the veil makes sense, and that she did so during the Shah's rule does not signify anything backward. It is a sign of faith. Yet this is how the feminist scholars Donadey and Ahmed-Ghosh characterize Nafisi's writing, "From the very first pages, Nafisi thus establishes a clear binary opposition between the enforced robe and headscarf as homogenizing symbols of women's oppression and the glorious individuality symbolized by diverse clothing and hairstyles" (629). That's a woeful misreading of the text. There is no binary opposition because Mahshid already wore the veil as a voluntary act and the revolution, not the author, homogenized women's public attire. "When the revolution forced the scarf on others, her action became meaningless" (Nafisi 13) not because she abandoned sexy, intricate hairstyles but because of faith. The opposition is between the veil as choice and the veil as mandate.

I want to briefly look at Chapter Two about *The Great Gatsby* to help students negotiate working with nonwestern texts. Donadey and Ahmed-Ghosh argue Nafisi's memoir reinforces the America way (643), but this argument has many unexamined assumptions as the critics claim Nafisi's memoir does. As the quintessential American novel, the story of the American Dream, gone awry, Gatsby is the perfect novel for America's secular values. Nafisi begins the chapter recounting her return to post-revolutionary Iran where she takes up a position teaching literature at the University of Tehran.

The homecoming prompts the writer to contrast her childhood in Iran with her student days in America. As a student at the University of Oklahoma, Nafisi participated in the radical Iranian student groups chanting and arguing against Western imperialism, but she never felt comfortable with such associations. She feels more at home with less radical, what she says were considered counter revolutionary writers like T.S. Eliot (87). There is a less a stance favoring the American way then there is a rejection of fundamentalism. "They [leftist movement] wanted the girls to cut their hair short or wear it in pigtails. They wanted us to avoid the bourgeois habits of studying" (86). Again, the author does not embrace liberalism so much as reject extremism. To see Iran as nothing more than religious fanaticism that oppresses women is highly reductive. Likewise, the counter argument that the American way is necessarily open minded and liberating for women is equally reductive. After all Nafisi wears "long dresses outside meetings" not miniskirts. Also one can hardly call studying bourgeois.

This brings up the facile charge against the memoir's book club structure. Criticism of Oprah's Book Club, which comes either explicitly or implicitly with this characterization of the memoir's organization, strikes me as ressentiment as Nietzsche would say. Is Oprah's success to be condemned as Western imperialism? Theresa Kulbaga makes such claims in an essay for *College English* (2008) arguing, oblivious of Oprah's history or career trajectory, that the female billionaire is a symbol of American privilege and Nafisi's memoir represents an "…edifying experience of difference while ultimately providing a life-affirming look in the mirror" (510). The critic's indictment of the "pedagogies of power and privilege" can just as easily, and reductively, be read as an envious projection of an academic's need for attention. On the simplest level, as a Professor of English, Nafisi teaches British and American literature. I teach the same and neither identify nor support imperialism anymore than I do fundamentalism. We need most of all to move students away from reductive readings.

*Gatsby* offers a contrast, in the author's view, between the revolutionary ferment in Iran and a story of personal betrayal. Nafisi dislikes political readings of texts. In this sense she is partly reductive, since no text exists in an apolitical vacuum, but she clearly knows her memoir is an indictment of Iran's theocracy. Nafisi opposes didactic reading of texts or seeing literature simply as an illustration of political praxis something like the Soviet's sponsorship of social realism. The veil inevitably became a symbol of the clerics' power (112) and that symbolism offers the opportunity to examine how politics entangles itself in culture to be absorbed and reflected upon through literature.

One of her students Mr. Nyazi makes the common, but mistaken claim about a novel's offering a political message, "…'what sort of dream is this? Does this suggest that we should all be adulterers and bandits?'" (127). Gatsby is not a didactic novel and Fitzgerald is not Brecht, but such moments allow for instructors to distinguish between writing in a democracy where freedom of speech is a right and a totalitarian regime, religious or otherwise, where such writing is banned. How does this change the author's approach to writing and affect his or her style and the text we end up with? You can also, in an education class, talk about why books are still banned in high school including *Persepolis*.[4] The naïve idea that the West has moved far beyond the backwardness of "third world countries" has limited validity given the recent #MeToo movement. The same with the veil.

In the end, Nafisi's chapter and her class does not represent *Gatsby* as a sign of American superiority or the "fictional heroes who defy circumstances in order to live their best lives…" (Kulbaga 508). How does that critic's statement describe Gatsby? Here is Nafisi's actual statement: "The reality of Gatsby's life is he is a charlatan" (141). Yes, the author can read Gatsby, and does, to critique a fundamentalist regime's restrictions on the individual, but she also reads the novel as a critique of Western dreams as well. In fact, her deepest reading of the novel suggests there is a connection between Gatsby's America and her students' Iran.

> What we in Iran had in common with Fitzgerald was this dream that became our obsession and took over our reality, this terrible, beautiful dream, impossible in its actualization, for which any amount of violence might be justified or forgiven. This was what we had in common, although we were not aware of it then (144).

This does not suggest any universalism, but rather shows a connection between two radically different cultures brought out by a great work of literature. Reading a novel, watching a film, or playing a game by a native artist who also has an equally strong foot in the West gives students a much fuller picture of "the other" than our media or textbooks present.

These kinds of classes can go a long way in challenging stereotypes and biases in both directions.

## WHAT SHOULD WE TEACH?

Academic critics of Nafisi provide a critical moment to reflect on what we should teach in college and, to a lesser but significant extent in the more regulated high school. Donadey and Ahmed-Ghosh argue that Nafisi's book and her course defend The Great Books Tradition, a version of core curriculum that represents male white authors as universal and essential reading for all students. They claim Nafisi promotes "…British and American canon as having universal value …" (637). That she claims her texts are great books is indisputably true, but that they are superior and universal she does not claim.

First, Nafisi teaches British and American literature, so why in the world would she teach say Naguib Mahfouz? She has not been assigned a class where Middle Eastern literature plays a role. The Western canon that even Harold Bloom clearly demarcates as Western does not claim universality.[5] It is a Western canon. A course on World Civilization would be different but that's not the case here. In my own situation, I have taught Introduction to Literature perhaps 30 times. Each time, I cover the major genres, and, as much as possible, the span of literature's history. Anthologies make such coverage relatively easy, but I have never been happyusiast asking students to purchase a 1,000-page textbook for $80–$100 knowing only a small fraction of the book can be covered. Additionally, textbooks reflect the preference of the editors and those preferences do not always correspond to the student body where I might be teaching at any point in time. Consequently, I make my own choices and they vary by year because of the changing student composition and the fact there is so much to choose from. Nonetheless, the one book I choose every single semester and which I consider essential to the course, *The Epic of Gilgamesh* (circa 2,100 BC) comes from the Middle East-ancient Mesopotamia. Thus, charges of Western superiority are projections of the critics. Granted the Great Books Tradition can be called conservative, but are we seriously supposed to jettison Plato, Augustine, and Dante or sticking to the English/American tradition, Chaucer, Melville, and Dickens because they are white males?

On the other hand, all courses in Western literature or civilization should be diverse. Consequently, the Western canon, or what we should teach, needs to be expansive. Teaching just white male writers does a disservice to tradition and to students. If Nafisi is in fact reinforcing "western, white, mostly male canonical literature" (Donadey and Ahmed-Ghosh 637), that's a legitimate criticism, but her course does not really require such scope. It is a more advanced and circumscribed scope than survey courses. She could have made different choices, and I would have, but I don' think she merits condemnation.

The bigger point for me remains what should we teach from the canon? Henry Louis Gates, Jr, (1992) makes the most cogent argument in response to this question calling the existing tradition of Great Books a reflection not of masterpieces but the master's pieces for the exclusion of African American voices, including slave narratives. As he writes, you cannot expect students to learn about the world when you "bracket 90 percent of the world's cultural heritage" (175). The canon must not be protectionist of "a great and inviolable 'Western tradition'" but nor can the canon just reflect demographic trends. Endless fragmentation Gates suggests takes us away from our common humanity (see pages 173–193).

In this regard, I maintain that including new media like the game *1979 Revolution: Black Friday* belongs in the curriculum just as much as film does. Likewise, *Persepolis*, a comic or graphic novel, also belongs. Comics may not be considered high literature, but how many times must we all be reminded that Shakespeare wrote predominantly for the Globe Theatre? The only way to prepare students for the globe is to bring them into contact and conversation with the diversity of the Humanities, games and comics included.

## NOTES

1. Iranians down with America chants have deep roots and are grounded in historical grievance that students need to be aware of when trying to understand the nuances of history. The coup that put the Shah in power, bolstering his rule as an absolute monarch, was engineered by the C.I.A. British and American strategists planned to bring down the democratic government of Prime Minister Mohammad Mosaddegh. It was an entirely antidemocratic action in response to Mosaddegh's nationalization of the country's oil reserves. In other words, Iranians wanted to control their own natural resources and British and American interests wanted to continue exploiting another country's resources. This antidemocratic initiative was

decided by two revered national leaders, Prime Minister Winston Churchill and President Eisenhower, respectively. Making students aware of this less savory aspect of American policy will give students a context for understanding the anti-American sentiments of the Iranian people and hopefully dispel stereotypes of the Middle Easterner as fanatic. We need balanced and accurate history if we are to overcome the polarized, biased thinking that perpetuates hostility.

2. The game's title provides a stimulating juxtaposition for American students to ponder. Opposition to the Shah often focused on his imperialist connections to Britain and the United States with their capitalist lifestyles, and economies, which many Iranians perceived as decadent and immoral. In this context, America's Black Friday symbolizes consumerism at its most brazen. Black Friday is the day after Thanksgiving, the official beginning of holiday shopping in the United States where citizens might line up and wait all night for a big sale on desired merchandise an evisceration of the holiday season's deeper spiritual message. Chanukah, and Christmas are too often reduced to tablets and tv. There is something unsettling about such consumerism that has no good defense. At the same time, as the revolution passes, Reza loses his idealism. Change can be harsh, and one kind of oppression can often result in another kind of oppression. Revolution, like most of history, has a fundamental moral ambiguity, a dark grey cloud that makes the sun's appearance too fleeting.

3. The most trenchant criticism of Nafisi has been Columbia Professor of Iranian Studies Hamid Dabashi who claims she is, "...at the service of the predatory US empire..." and her memoir gives justification for military aggression against Iran ("Native Informers and the Making of the American Empire," *Al-Ahram Weekly*, June 1, 2006). That argument has no validity. Nafisi offers a personal critique of the Islamic Republic she does not advocate, allude to, or even write about any military intervention. She neither dismisses Iranian culture nor Persian literature. Nafisi teaches English and American literature! Am I supposed to teach Rumi in a course on Modern American Poetry? Similarly, to designate a Professor of English as a native informer as if she is a cultural anthropologist simply stretches credibility to make Dabashi's own doctrinaire political point. For a balanced overview of the battle around Nafisi see DePaul, Amy. "Re-Reading *Reading Lolita in Tehran*." MELUS, Volume 33, Number 2 (Summer 2008).

4. *Persepolis* was banned by Chicago Public Schools in March 1993 apparently over a couple of images pertaining to torture. Banning books serves no one well. Schools need to exercise judgment in making sure material is grade level appropriate. Obviously, some works of art are too mature for a public school environment but Persepolis is not one of them.

5. Harold Bloom argued in favor of some clearly defined masterpieces in *The Western Canon: The Books and School of the Ages* (Harcourt Brace 1994). Although Bloom's title stresses Western Canon he does list outside

the book numerous ancient classics from India, the Ancient Near East, and so on. Bloom's problem concerns his dismissal of many diverse voices as being simple reflections of political trends, the product of resentment. They are not. I don't dispute Bloom's choice of great books, but they are not The Great Books. The aesthetic consideration Bloom applies to judging literature oddly fails to acknowledge that the aesthetic has always also been political. Great texts may prove to be timeless, but they are always of a time as well.

## GAME

*1979 Revolution: Black Friday.* Developer and Publisher: iNK Studios with assistance from N-Fusion, Designer: Navid Khonsari, Publisher:

## LESSON IDEA

I would take any of the exercises or activities in the Brown University Choices packet listed below and pair that activity and its historical context with the game, especially the role-playing activity. There are many excellent curricular materials listed below for teaching texts about the Middle East in the context of Middle Eastern culture as opposed to European-American culture.

## RESOURCES

Primary Texts

Satrapi, Marjane. *Persepolis, Volume I: The Story of a Childhood* (Pantheon Graphic Library, 2000) and *Persepolis, Volume II: The Story of a Return* (Pantheon Graphic Library, 2002) originally published in France by L'Association in 2000 and 2002, respectively. The English translations were published by Pantheon in 2004 and 2005, respectively.

This award-winning graphic memoir tells of Marjane's experience as a child at the time of the Iranian Revolution. It is a child's perspective from the adult Marjane's memory. In other words, you have a dual consciousness representing the revolution from a female perspective. The second volume begins with Marjane's exile as an adolescent. The story is well established in public schools and used as early as 7th grade but should be paired as suggested above with authentic historical documents. The graphic format compares well with 1979 which also uses a graphic novel style of storytelling.

Nafisi, Azar. *Reading Lolita in Tehran: A Memoir in Books*. Random House, 2003.

Another memoir about living in Iran during the revolution, but this time entirely from an adult perspective. Nafisi also went into exile, but as an adult, whereas Marjane was sent to Vienna by her parents. This book is only appropriate for higher education. Like *Persepolis*, you can use the autobiographical female perspective of the revolution as a comparison with Reza's male perspective, given that character is filtered through another Iranian expatriate, the game's designer Navid Khonsari, who was ten at the time of the revolution. Place these texts in conversation with Brown University's material on women's role during the revolution makes for very deep thinking about a world changing event from the eyes of Middle Eastern natives living in the West.

Websites/Organizations/Curricula

*Banned & Challenged Books. The American Library Association.*

https://www.ala.org/advocacy/bbooks

Comprehensive information about banning books in public schools, along with legal and advocacy information. It is an essential project given the recent turn of many deeply conservative states to ban books in support of political agendas that have nothing to do with the books most critics have not even read.

*Challenging Perceptions: Persepolis Beyond the American Lens*, Yale National Initiative.

https://teachers.yale.edu/curriculum/viewer/initiative_13.01.10_u

An exceptionally rich curriculum on understanding *Persepolis* from a non-Western perspective put together by Amanda Targgart.

*Reading Persepolis: Defining and Redefining Culture*, a seminar about "The Middle East Through the Eyes of Women" by Tara Ann Carter from John Bartam High School, provided by The Teacher's Institute of Philadelphia.

An excellent interdisciplinary curriculum unit on *Persepolis*.

*Teaching Persepolis*

> https://teachingpersepoliseng434.weebly.com/teaching-resources.html

> A compendium of resources for teaching the graphic memoir in high school.

*Why did Iran become an Islamic republic in 1979?* Fourth edition, July 2019. *The Choices Program.* Brown University.

> https://www.choices.edu/curriculum-unit/the-iranian-revolution/

> A truly excellent history resource on the 1979 revolution with timelines, videos, background information, maps, and primary documents along with a full curriculum including graphic organizers, activities, role plays, and lessons.

Books

Said, Edward W. *Covering Islam: How the Media and the Experts Determine How We see the Rest of the World.*
A close consideration of how western news organizations represent the Middle East from a highly biased perspective.

Said, Edward W. *Orientalism*. Pantheon Books, 1978.
Published during the Iranian turmoil this book should be a must read for any faculty member interested in understanding how the West has historically perceived and represented Middle Eastern societies as inferior, backward, violent, despotic, and irrational. Although controversial, as most thought-provoking works are, Said's text pioneered the field of Post-Colonial Studies and opened Western thinkers and historians to the imperial nature of its devaluation of the East. Professor Said was one of my professors at Columbia. I admired his convictions, his public role, and his immense erudition. Said was a true Man of Letters.

# CHAPTER 21

# Teaching about Pandemics During a Pandemic

N O EVENT OF THE 21st century has had more of a global impact that emergence and spread of COVID-19. The novel virus emerged in China and moved quickly across the entire globe causing massive fatalities, bringing public health systems to the breaking point, tearing at the fabric of societies, destroying businesses, closing schools, and leading to a rearrangement of how everyone conducts our lives. Variants have extended the virus's impact longer than most countries expected and challenged our collective fortitude.

COVID-19 might be novel, but epidemics are not. Contemporary society has suffered many epidemics such as Ebola, HIV, and H1N1 in just the last 40 years. Society and individuals have had to learn and adapt on the fly. The novelty of such a world-changing epidemic also presents opportunities for innovation, and new ways of learning, acting, and teaching. In this concluding chapter, I will discuss some ways to teach about pandemics in the middle of one by using art from an interdisciplinary fashion. Fiction, creative nonfiction, board and video games, and film will serve as case studies for a pandemic curriculum.

DOI: 10.1201/9781003201465-26

## *A JOURNAL OF THE PLAGUE YEAR*: TEACHING HISTORY AS THE PRESENT

The best way to understand the present and prepare for the future remains the study of the past. Daniel Defoe's *A Journal of the Plague Year* presents the ideal text for learning from the past through the creative imagination. Defoe's text shatters genre classifications and challenges readers to think outside closed systems. The journal obeys its title as a personal form of writing. Journals are normally nonfictional observations about current events from a first-person perspective. However, this journal about events during the great London Plague of 1665 does not bear the imprint of Daniel Defoe. Rather, the journal writer is one H.F. We have no name, just initials. Fictional initials, or maybe "real" initials, Defoe's Uncle Henry Foe. From the beginning, the story plays with classifications and definitions. Defoe writes as a journalist, which he was, and reports events as he sees them. He gives exact dates, and recounts precise events as if he were on the scene. However, Defoe published the text in 1722, not 1665. Consequently, the journal must be fictional, a simulation of journal writing, but one with historical veracity. You have a text vacillating between a historical novel and what we now call creative nonfiction. Finally, the great plague that occupies the text's narrative may have occurred in 1865, but Defoe writes the text during the appearance of another plague in 1720. The narrative then serves as a "real" journal of 1720 while simulating a journal of 1865. Fiction and nonfiction dance around each other in this complex narrative that, like the virus itself, dissolves boundaries.

The text's purpose as Roberts (2010) suggests has three dimensions. First, there is a survival narrative something akin to Defoe's recently published novel *Robinson Crusoe* (1819). Second, playing on top of the survival narrative is the practical handbook of how to survive, and third, a conduct manual. A novel mixed with self-help and how-to. *A Journal of the Plague Year* takes a major turn from *Robinson Crusoe*. "Where Crusoe articulates a 'foundation myth' that shows Western Man asserting his autonomy and dominance as if from scratch, the *Journal* charts his encounter with a phenomenon he cannot understand or control. *Crusoe* celebrates the resourcefulness needed to create a world from new; the *Journal*, the endurance to watch it fall apart" (Roberts ix).

As I discuss below, the plague or pandemic crushes efforts at individual heroism. Pandemics require collective narratives and community, and community is precisely what the plague tears apart. Inevitably, in writing about a plague/pandemic you have the framework of a disaster narrative. Rather than simply talk about fake news, you can have your class discuss the complications of representing the truth in language through Defoe's stylistic inventiveness. You can even go further and spend some time with Erich Auerbach's concept of figura as a way of reading (1938).

Auerbach outlines three major rhetorical modes: allegorical, symbolic, and realistic (i.e., mimesis). In allegory, one reality substitutes for another. Everett Zimmerman's essay in *PMLA* (1972) points to this reading, "Defoe ordered his factual material to suggest the spiritual reality that lies beyond the physical one" (295). True enough Defoe's story has numerous Biblical references and H.F. returns to religion's promise of salvation as the only possible way to survive the plague's random destructiveness. The symbolic reading resonates most profoundly with Defoe's text. Following the Church Fathers, Auerbach describes and analyzes how religious scholars read the Old Testament as a prefiguration or prediction of the life of Jesus. A past historical event as a figura of a future historical event. In the symbolic reading, the Great Plague of 1665 acts as a figura for the plague of 1720, but even more, and this would be the focus of class readings, for 2020. A 1720 narrative about 1665 as a symbol for 2020. Finally, Auerbach describes the evolution of realistic writing, subject of his masterpiece *Mimesis*. Clearly Defoe's "mechanics of truth inquiry" to quote Roberts represents the plague in a highly realistic, even historical fashion.

I would take the concept of figura and ask students to find parallels between what Defoe describes and what they observe regarding the COVID-19 pandemic. This exercise helps students learn how the past can be read as a lesson for the present and simultaneously show how many experts in our society have failed to read or listen to the past. Let me point to a few pertinent examples of why *A Journal of the Plague Year* speaks to us so powerfully 300 years after its publication.

## Preparation

The British government had forewarning of the plague's visitation upon news from Marseilles, its alleged point of origin, and spread to Holland where England received many shipments of goods. How does the plague impact social stratification and personal decision making as well as government policy? England shut its borders and forbid international travel just as governments have had to do today. The Quarantine Act of 1721 took further action similar to what governments have enacted today.

## Social Stratification

Time and time again Defoe describes how the wealthy vacate London for the perceived safety of the English countryside leaving the poor to fend for themselves. The poor have no place to go and few means to provide for their families when businesses shut down and provisions are meager (126–127). When the plague does hit full force and the poor need to run for survival, they end up living in any hut or covering they can find (129–130). In other words, the plague puts in sharp relief the social hierarchy and the privileges of wealth in a time of disaster. Part of Defoe's greatness, as Maximillian Novak (1977) observes (303), concerns his sympathy and identification with the poor. The working class and underclass serve as the story's true hero.

We see the class hierarchy everywhere today. The rich can stayed shut up in their penthouses and mansions with provisions for months. When New York City was hit the hardest the wealthy fled from Manhattan to the Hamptons and other suburban enclaves just as the rich fled London in 1665.

## Statistics as Truth and Lying

In Defoe's time, the weekly Bills of Mortality publicly announced fatalities just as our nightly newscasts do today. Statistics make clear the gravity of the virus and challenge disbelievers and deniers. At the same, time statistics and deaths can be underreported for political reasons. In New York State, former Governor Andrew Cuomo underreported deaths in nursing homes giving a false impression of the state's health. H.F. shows how the Bills of Mortality distorted the plague's gravity by attributing deaths caused by the plague to other causes such as Spotted-Fever. From May 23–30, 1665, of the 53 recorded deaths 9 were attributed to the plague but investigation revealed the attribution of 20 more deaths attributable to the plague, so in fact 29 of 53, more than half of that week's fatalities, were the result of the plague (7).

## Social Dilemmas

COVID-19 has forced hard decisions between keeping businesses open and keeping the public safe. During lockdown periods, many businesses went bankrupt or lost considerable revenue and many individuals lost their jobs. Depression increased significantly. Defoe, through H.F., crystallizes this dilemma in his own life. As a saddler he has a business and leaving London would put his business at risk (9).

## Contagion

Defoe spends many pages discussing how the disease can be spread by asymptomatic individuals and the risks this poses for the community. Today, this allows for discussion about mask mandates and vaccination, which in turn leads to critical existential questions about individual responsibility (64).

## Existential Choices

The honor system of trusting that individuals are vaccinated almost seems like playing Russian Roulette. We see people committing violence on plane flights and fighting in stores because they don't want to be told to wear a mask. They put self-interest above the public good. Under such circumstances how can an honor system possibly work? The idea of holding super spreader events where large crowds gathered without masks against public health advice would have abhorred Defoe. Nothing roused his anger more than the fact of people deliberately transmitting the disease and putting others at risk. H.F. vents his spleen at these evil doers.

## Quackery and Science

Like today, quackery proliferated in 17th-century England. Social media permits and affords the spread of misinformation. The former president and others touted drugs like Hydroxychloroquine, which medical science had shown to be ineffective in treating COVID-19. Defoe has some fun with preposterous claims of the mid-17th-century "Quacks," "Wizards," and "Fortune-tellers." "INFALLIABLE preventive pills against the Plague." "SOVERAIGN Cordials against the Corruption of the Air" (27).

## Dead Bodies

Defoe provided detailed descriptions of the "dead-carts" and the endless burials and mass graves including the giant pit in the churchyard of Aldgate "40' × 15' 20'" (52, 55, 170).

## Surveillance

COVID-19 has necessitated more surveillance of the population. The government must contact trace infections and require vaccination cards for individuals to enter buildings and events. Defoe catalogs the entire group of people who deal with the plague: Examiners, The Examiner's Office, Watchmen, Searchers, Chirurgeons, and Nurse-keepers (34–36) as well as marking infected houses and much more. All this tracking leads Defoe to the powerful observation that the city had become a "Prison without Barrs and Bolts" (47–48; see Bender 318–335).

### Self-Indulgence and Impatience

Finally, and most relevant to the 21st century, Defoe spends a significant time describing human behavior during the time of the plague's decline. As soon as people see a relaxation of mandates, and a drop in fatalities or infection rates, they drop their guard, throw caution and common sense to the wind and celebrate as if the incurable disease has simply disappeared. H.F. details the warnings and directions of doctors, "advising the People to continue reserv'd, and to use till Caution in their ordinary Conduct...," "But it was all to no Purpose..." (194) stores opened, people mingled, taverns filled up. Defoe's description could be written today in London or New York City and many other places. The nasty consequences of such human foolishness in 1665 is no different than today, "The Consequence of this was, that the Bills encreas'd again Four Hundred the very first week in November, and if I might believe the Physicians, there was above three Thousand fell sick that Week, most of them new Comers too" (195).

We listen no better today. Thankfully we have much better medicine and more tools to fight such a virulent disease. Nonetheless, as I write this chapter strains of COVID continue to infect millions of people. Teaching and thinking about such diseases from an interdisciplinary perspective helps students understand the wide-ranging effects of an epidemic in a globally connected environment. The disease impacts every aspect of the world we inhabit so students and teachers alike benefit from the wisdom and experiences of others.

## PARTYING DURING THE PLAGUE: *THE MASQUE OF THE RED DEATH*

Edgar Allan Poe's *The Masque of the Red Death* (1842) uses fictional horror to explore the very real horror of plagues and epidemics. He sets the story during The Black Death of medieval Europe, Italy, to be specific. History always provides lessons for the present, if we listen, and great fiction speaks across the years as well. In Poe's story, the plague is ravaging the country, a "horrendous pestilence" that takes no hostages. Prince Prospero, surely, an allusion to Shakespeare's character in *The Tempest*, decides the best offense is a great defense. He will wait out the plague.

The prince gathers 1,000 members of his court and they shut up in Prospero's "castellated abbey." Enough provisions are made available, and the guests even have splendid entertainment with dancers, musicians, comedians, and theater. A banquet fit for royalty. The scene makes me think of a big bash, COVID be damned, in the Hollywood Hills or maybe the Hamptons on Long Island or even Palm Beach in Florida. The rich can run to second homes and estates while the poor and middle class are infected, killed, buried, if fortunate, and mourned. "A thousand securely were within. Without was the Red Death."

Prince Prospero wants to wall out the plague, but our first lesson must be that you cannot wall out illness. Walls do not keep the bad element out; they trap it within. As in Jean Paul Sartre's famous play "Huis Clos," there is no exit when you are walled in and the haven of seclusion and privilege inevitably becomes the hell of narcissism and death. Around 6 months into the prince's experiment with his self-sustaining pleasure palace, he throws a masquerade ball. Venice, of course, is famous for masquerades, and here the play on mask and masque takes effect. A mask hides one's identity. It is a sign of secrecy; I am not who I appear to be. A masquerade is a ball, a lavish full out party, New Year's Eve style, with maskers at the masque. During COVID-19, a mask has other meanings than in Poe's story. A mask does not hide one's identity, but rather arms one's fellow humans against spreading infection. It is an inversion of Poe's masks, but in both cases, there is a relationship between masks/masques and death. A Spring Break party could serve as one instance of a contemporary inverted masquerade, nearly naked not fully clothed, beach and bar revelers celebrating. In celebrating an assumed immunity, the partiers can only spread what they try to keep away. No mask, no distance. We are, like the courtiers, special. The plague, the virus is elsewhere, not here where life goes on as life should go on. Denial, another lesson to learn, never succeeds. You cannot deny a biological reality out of existence. Even if you cannot see the virus, you know that microscopic droplet might carry the disease. Magic does not work outside magic shows. We need to listen to science, accept unpleasant realities, and work on changing them, not wishing them to disappear.

At every hour, the narrator tells us, the large ebony clock sounds loud and foreboding. The orchestra stops and everyone pauses—a still moment in the whirlwind of indulgence, "… the aged and sedate passed their hands over their brows…." Think of the abbey as a nursing home. The enclosure acts as a breeding ground, a kind of hot house, for the virus's spread. The pause is but for a moment. The party continues. Yet another lesson, listen to alarms and warnings. When the clock strikes take stock of your situation and make smart decisions. But no, the partiers fail to listen. The masquerade is just that, a masquerade, an escape from reality and the courtiers, like many of today's political leaders, exist in a morass of inaction. The prince feels secure. He is immune. He, like Shakespeare's Prospero, will manipulate reality to fit his design. However, nature does not do human bidding. Lesson 3: arrogance will reap disaster. The ancient Greeks knew that lesson well. A plague struck Thebes, and King Oedipus, the savior, brought ruin. He who thinks he knows too much knows too little.

Finally, the gigantic clock strikes midnight, and the year turns, but not for a new year in Poe. For Poe, the midnight hour brings the end. It is imminent. The revelers became aware of the "presence of a masked figure which had arrested the attention of no single individual before." As one expects with Poe, this stranger is dressed "in the habiliments of the grave." The language is clear, the stranger has been there all along, but no one paid attention. No one took note. He seemed invisible, but he was there, like a virus, everywhere. The invisible enemy. The revelers fall dead one by one. Death is imminent. You cannot wall death out. It is always already inside. Like COVID-19, the stranger is "untenanted by any tangible form." Substitute COVID-19 for the "masked figure which had arrested the attention of not a single individual before," and you have an allegory for our time. Of course, we have seen the virus before, in the form of HIV, polio, the Spanish flu, but we humans, us Americans resoundingly included, don't often take notice in time, the ebony clock strikes and we dance on, until "…Darkness and Decay and the Red Death held illimitable dominion over all."

As with most of Poe's stories, *The Masque of the Red Death* has symbolism rich with meaning. He is the acknowledged master of the horror genre, and in the time of COVID-19 we are living a horror story. The fantastic has become real. Have students from 9th grade through college re-read this story and you have a text for our times.

## PLAYING THE ENEMY: *PLAGUE, INC.*

*Plague, Inc.* (Ndemic Creations, 2012) gives us a perfectly congruent game for COVID-19. The mobile game takes a unique angle to pandemics. You play the virus with the goal of infecting the entire globe. Critics sometimes note evil characters can be more interesting than good characters. Milton's Satan in *Paradise Lost* gets much more scholarly attention than the Jesus of *Paradise Regained*. However, playing as a virus bent on ravaging the globe during a pandemic has a very unnerving effect. We have seen how COVID-19 rapidly spread west laying waste to so many thousands in country after country. Playing the pandemic from the inside as a nefarious, fatal disease gaining power can raise a player's awareness of just how deadly COVID-19 has been.

There is tremendous value in requiring students to play the opposite side of an issue. When I hold classroom debates, I prefer requiring students to take a position contrary to their own personal belief. It requires students to see another perspective and, consequently, builds genuine understanding. Our current Congress (2022) has been unable to practice this basic principle of critical thinking and the result has been catastrophic and paralyzing.

You begin play by choosing a disease and a ground zero for the disease. My last play through I chose China for some hyperrealism, but the next time I selected Algeria. As you infect people your DNA points accumulate. You use these points like you would in a combat game to strengthen your attack. The virus can be enhanced by methods of transmission, and symptom generation, i.e., making the disease more lethal. You can also frustrate attempts at a cure. As things get rolling, humans, your enemy, finally wake up as they watch the body count climb. The screen will tell you the death count just like the Nightly News' running tally of deaths from COVID-19. The game now becomes a race between your spreading the infection and countries' race for a cure (Figure 21.1).

The game's colors are classic Poe. Death is black. Red signifies infection. The red death claiming more and more victims in front of your eyes. The visual effect makes the denial practiced by some political leaders almost impossible. It is hard to deny what stares you in the face. This proves a great learning moment. The more leaders try and push COVID-19 out of the headlines the more people are likely to die. On a certain level denial serves to spread what the defense mechanism is meant to deny. Students might be more apt to put on a mask after playing this game.

The game's use of maps and graphs provides excellent tools for students to analyze, interpret data, and identify trends. This improves both students' visual literacy and information literacy. It also drives home the stark reality of infectious diseases and the necessity of a global response. At any point, you can pull up a country map to see the health status of that country. Toward the end of play I pulled up Australia, an island country geographically distant from other advanced countries and hence not easy for transmission to reach (Figure 21.2).

FIGURE 21.1 World pie chart of the virus's progression. (Image courtesy of Ndemic Creations© Used with permission.)

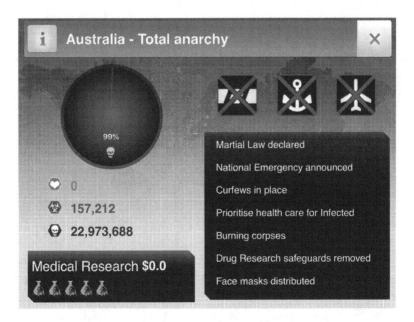

FIGURE 21.2 Graph of Australia destroyed by the virus. No place is safe. (Image courtesy of Ndemic Creations© Used with permission.)

Moreover, the country is resource wealthy and offers advanced medical care and top-notch research centers. Regardless, the plague's devastation spares no place. In today's global world, more than the medieval world struck by the Black Plague, transportation, business networks, and tourism shrink the globe into a small test tube perfect for incubating viral destruction. Comparing game maps with maps of COVID-19 spreading across southeast Asia into Europe across the Atlantic and everywhere else give students a graphic picture of how a virus spreads. Data from the Center for Disease Control (CDC) can be used to draw parallels with the in-game data to discuss response to the pandemic, both by country, and, with the United States, by state. This, in turn, produces a forum for talking about state politics, the relation between state and federal response, and national and international responses. Is the United States' dismissal of the World Health Organization a good strategy amid a world health crisis? The game answers that question for students.

The game also offers frequent updates like a "Fake News" scenario. For my most recent game play, I selected the Science Denial scenario (Figure 21.3).

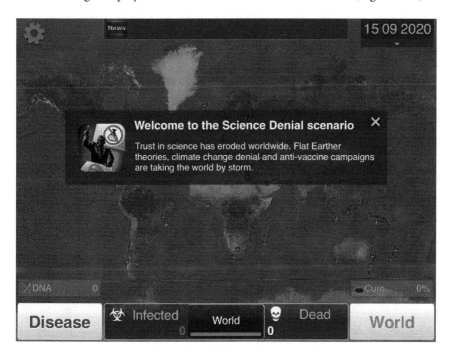

FIGURE 21.3 The Science Denial scenario: Eerily real. (Image courtesy of Ndemic Creations© Used with permission.)

What an excellent opportunity this scenario presents for students to talk about the implications of ignoring science and research. Conversely, such discussions might also push students to pursue research as a necessary step to solving any public health or other health-related problems ranging from the opioid epidemic to breast cancer.

## DARKNESS AND DECAY OR COOPERATION AND HOPE?

In addition to the rich discussion of a critical public health issue, these two texts offer less evident, but important political messages. Prince Prospero rules as an authoritarian leader. He may or may not be a benevolent dictator, but for sure he alone makes decisions. When he closes his principality, he chooses to protect or try to protect only the members of his court, i.e., the wealthy. How do authoritarian regimes handle a crisis vis-à-vis democratic countries, i.e., China and Russia as against say Italy and the United States? What happens to a democracy when checks and balances are eroded, and a crisis presents greater leeway for a leader to make unilateral decisions? Can one person make fair and balanced decisions for the

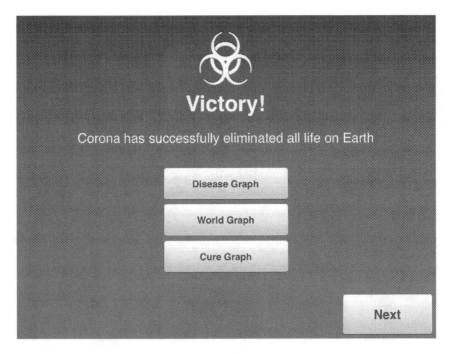

FIGURE 21.4 Game over screen. The disease has won! (Image courtesy of Ndemic Creations© Used with permission.)

many? Finally, in a global crisis that demands a coordinated international response between different forms of government, including adversarial governments, what will happen when some countries isolate and pull in their boundaries like Prince Prospero? I provide the answer with my Game Over Screen below (Figure 21.4).

We are living in a time where many problems are global and need a cooperative approach like that required by the board game *Pandemic*. At the same time, in the United States, partisan self-interest at the expense of the common good seems more prevalent than ever and ethical decision making has virtually disappeared. The United Nations issued an absolutely shameful report on the world's failure to meet a single biodiversity goal in stopping the destruction of nature.[1] Moreover, COVID-19 has interrupted progress on sustainability goals leaving greater equity gaps than ever before and an actual increase in world poverty.[2] It is imperative we help students think critically, make ethical decisions, and act in a global context or the result will be as inevitable as the fate of Prince Prospero's kingdom.

## HEAVENS TO BETSY: TEACHING *OUTBREAK* IN AN OUTBREAK

The release of the film *Outbreak* in 1995 dramatized the Ebola outbreak of 1976. It was based on the bestselling nonfiction account of the outbreak in Richard Preston's *The Hot Zone* (1994). Real-life suspense combined with major Hollywood stars like Dustin Hoffman, Kevin Spacey, and Morgan Freeman made the movie both socially relevant and a blockbuster hit. The Hollywood treatment keeps the viewers on the edge of their seats with fast-paced action, and tense drama in a race against time. COVID-19 has naturally enough returned people to this film from quarter of a century ago, but now much closer to home than the African continent.

The film conflates two aspects of the Ebola crisis in a dramatic way. The actual Ebola crisis erupted in Zaire (The Democratic Republic of the Congo) and Southern Sudan. That remains true in the film. The disease had an 88% fatality rate. At the time, the deadly disease was confined to Africa, but interestingly a strain of the virus was discovered in Reston, Virginia, just outside Washington, D.C. This strain of the virus (now named Reston ebolavirus) appears to have entered the country through infected monkeys from the Philippines. This virus turned out not to infect humans, but the fact a virus could be easily transmitted between countries made ripe material for the movie.

In the film, a veterinarian technician named James Scott (Patrick Dempsey) smuggles a monkey into Northern California. The monkey turns out to be the reservoir host of the Ebola-like virus called Motaba in the movie. The Level 4 disease (meaning highly contagious, fatal, and virtually unpreventable) spreads through the town of Cedar Creek, California. The entire town must be quarantined. Meanwhile the monkey ends up near the Jeffries family where their young daughter Kate makes a "friendship" with the monkey (by distance, but rather close distance). Kate (Kara Keough) names the monkey Betsy. The plot becomes rather convoluted with the military wanting to bomb Cedar Creek sacrificing the town to preserve the rest of the nation while also testing a biological weapon. Dustin Hoffman's Colonel Sam Daniels and his team undertake a race to find the host monkey and develop antibodies to the disease.

Major General McClintock (Donald Sutherland) wants to implement the Army's Operation Clean Sweep as a solution to the Cedar Creek "hot zone." Clean sweep refers to erasing Cedar Creek's population by bombing it, i.e., incinerating the entire village to ensure the virus does not spread. It's a purely utilitarian solution, sacrificing a small number of citizens for the larger U.S. population ("2,600 dead or dying Americans. If the virus gets out there, 260 million Americans will be dead or dying," as the Major General puts it to Colonel Daniels). However, the plan also hides a more sinister military conspiracy around the desire to develop and deploy a biological or germ warfare weapon.

Tseng and Wang (2021) have used the film to illustrate the differences between Major General McClintock's utilitarian philosophy and Colonel Daniels's deontological position, i.e., maximum good for maximum citizens versus do the right thing and, hopefully, save everyone. This is an effective way to teach the film with respect to ethical decision making in a public health crisis and extend the film to less Hollywoodized scenarios with respect to COVID-19.

For example, the debate between locking down the country in 2020. This debate represented a dilemma that the film gets at effectively. The failure to lockdown risks more and more fatalities, but locking down the country too long causes bankruptcies, depression, unemployment, and so on. Indeed, the debate between individual freedom and the public good has become acute in the United States, as Kristine Jenes (2020) writes, "The pandemic has been an urgent wake-up call for high income countries where survival now depends on limiting individual-centered desires for the benefit of others." The fact we have violence because stores require a consumer to wear a mask shows what a difficult time many Americans appear to have with respecting their fellow citizens.

In a final point about conflict between individual and group, *Outbreak*'s resolution depends on a very Hollywood story or myth, whereby Dustin Hoffman's Colonel Daniels performs heroic acts, including a crazy wild helicopter "dogfight" in the name of doing the right thing by finding the reservoir host monkey Betsy, retrieving her, developing an antiserum, and defeating Major General McClintock (an act of subordination that risks his career). That makes a great story, a blockbuster movie, but a counterproductive fantasy. Individual heroics will not save us from a pandemic, only cooperation and group unity required in the games discussed below can do that.

## A NOTE ON TEACHING INTERDEPENDENCE

Teaching the importance of cooperation and public good goes well beyond national borders as *Outbreak* and COVID-19 both demonstrate. Ebola originated in a small poor rural village in Africa. SARS-CoV-2 originated in a densely populated Chinese city in a country known for secrecy. Yet in both cases the public health threat spreads through global travel at an alarming rate threatening people everywhere.[3] But our global interdependence goes deeper. Ebola appears derived from fruit bats, the Reston version from monkeys imported from the Philippines, HIV possibly from chimpanzees, and COVID-19 probably from bats. We are linked not just transnationally, but interspecies as well. The globe is one and destruction or unbalancing one part of the global ecosystem unbalances the entire system until it readjusts, but the new "normal" or homeostasis most likely will be worse than the previous state of homeostasis.[4] *Outbreak* hints at this delicate balance in an early scene where a native tribesman who stresses how deforestation, expressed as a violation of the sacred, will have deadly consequences. Western science proves how this shamanic vision speaks the deepest truth, but we are not listening. Reston's torrid prose makes this intimate connection between man and environment clear in his essay and book. The alarm needs to be responded to in a much more proactive way. We cannot expect Superman to save us. Help students learn the value of teamwork, collaboration, and cooperation across boundaries of all kinds. Interdependent learning is a major step forward in that direction. Disaster movies are no longer just movies, so teaching is more urgent than ever.

## COOPERATION IS THE ONLY THING: *PANDEMIC*

The award-winning board game *Pandemic* (2008) has become very popular during COVID-19. It is an excellent fast-paced game that can be played in a single class period. Although necessarily abstract, *Pandemic* affords excellent teaching points for public health and related crises of international scope.

The game board represents a map of the globe with major urban infection centers. Players take on specialized roles crucial for fighting a global pandemic: Medic, Scientist, Dispatcher, Quarantine Specialist (specific powers are listed on the back of each specialist's card). The Quarantine Specialist is a new addition to the game reflecting our growing understanding of how to treat diseases. There are four disease cubes of different colors, four cure markers (vial shaped with colors matching the four disease colors), an outbreak marker (green with a circle and outward pointing arrows), and an infection maker (biohazard symbol). You draw from the infection deck to infect the initial cities. Initially 18 cubes will be on the board.

In a four-player game, which is ideal, each player gets two player cards. You are allowed a maximum of seven cards at any one time. A game's difficulty can be adjusted by adding more epidemic cards. Each turn a player takes up to four actions out of a possible eight. Four actions are flight related and the following four are fight oriented: Build a Research Station, Treat a Disease, Share a Knowledge, and, best of all Discover a Cure. A cure happens when you reach a research station and discard five player cards of the same color. Once there are no cubes of a cured disease left, that disease is eradicated. You win the game when all four diseases have been cured. Not easy.

Three major phases make up the game play: Players Action, Draw Cards (Epidemic Cards/Event Cards), or Infect Cities. Play starts in Atlanta, home of the Center for Disease Control. Obviously, you want to prevent an outbreak that occurs when a city already has three cubes of the same color. You move the outbreak marker to the next spot on the outbreak track and place a disease cube on each city connected to the original city that had the outbreak. Outbreaks happen fast and cures do not. If you reach the last space of the outbreak, track your loss. An uncontrollable outbreak signifies our worst fears, and these are fears COVID-19 has raised for many of us.

In a fascinating development, Matt Leacok designed a legacy version of the game *Pandemic: Legacy* (2015). A legacy game refers to an ongoing game, something like *Dungeons and Dragons* where you have monthly meetings of an ongoing game. In *Pandemic Legacy* the results of one game carry over the next game. What fascinates me about this concept is that the game parallels the reality of COVID-19 in a key respect. When we think we have achieved a measure of control over the virus with vaccines, containment measures, and so forth, a new strain erupts, Delta and, as of this writing, Omicron. The virus rages, hospitalizations increase, and social disruption continues at a high level. Consequently, the legacy game asks for the kind of long-range planning necessary in actual public health practices.

When asked by a reporter from the *Chicago Tribune*, "What's the biggest mistake people make when they play Pandemic?" Leacock answers, "They focus on short-term opportunities. They run around and try to put out local fires without thinking about a long-term goal, which is the only way they can win" (Borrelli, 2020). The same can be said about global governments' response to COVID-19. You cannot beat *Pandemic* without cooperation. You win together or lose together. That's also a message for today's policy makers.

When you move from the game to reality cooperation presents as a challenge. My students respond positively to the game, but they usually lose their first couple of rounds until they learn the lesson of playing and planning cooperatively. Public health demands many levels of cooperation. International cooperation to fight a globally spread disease, and implement needed travel restrictions, intergovernmental planning between federal, state, and local governments. The United States does not do well in this regard. Differences between Northern and Southern states mirror political divisions and make a unified national policy difficult to achieve. There are even conflicts within a state, like between the City of Houston and the state of Texas. Private industry must cooperate with public policy despite significant revenue loss and layoffs, and finally, cooperation at the individual level, a major challenge, is also necessary. In some sense our highly individualistic culture with its emphasis on individual freedom undermines the public contract necessary for an effective response to the disease and its rapid, often fatal, spread. Megan Garber makes this very point in writing about the film *Outbreak* which I discussed above, "*Outbreak* gets a lot wrong, but it gets one of the broadest things right. It understands that, in America, one of the biggest threats to public health can be American culture itself." In all, *Pandemic* is a superb game for introducing the importance of cooperative play and long-range planning.

## A POX ON US ALL: BOARD GAMES FOR VACCINATION

Like *Pandemic* discussed above two absorbing games from Tilt Factor also require cooperative play to defeat a public health crisis. *Pox: Save the People* (2011) and *ZombiePox: Save the People* (2012) have the added advantage of being designed specifically for a public health outcome and very targeted outcome at that. *POX: Save the People* (hereafter just POX) was designed by Mary Flannagan's Tilt Factor Studio at Dartmouth College to address Martin Down's (Director of Public Health) and the Mascoma Valley Health Initiative's (in New Hampshire, home of Dartmouth) need for better public education about vaccination. An admirable outcome, increase vaccination rates in a specific region of a state.

The extraordinarily fast development of COVID-19 vaccines hit something of a stonewall with American's resistance to vaccination. The anti-vaccination movement has a strong voice and some celebrity endorsements as well. Additionally, social media today has a propensity to spread misinformation about vaccinations. Finally, certain extremist voices fueled by conspiracy thinking, a distrust of science and government, and a radical political agenda have frustrated vaccination efforts that were not present during vaccinations over polio or measles for instance. Given the fact, vaccination rates are the best defense against the spread of a virus such a game has a an immediacy not many games have.

POX is a fast-paced game (half an hour play time) for 1–4 people. Two disease drop points (patients zero and 1) begin the game. Players must stop the disease's spread and increase vaccination rates. The game plays on large game mat. There are 50 blue vaccination cards, 40 red infection chips, 20 spread cards, 8 outbreak cards, and 5 black death chips. The POX cards determine the direction of the disease's spread or an outbreak. For example, if a card says spread the disease north, you put two red chips upward on the mat. If a person in the spread path has been vaccinated, then they are protected. Players are also presented with a choice between vaccinating three uninfected people or curing and vaccinating one person. These decisions constitute a key aspect of strategic thinking. Into the mix, you must consider the yellow chips scattered around the mat. These chips are present at the start of play and represent vulnerable populations like infants. It is imperative to protect these people, which immediately transfers to COVID-19 prioritizations in vaccinating the elderly, those who are compromised by certain illnesses like heart disease and so on. In this game, the vulnerable cannot be vaccinated so they are disease targets.

If an infected person is surrounded by other infected people that person dies, and the chip becomes black.

As play continues the disease spreads more quickly. You need to use a containment strategy. There is always a chance you will draw an outbreak card. In this event you must match the picture on the card with the same looking person on the mat. An outbreak can occur in a healthy area of the mat making containment difficult. Players can also set the game's difficulty level by determining how many deaths are allowed before you lose the game. That decision is quite strategic. A win state requires a total containment of the disease. The more vaccinations the greater the opportunity for herd immunity, and the more likely the virus will evaporate, but as proves true with diseases we thought to have been eradicated, a falloff in vaccination rates can result in the return of long dormant diseases.

Cooperation is key. Vaccinate a neighborhood so no disease can find room to spread there, and you are rewarded with the ability to vaccinate twice as many people. As with *Pandemic* you live or die as a team, a neighborhood, a nation, a world. A final important point covers the inverse relationship between cooperative play and heroism. As I discussed above, the movie *Outbreak* stressed heroism, the individualism of Lt. Colonel Daniels. That's an American myth, comforting, but fantasy. You cannot beat an outbreak accept as a group, a design point emphasized by Dr. Flanagan (2011), "focusing on the vexing question of how to reward players in collaborative and co-operative games, we had to decided early on that it would be inappropriate for the game to feature a 'hero' character or some other individual who would 'win' by preventing disease in the community" (p. 3). This is one case where a game speaks better than a movie about the realities of public health. A collective hero. That is what the game strives for and that's what we need to strive for during a pandemic.

*ZombiePox* is basically the same game as *POX: Save the People* with a literary horror twist, but an important twist. The earlier public health game is now framed by a fictional world consonant with today's zombie-obsessed audiences. This fictionalization of the game supports Tiltfactor's model of persuasive game design where an indirect approach to changing attitudes or behaviors works better than a direct impact game that raises players' self-defenses and mitigates against actual change. In fact, Flanagan (2016) states,

> ...the use of a more distanced, metaphoric representation of disease was not only effective in shifting attitudes toward a real-life

> health policy issue, but indeed, even more effective than the less distanced, realistic narrative at forging a bond of compassion between players and the real-life individuals symbolized by zombies in the game (187).

There is also something refreshing about fighting zombies as a medical team with vaccinations as a weapon instead of gun-toting soldiers or citizens gone wild.

## CONTAGION, COVID-19, AND THE FUTURE

No work of art has generated more commentary during COVID-19 than Steven Soderbergh's *Contagion* released over a decade ago in 2011. Unlike *Outbreak*, *Contagion* is grounded in science; Dr. Ian Lipkin from Columbia University being one of the film's primary advisors (Offit, 2011).[5] Even the familiar Dr. Sanja Gupta, CNN's chief medical correspondent appears in the film as himself. The film climbed into the top ten rentals on iTunes (Kelly 2020). A mixture of fascination and fear seems to attract the large audience seeking comfort and understanding of the COVID-19's menace. Part disaster movie, part medical drama, and part apocalyptic science realism, the movie provides a perfect vehicle for classroom discussion about pandemics: how they emerge, their human impact, how to cope with them, and how to defeat such a gargantuan foe.

The film's fictional MEV-1 (meningoencephalitis virus-1) virus is modeled on the actual Nipah virus discovered in Malaysia among pig farmers (Andi-Lolo, 2021). This realism has a very unsettling effect on the audience. The film begins with a black screen- a horror film trope, as we hear a cough. This could be us, out in public, not knowing who has the virus. The invisible threat in hearing distance, the cough a warning, war's alarm, or just an everyday cough? No, this is a cough of distress, an ill person suffering from a respiratory ailment. The camera slowly reveals Beth Emhoff played by Gwyneth Paltrow sitting at a Chicago airport. Chicago is middle America, the crossroads of the country, one of the world's busiest airports, a place of maximum human traffic. The slow-motion camera work dramatizes the threat Beth unwittingly represents to the people running about or lingering in this congested space. She is patient zero, the index patient for the disease and her hand reaches for peanuts, takes out a credit card, and passes it to the cashier. She has just gotten off the phone with a lover, and all these contacts and touches pose imminent danger to others. Soon

Beth will return home to Minneapolis where she passes the disease to her 5-year-old son. Beth soon passes. A major figure already gone just minutes into the film. This tragedy strikes home.

The camera's slow progression between objects stresses how much COVID-19 brings us back into a relationship with our bodies. As Annu Dahiya discusses (2020), contagion is a phenomenology of touch. Our safety resides in social distance from others, in constantly washing our hands, not touching surfaces unless they are thoroughly sanitized. In the classroom, if we were in a classroom, papers would not be passed up from students or handed out by instructors. Every contact displaced to the virtual world of a Learning Management System. In one of the film's staged instructional scenes, epidemiologist Dr. Erin Mears played beautifully by Kate Winslet, talks to officials in the Minnesota Health Department about fomites. A fomite is a surface that has been contaminated and can become a transmission site for the virus. We also learn how often we touch our face, a few thousand times a day. Again, the virus makes us acutely aware of the embodied self. A philosophy class could spend a few weeks discussing this film through the lens of Maurice Merleau Ponty's brilliant, but underappreciated *Phenomenology of Perception* (1945).

Another early moment in the film, where Soderbergh's skill plays such a prominent role, is the editing. After disclosing Beth's touch of death in slow motion the film cuts between various urban centers, mega cities—hubs, or in this case, hot beds of contagion. These are potential super spreader sites: Tokyo, Hong Kong, Minneapolis, London, and so on. This cutting between urban hubs reinforces the global nature of the world and how rapidly a virus can spread from Asia to North America to Africa and South America. The world has shrunk, and we are all living in a potential hot bed of contagious disease.

Additionally, the global network is susceptible in other ways. As we know all too well, COVID-19 has severely disrupted supply chains resulting in a scarcity of goods and high prices. Although COVID-19 has not led to the social chaos represented in the film by wild looting of stores, it has brought to the surface unpleasant social realities. For one, the high number of people who falsely think not wearing a mask is a civil liberty putting others at risk, including their own families. Likewise, the anti-vaxers, uninformed, and dangerous. In terms of scarcity, the virus, like in Defoe's time centuries before, shows how easily the wealthy can escape to their bubble of entitlement—running to the Hollywood Hills or

Hamptons while most of us must fight the realities our lack of privilege does not shelter us from. When we shelter in place we are not surrounded by stockpiles of food and a short stroll to the pool. These two points should be central to class discussions: the rights of the individual vs. the safety of the public, and the privileged few vs. the vulnerable many. In both cases, as Owen Gleiberman (2020) observes, the virus is "…eating away society from the inside." The virus contributes to social implosion showing the internal weaknesses hidden from 'normal' everyday social functioning.

Three more aspects of the film allow for rich discussions. First, there is the central role played by rogue blogger Alan Krumwiede (Jude Law). Krumwiede anticipates the prominence of new entertainers like Alex Jones and Tucker Carlson with their propensity for spreading misinformation. Krumwiede is a charlatan. He feeds on sensationalism and social dissension, always seeking attention; a snake oil salesman who doesn't use his own product (a phony homeopathic "cure" forsythia). Krumwiede personifies the social media's misinformation engine. In a debate with CDC head Dr. Ellis Cheever, Cheever, played by Laurence Fishburne, calls out Krumwiede's fear mongering, "In order to get scared, all you have to do is come in contact with a rumor, or the television, or the internet. I think what Mr. Krumwiede is is far more dangerous than the disease." Indeed, misinformation infects minds, which in turn, infects behavior that threatens the entire public's safety.

Alissa Wilkinson, writing for *Vox* (2020) perfectly characterizes how the film represents social media's danger. "*Contagion* reminds us that the structure of the internet allows bad information to spread in a way that uncannily mimics a very contagious virus." That statement applies just as well to COVID-19. We are fighting two formidable foes, the virus and the communication platforms enabled by the Internet.

A second, much more positive aspect of the film addresses and reevaluates the nature of heroism. Western society since the Middle Ages, and most emphatically in American society, props up the individual, not the group. The great hero saves society. The superhero who rises above all obstacles in a heroic effort that brings the world back from the brink of chaos to safety and health. *Outbreak*, discussed above, caters to this myth in typical Hollywood fashion with the wildly unrealistic heroism of Dustin Hoffman's Colonel Sam Daniels.

Students will see these heroes on television, in movies and video games, novels, comic books, and sports fields, but what they rarely see is the community as heroic. During COVID-19 we finally acknowledged the true heroes as the front-line medical workers with their superhero costumes of hazmat-like protection as they risked their lives to help save others. In New York City, the windows of skyscrapers opened as people cheered the EMT workers, the nurses, physicians, and many others who allowed the world to go on. Behind the scenes, scientists and researchers developed vaccines in an astonishingly short time. The same in *Contagion*. Although operating outside protocol, the scientist Dr. Ian Sussman (based on Columbia University's Dr. Ian Lipkin) played by Elliot Gould shows the potential for developing a vaccine to defend MEV-1 and Dr. Ally Hextall (Jennifer Ehle) tests the vaccine on herself. Dr. Jonas Salk did the same with his polio vaccine miracle. The true heroes of *Contagion* are the medical workers, the scientists, and the government workers who cooperate and put the health of others over self-interest. It's a rare message, but a message students should hear loud and clear. The public good needs the good of the public.

Finally, the film concludes by asking us to move out from the human community of cities and nations to the entire globe. We are not just a global human community, but also a global community. Our relationship with other species is one of interdependence. We are a global ecosystem, and the delicate balance of life requires a recognition and application of that interdependence which we currently do not have. That is something students need to acknowledge and act upon or the balance of life that we tightrope along will be thrown off the tightrope into the void.

A bat drops a piece of food into a pig pen. The pig eats the food containing the bat's virus. The genomes recombine. The pig is sold into the voracious food chain. He is butchered and served at a casino where the chef shakes hands with Beth and the contagion kicks off its path of destruction. The bat's food ended up in the pig pen only because its natural habitat had been disturbed by yet more human development, more churning up the earth's finite resources. It is Beth's company that ultimately unleashes the terror and there is a terrible poetic justice to that fact. We have become the executioner of our own death sentence. As 2022 progresses, we are being brought up to the gallows. Human arrogance and shortsightedness no longer work. Selfish consumption will end with us choking on our own self-interest, sooner, not later. Let's hope the world has an ending like the movies, but we know Hollywood endings are fictions. We will need today's students to work like the front-line professionals and dedicated governmental servants of *Contagion*, or the roulette wheel we have spun will not land on our number.

## NOTES

1. Celebrities have influence on the public's perception of issues. Although they are not obligated to take any position, they are ethically obligated to act in a responsible way. In other words, as Stan Lee authored way back in 1962, "With great power comes great responsibility." Three superstar athletes' unvaccinated status present an interesting discussion for classes. Brooklyn Nets superstar guard Kyrie Irving is the only one of the three that appears responsible vis-à-vis the public. He accepted the team's decision that he was not allowed to play in any games until he was vaccinated, or New York City vaccination requirements changed (see, Axson, Scooby. "What we know: Brooklyn's Kyrie Irving explains vaccination status in Instagram live post." *USA Today*, October 14, 2021). At the same time, Irving acknowledged that he was not really prepared for the consequences. This changed mid-season 2021–2022 because of the team's active player shortage; however, Irving has remained true to his beliefs without making any public pronouncements. Tennis superstar Novak Djokovic, on the contrary, hosted an unsanctioned tennis mini tour, The Adria Tour, where he and several others including his wife tested positive (June 23, 2020). He also asked for a medical exemption to play in the Australian Open (January 2022), using his status to achieve special treatment (see Layton, Jeremy. "Novak Djokovic making things 'awkward' after arriving at Australian Open." *New York Post*, 1/11/2022; ultimately the Australian government revoked his visa and Djokovic did not play). Finally, Green Bay Packer's sensational quarterback Aaron Rodgers, who also appears in many high-profile commercial advertisements, tried to defend his unvaccinated status on public radio and elsewhere with misinformed information bordering on quackery. Rodgers was tested positive and missed one game during the 2021 season. See, Rivera, Joe. "Aaron Rodgers COVID comments: Timeline of Packers QB's vaccine drama from 'immunized' to COVID toe'." *Sporting News*, 12/25/2021. See the Lesson Ideas below for a way to incorporate ethics and responsibility in a lesson.
2. Measles had been declared eradicated in the United States in 2000, but by 2019, the United States reported 1,282 cases. Measles has been imported from travel abroad, but communities of unvaccinated people can also cause outbreaks of this resurgent disease (Center for Disease Control report on Measles, https://www.cdc.gov/measles/cases-outbreaks.html).
3. "World fails to meet a single target to stop destruction of nature – UN report," *The Guardian*, 15/09/2020, retrieved from https://www.theguardian.com/environment/2020/sep/15/every-global-target-to-stem-destruction-of-nature-by-2020-missed-un-report-aoe, 9/16/2020. Web.
4. "Sustainable Devolvement Goals Report 2020," *The United Nations*, retrieved from https://unstats.un.org/sdgs/report/2020/, September 18, 2020. Web.
5. In addition to Dr. Offit mentioned above, several experts have weighed in on the comparison between MEV-1 and COVID-19. These articles provide material for informed class discussions. See, Garry, Robert F. "*Contagion* (the movie) Reconsidered in the Time of COVID-19." March 19, 2020, *Sloan Science & Film, The Museum of the Moving Image*, http://www.scienceandfilm.org/articles/3294/contagion-the-movie-reconsidered-in-the-time-of-covid-19

and Rogers, Kristen. "'Contagion' vs. coronavirus: The film's connections to a real life pandemic." *CNN Philippines*, April 3, 2020, https://www.cnnphilippines.com/entertainment/2020/4/3/contagion-movie-versus-coronavirus.html. Web.

## LESSON IDEAS

My primary recommendation here is to use any of the games, novels, nonfiction, or films in juxtaposition to COVID-19. There pairings will add depth and context to our ability to understand and cope with contagious diseases which will continue, and most likely, intensify in the future.

1. Consider having students write their own "Journal of the COVID Year" or now in retrospect, write an account of their experience in the style of Defoe on "Reflections on my year during COVID-19."

2. Have students rotate between playing *Pandemic* and *Pox: Save the People* then compare their experiences followed by a reflection on the importance of cooperation in problem solving.

3. Write about quarantine in relation to Poe's story or connect the story to stories of Spring Break at the height of the pandemic. Finally, how does wearing a mask contribute to our sense of self during a pandemic?

## GAMES

*Pandemic.*

> Developed and designed by Matt Leacock and published by Z-Man Games, Inc., 2008. Board game for 2–4 players, approximately 45–60 minutes playtime.

*Pandemic Legacy.*

> Designers: Rob Daviau and Matt Leacock. Publisher: Z-Man Games, Inc., 2015. 12–24 sessions 60 minutes each for 2–4 players.

*Plague, Inc.*

> Ndemic Creations, 2012. Video game. Fast paced mobile strategy game with multiple scenarios.

*POX: Save the People.*

> Designed by Zara Downs, Mary Flanagan, Max Seidman, 2011. Cooperative strategy board game for 1–4 people.

*ZombiePox.*

> Developed and published by Tiltfactor. Designed by Zara Downs, Mary Flanagan, Max Seidman, 2012. Cooperative strategy board game for 1–4 people.

## RESOURCES

### Primary Texts

*Contagion.* Directed by Steven Soderbergh. Warner Brothers, 2011. Film.

Defoe, Daniel. *A Journal of the Plague Year.* Edited with Notes by Louis Landa. Oxford World's Classics, 1990, Revised edition, 2010. Originally published in 1722. Print.

*Outbreak.* Directed by Wolfgang Peterson. Warner Brothers, 1995. Film.

Poe, Edgar Allan. *The Masque of the Red Death*, in *The Short Fiction of Edgar Allan Poe: An Annotated Edition*, edited by Stuart Levine and Susan Levine, University of Illinois Press, 1950.

### Website

*Tilt Factor*

> https://tiltfactor.org/

> An excellent game studio led by Distinguished Professor Mary Flanagan based at Dartmouth College. The studio specializes in evidence-based games for social and behavioral change.

### Books and Articles

Andi-Lolo, Indah. "Nipah Virus Inspired the Film *Contagion*." *PATH*, November 1, 2021. https://www.path.org/articles/nipah-virusfilm-contagion-vaccine/.

Camu, Albert. *La Peste.* Gallimard, 1947. English translation by Stuart Gilbert, Vintage, 1991.

A brilliant novel about a plague spreading across Algeria. Camu's text is a profound meditation on the human condition and morality.

Defoe, Daniel. *A Journal of the Plague Year*. Norton Critical Edition. Edited by Paula R. Backscheider. W.W. Norton & Company, Inc., 1992.
The Norton Critical edition has many primary documents related to Defoe's text and the period he wrote about.

Illing, Sean. "What Camus's *The Plague* can teach us about the Covid-19 pandemic." *Vox*, July 22, 2020, https://www.vox.com/ future-perfect-podcast/2020/7/22/21328295/albert-camus-the-plague-covid-19-robert-zaretsky
A conversation about Camus's famous novel with philosopher Robert Zaretsky.

Lepore, Jill. "What Our Contagion Fables Are Really About." *The New Yorker*, March 23, 2020, https://www.newyorker.com/magazine/2020/03/30/what-our-contagion-fables-are-really-about.
An excellent analysis of plague stories by an eminent Harvard historian.

Tseng, Po-En and Wang, Ya-Huei. "Deontological or Utilitarian? An Eternal Ethical Dilemma in Outbreak." *International Journal of Environmental Research and Public Health*, Vol. 18, No. 16, 8565. https://doi.org/10.3390/ijerph18168565

# Conclusion *A Short Hike* to the Top of the Mountain: Teaching the Transcendent or Walking the Dog

MY CONCLUDING CHAPTER POSED a non-rhetorical essential question about the existential choice between hope and despair. We seem like a country, a world, and a species suspended between these two choices, somewhat like T.S. Eliot's evocation of limbo in "Hollow Men."[1] After two years of COVID-19, the world seemed to echo Eliot's prognosis that the world will end by a whimper. In other words, we collectively fade into extinction. We would just slowly stop breathing, the oxygen gone. However, 2022 has seen a diminishment of COVID's impact on society and a resumption of somewhat normal activity. Then, suddenly, but somewhat predictably, a monstrous tyrant of unspeakable evil launched an invasion of Ukraine, a peaceful, democratic nation, throwing the world back some 77 years into a maelstrom of horror. Maybe Eliot was wrong; the world will end in a bang after all, the bang of nuclear apocalypse. We have arrived at the heart of darkness, Mr. Kurtz's words in our ear, but praying that when this manuscript goes to press darkness will have lifted and we can all climb out of war's chaos and ascend Dante's Mount Purgatory rather that descend farther into the deepest circle of his Inferno.

A very small, very engaging, and potentially transformative game can help us make the climb upward, a game of beauty and hope, playable in two hours. The tragedy in Ukraine has rallied most of the world in defense of freedom. As we have seen last chapter, games that teach cooperation show us the indispensable value of working together to solve complex, global problems. Change begins at the individual level, and so this game, *A Short Hike*, allows students to explore a small, open world in search of transcendence, a view of the world from the mountain top: solitary, at one with nature, removed from conflict, connected to our inner self.

## THE VIEW FROM THE TOP

Reaching the mountain top brings clarity of thought not possible when surrounded by the world's noise. Hiking through the mountains we are in the realm of birds, part of nature, and close to the sacred. In the mountains we find freedom, and discover peace no money can purchase, no power can claim. The Swiss Alps, in Davos, is where Thomas Mann's Hans Castorp made his way up *The Magic Mountain* (1924) to visit the Berghof Sanatorium where his cousin Joachim Ziemssen sought a cure from the choked world below. In these same Alps, Sils Maria to be precise, Nietzsche discovered his prophet Zarathustra among the clouds. Moses ascended Mount Sinai where he received the Decalogue (*Exodus* 20: 2-17; *Deuteronomy* 5:6-21) and Jesus climbed the Mountain of Beatitudes in Northern Israel (*Mathew* 5: 1-2) where he delivered his most powerful sermon (*Mathew* 5-7); these two moments give the Jewish and Christian faiths their moral grounding. In Islam, the sacred Kaaba represents the center of the world. Mount Meru speaks to both Hinduism's and Buddhism's most sacred beliefs (Figure A.1).

The Incas built the extraordinary 15th-century city of Machu Picchu on top of the Andes overlooking Valle Sagrado de los Incas/Willka Qhichuu (SacredValley) (Figure A.2).

In Nepali, Mount Everest or Sagarmatha translates as "Goddess of the Sky," and in Tibetan, Chomolungma or "Holy Mother" (Keay, 2000). These mountains are sacred because, as the great religious historian Mircea Eliade (1991) explained many years ago, the mountain is an "axis mundi" or "the world's navel" where we can both descent to the underworld and ascend to the heavens.

In *A Short Hike*, you move upward. This game helps you explore the sacred, and no better protagonist for that journey than the bird Claire.

FIGURE A.1   Cosmological Mandala with Mount Meru. (author, Public Domain, via Wikimedia Commons, https://uploadMetropolitan Museum of Art, CC0, via Wikimedia Commons.wikimedia.org/wikipedia/commons/1/1c/Cosmological_Mandala_with_Mount_Meru.jpg.)

FIGURE A.2   Machu Picchu main square. (CEllen, CC BY-SA 4.0 https:// creativecommons.org/licenses/by-sa/4.0, via Wikimedia Commons https:// commons.wikimedia.org/wiki/File:Machu_Picchu_main_square_2.jpg.)

Only birds fly to the mountains, we humans must climb. Claire is a personification for sure. As Claire, we learn various helpful human skills and obtain important tools that man must have to ascend the mountain, but we also experience the freedom of flight. We run, jump, climb, but best of all, we can glide. To glide is truly to be untethered by worldly concerns, the demands of materialism, the grip of the secular. You ride the wind, at one with nature's spirit (Figure A.3).

The game takes place in Hawk Peak Provincial Park on a small island. Like in *Alba*, this is a friendly world, a world populated by animals you can help and learn from. Again, like *Alba*, this world has no clock. We are in Shakespeare's Forest of Arden (*As You Like It*, III ii), as we wander about and leisurely explore; you get there when you get there and where you get to is where you end up. This is a pastoral landscape where time proceeds according to nature's rhythms not man's impositions and schedules. A reviewer for *Eurogamer*, Christiaan Donlan (2019) captures the game's essential paradox, "…getting somewhere by going nowhere." The island's world is akin to Wordsworth's Lake District, a world of childlike wonder. Ironically, Claire's mission is to reach the island's mountain top so she can get cellphone reception. A game about nature with a technological objective? Nothing tethers people more today, inhibiting any experience of transcendence, than the ubiquitous cell phone sutured to people's hips and ears. Claire is waiting for an important call, so she needs reception. Or does she?

No. For me the cell phone is a metaphor. The call comes not from the secular, but the sacred. That's why the mountain matters. Today, students

FIGURE A.3  The freedom of gliding. (Image courtesy of Adam Robinson-Yu. Used with permission of adamgryu©.)

can get a simulated sense of transcendence by playing this game on their phone, but then the phone must be put down. The phone and the game enable an experience that transcends both. Claire waits for a call—a call from the clouds if you will. I am reminded of the distinguished philosopher/theologian Cornell West (2022) who recently differentiated a call to a vocation from a commitment to a job.

**Cunningham:** **Is it the personal dimension that then creates, not an escape hatch, but sort of a parallel current to that?**

West: Part of it is that, when you have a vocation, as opposed to just a profession, and a calling as opposed to a career, then you're really trying to proceed in the spirit of integrity, and you're going to find persons who also have that same sense of vocation, no matter what color they are.

West criticizes the academic world for its thoroughly secular materialism. Professors who work a job, manage a career, and compulsorily publish are professionals, but insular. How different is a calling, a vocation? In a vocation, you do not publish an article to achieve tenure or promotion, you deliver a message.[2]

If nothing else, I can say I have never acquiesced to the career, the compulsion to publish, the "tenure track," the immersion in the politically correct trend of the day. I have been more like Nietzsche, though necessarily far less profound (that goes without saying), a nomadic scholar— a wanderer and his shadow—and sometimes social worker.[3] Although I have lived many of my years near the Adirondack Mountains, I did not discover my transcendent experience on the mountains of great literature. My walking stayed on the flat terrain of local nature preserves.

When walking or hiking, what matters is that you are outside and away from the clamor of classrooms and offices, the scheduled life, the tic toc of semesters or quarters, the Kafkaesque bureaucracy of administrative dictates. Frederick Gross describes the departure from society's "thou shalt" (see *Thus Sprach Zarathustra's* prologue) so well in *A Philosophy of Walking* (2014), "You choose to leave the office behind, go out, stroll around, think about other things. With a longer excursion of several days, the process of self-liberation is accentuated: you escape the constraints of work, throw off the yoke of routine."

For Henry David Thoreau, walking was sustenance, "I think that I cannot preserve my health and spirits, unless I spend four hours a day at least—and it is commonly more than that—sauntering through the woods and over the hills and fields, absolutely free from all worldly engagements." Thoreau discusses the etymology of sauntering as a wanderer roaming the countryside asking charity by feigning he is on journey to the Holy Land, while in reality the wanderer is just walking, a homeless, vagabond of sorts. However, the good wanderers, as Thoreau invokes them, may be without home "sans terre," but only the fixed sense of home. The good wanderer is at home anywhere. "For every walk is a sort of crusade, preached by some Peter the Hermit in us, to go forth and reconquer this Holy Land from the hands of the Infidels." The Holy Land is nature, the wilderness, the mountains, the pond, the lake, the river. It is not the school room, the lecture hall, the office building, the tavern, sports arena, or shopping mall.

For me walking my pug, Roderick has been a transcendent experience, self-liberating in a way that goes beyond the secular struggles of academia

FIGURE A.4  The author walking his beloved pug, Roderick. (Photograph courtesy of Beth Tedford©. Used with permission.)

and life more generally. With Roderick, there is no deadline. You smell the roses and everything else; the walk is a serendipitous journey with no destination. It's all about the journey, the walk. No need to impress anyone or answer to anyone. Roderick could care less if you have money—if the car window can open, he is happy. Whether that window belongs to a Mercedes, or a jalopy does not matter. He has no mean bone in his little body. Roderick loves me unconditionally as I love him. He is truly a gift that has no exchange value. He is invaluable. Roderick is simply "being there" "Da-sein" as Heidegger would have it. Simply being present and attentive. I am grateful for that (Figure A.4).

How do you teach this unteachable realization? This epiphany? The act of being present? You can't teach it. You enable the experience, create the conditions of possibility, not by administering a test or implementing a curriculum, but by suggesting, students play, perhaps, *A Short Hike* on their phone, then ask them to put the phone down and take a short walk, on their own, like Henry David Thoreau, and see what comes of it.

## NOTES

1. Eliot's poem implies that men are hollow because they are spiritually dead. For Eliot, living without spirituality meant living without purpose, devoid of any transcendent reality. The poem is in the same vein as *The Waste Land* (1922) in its apocalyptic tone and complicated imagery. The epigraph from Joseph Conrad's *Heart of Darkness* published in 1899 reiterates the novel's apocalyptic imagery, but in any case, both texts emphasize spiritual decay. For Eliot, World War I signaled a collapse of order and reason. Without a sense of the transcendent to fill the void left by a destructive, meaningless war man was doomed to an unfulfilled existence. For Conrad, the void signaled the aftermath of colonialism, a world ravaged by greed leaving only the internal horror of an absurd world.
2. Cornel West has been a strong critic of the establishment and his letter of resignation from Harvard sounds his discontent with what he perceives to be Harvard's institutional inertia, biases, market-driven practices, and politically correct thinking. You can read Dr. West's resignation letter to Harvard on his Twitter account, @cornelwest from July 12, 2021, at 9:56 PM.
3. Nietzsche published "The Wander and His Shadow" as the third part of *Human All Too Human* in 1880. He composed the book of 350 aphorisms during his walks in the Swiss Alps. Nietzsche often walked six or more miles a day during this time. The wanderer is a prototype for his free thinker. Nietzsche notes how a wanderer unlike a traveler has no ultimate

destination. He lives outside any telos, and the free thinker is a person who thinks as he walks, untethered by culture, convention, partnerships, family, or the academy.

## GAME

*A Short Hike.* Developed and published by adamgru, 2019. Designer: Adam Robinson-Yu. Single player, casual adventure game.

## RESOURCE

*Everest VR.* Developed and published by Solfar Studios, 2016.

Thus is an excellent virtual reality experience where you get to feel what climbing Mount Everest must be like.

# Index

Note: **Bold** page numbers refer to tables; *Italic* page numbers refer to figures and page numbers followed by "n" denote endnotes.

Printed in the United States
by Baker & Taylor Publisher Services